ZEW Economic Studies

Publication Series of the Centre for European Economic Research (ZEW) Mannheim, Germany

Sebastian Hauptmeier • Friedrich Heinemann
Marcus Kappler • Margit Kraus
Andreas Schrimpf • Hans-Michael Trautwein
Qingwei Wang

Projecting Potential Output

Methods and Problems

Physica-Verlag
A Springer Company

ZEW
Zentrum für Europäische
Wirtschaftsforschung GmbH

Series Editor
Prof. Dr. Dr. h.c. mult. Wolfang Franz

Authors
Sebastian Hauptmeier mail@sebastian-hauptmeier.de
Dr. Friedrich Heinemann heinemann@zew.de
Dr. Marcus Kappler kappler@zew.de
Dr. Margit Kraus kraus@calculas-consult.com
Andreas Schrimpf schrimpf@zew.de
Prof. Dr. Hans-Michael Trautwein michael.trautwein@uni-oldenburg.de
Qingwei Wang wang@zew.de

Centre for European Economic
Research (ZEW)
L7, 1
68161 Mannheim
Germany

ISBN 978-3-7908-2176-5 e-ISBN 978-3-7908-2177-2

DOI: 10.1007/978-3-7908-2177-2

Library of Congress Control Number: 2009921248

Cover design: WMXDesign GmbH, Heidelberg

Printed on acid-free paper

springer.com

Table of Contents

1 Introduction

The concept of potential output has played an important role in economic analysis and policy debate at least since the 1960s. Usually defined as the productive capacity that would be feasible under full utilisation of all factors of production, it is a central reference variable in economic theories and provides the starting point for analysing the current status of the economy. Potential output is also a key reference variable in empirical economic research and is regularly employed by national and international economic research institutes and economic advisory boards to analyse the business cycle. Potential output is of importance in economic policy for disentangling structural problems and business cycle phenomena, in medium-term budget planning and especially for providing an orientation variable for monetary policy. The potential growth concept also plays a pivotal role at the European level in the context of the Lisbon Agenda and, at the German level, in the definition of necessary reforms and reform priorities.

In spite of the widespread use of the concept of potential output in economic theory and empirical applications as well as in economic policy debates, the historical background and the assumptions inherent to the concept of potential output regarding economic relationships as well as concerning epistemological perspectives are rarely made transparent, let alone critically questioned. Apparently well-defined and unequivocal potential figures are quoted and used in empirical practice and economic policy debates as a matter of course and with a confidence that cannot be taken for granted given the assumptions and limitations of conventional methods. It is doubtful, for example, whether some of the fundamentally retrospective empirical procedures often used to determine potential output, such as univariate filter-based methods for example, can be appropriately applied in the context of a genuinely forward-looking concept (i.e. the future growth perspectives of an economy measured in terms of potential output). It is also doubtful whether labour input in production function-based methods can be reliably projected into the future given that such volumes are influenced in their turn by changes in labour market structures, technological trends or macroeconomic developments.

Against this background this study sets out to determine the extent to which the concept of potential output rests on clearly defined theoretical foundations and how far prevailing empirical quantification methods really provide truly reliable insights into potential growth of an economy. With this aim in mind the study aims at making the concept of potential output and its underlying explicit and implicit economic and system-theoretical assumptions transparent. The theoretical assumptions, the data requirements as well as the methodological strengths and

S. Hauptmeier et al., *Projecting Potential Output*, Zew Economic Studies,
DOI: 10.1007/978-3-7908-2177-2_1, © Physica-Verlag Berlin Heidelberg 2009

weaknesses of prevailing methods of determining potential output and growth are subjected to critical analysis. The study also aims at analysing how conceivable it would be to extend the current spectrum of methods by drawing on procedures that exploit the information provided by the yield curve in relation to anticipated future economic growth.

The study consists of two main parts. The theoretical part of the book examines the origins and historical background of the concept of potential output and discusses its epistemological foundations. Chapter 2 begins by tracing the way different historical economic schools of thought have developed over time that are relevant to the potential output concept. This historical outline is followed in chapter 3 by an analysis of the determinability of key aspects of potential output (the concept of an aggregate production function, the dichotomy between growth and the business cycle, the concept of non-inflationary unemployment and the role of monetary policy). The theoretical part of the book epistemologically concludes with a consideration of aspects relating to system theory (chapter 4).

The second part of the study focuses on empirical methods and begins in chapter 5 with a review of the most important univariate and multivariate methods of identifying potential output and a quantitative appraisal of the empirical distinctiveness and forecast precision of these methods. Chapter 6 briefly deals with the causes of weak growth in Germany as identified in the literature. Chapter 7 then focuses on the strengths and weaknesses of yield curve procedures that might appropriately supplement conventional methods of precisely estimating potential output since they exploit anticipations regarding future economic growth. Chapter 8 ends with conclusions for economic policy and empirical macroeconomics.

THEORETICAL PART

2 The Concept of Potential Output: A History of Origins

2.1 Introduction

This chapter outlines the economic conditions and theoretical ideas prevailing at the times of origin of the concept of potential output. In general, Okun (1962) is considered as the starting point for the development of methods for calculating potential output and output gaps (Section 2.2). However, the standard methods have been heavily criticised by proponents of the New Neoclassical Synthesis who in turn refer to Wicksell's theory of interest rate gaps, which dates back as early as 1898 (Section 2.3). Accordingly, this chapter outlines the extensive history of potential output concepts before Okun (1962), especially with respect to the development of Wicksellian and Keynesian "gap theories" since the late 1920s (Section 2.4). Since controversies about the existence of a trade-off between full employment and price-level stability are of central importance for the discussion of potential output, the different stages of the Phillips curve debates are described in Section 2.5. The development of systems of national accounting, which began in the 1930s and culminated after World War II, did also play an important role. Based on national accounting, numerous methods of calculation have been developed since the 1960s for purposes of political advisory. At the end of this chapter, it is discussed to what extent connections can be made between concepts of potential outputs and the macroeconomic framework conditions prevailing at their respective times of origin (Section 2.6). When gap theories were developed around 1930, circumstances were, after all, very different compared to the heyday of potential output concepts in the 1960s and 1970s. The corresponding macroeconomic framework conditions are captured in terms of growth regimes that give priority to the relationship between real growth rates and real interest rates – two key determinants of investment.

The various strands of evolution presented in chapter 2 amount to a chronological survey. Against this background, chapter 3 analyses key positions and controversies revolving around concepts of aggregation, the notion of non-inflationary unemployment, the interaction of growth trends and business cycles and the neutrality of monetary policy. It should be noted that in both chapters the history of economic thought is employed as a map that helps to determine the present state of theory. On the basis of earlier positions and controversies, crossroads in the

S. Hauptmeier et al., *Projecting Potential Output*, Zew Economic Studies,
DOI: 10.1007/978-3-7908-2177-2_2, © Physica-Verlag Berlin Heidelberg 2009

evolution of economic thinking are identified. Not all turn-offs that have been abandoned by *mainstream* economics have been convincingly proven to be dead-ends or detours. Some alternative routes that have been discovered but only partially explored in the past may still contribute to further advancements in the determination of potential output. The current reconsiderations of Wicksellian gap theories indicate that investigating theoretical developments of the past need neither be an end in itself nor worship of ancestors, but may prove to harbour valuable analytical potential.

2.2 Okun's Contribution

It is commonly held that the concept of potential output was born at the annual conference of the American Statistical Association in 1962, when Arthur Okun, the US President's chief economic adviser, spoke on the significance and measurement of potential GNP.[1] Okun defined potential output as the level of macroeconomic output attainable without triggering inflation. He, thus, linked the idea of maximum potential output with the criterion of an unemployment rate consistent with zero inflation quite a number of years before the term NAIRU became popular.[2] In the same essay, Okun devised the well-known "Okun's law", assuming a linear negative relationship between the GNP growth rate and the change of the unemployment rate as an empirical regularity. When economic growth recedes, unemployment increases and vice versa (Okun, 1962, 1983: 148f).[3]

Okun's law was actually a by-product of Okun's key proposition concerning the relationship between current output and potential output: If current output diverges from potential output, output gaps emerge from over- or underutilisation of productive capacities. Potential output becomes the pivotal factor of orientation for stabilisation policy because the existence of gaps implies macroeconomic inefficiency. As today's current output affects tomorrow's potential output, the dynamics of the inefficiencies require special attention. In the case of negative gaps (underutilisation), entrepreneurial profits and household incomes, and with them long-term oriented investments in production facilities, instalment, research and development, fall short of the level attainable in a situation of full utilisation. In the case of positive gaps (overutilisation), replacement investment for extra wear-out of personnel and material reduce the scope for net investment. Consequently, an effective stabilisation policy not only mitigates cyclical fluctuations in the utili-

---

[1] See Okun (1962); with respect to Okun's work in the Council of Economic Advisers and the application of the concept of potential output during the early stages see Prachowny (2000, ch. 2).

[2] The term NAIRU is the abbreviation for "Non-Accelerating Inflation Rate of Unemployment".

[3] Okun's law, amongst other things, allows the determination of so-called employment thresholds, i.e. GNP growth rates that need to be transcended before an increase in employment can occur.

sation of the current output potential but also furthers economic growth (Okun, 1962, 1983: 147).

Okun's 1962 essay drew up a double-track approach for assessing potential output. On the one hand, Okun's characterisation of output gaps as cyclical deviations from the growth trend fostered the application of statistical methods for trend adjustments, for instance, by applying so-called filters. On the other hand, his benchmark of an unemployment rate that is consistent with stable inflation formed the basis for estimating production functions or Phillips curve equations. Both types of methods are criticised as inappropriate by proponents of the "New Neoclassical Synthesis", the current mainstream of macroeconomic theory.

2.3 The New Neoclassical Synthesis

The critique of common practices for calculating potential output is best illustrated by taking recourse to Michael Woodford's "Interest and Prices" (2003) – a standard reference on monetary theory that has advanced to the position of a "bible for central bank economists" (Green, 2005: 121). The core model of this book is a special version of the New Neoclassical Synthesis' three-equations system. In comparison with the traditional synthesis as represented by the IS-LM model, its major differences are considered to be the micro-theoretical foundations of macroeconomic relationships as well as the endogenisation of aggregate supply and of monetary policy. The core model of the new synthesis can be labelled as an IS-AS-MR model describing the dynamics of short-term fluctuations of production, inflation and interest rates:[4]

- The *IS equation* describes a negative relationship between the output gap and real interest rates, resulting from the intertemporal optimisation of the representative household. It is assumed that the household has rational expectations concerning the development of future income and inflation levels. If income is expected to rise, current demand for goods also increases. By contrast, rising real interest rates (nominal interest rates net of expected inflation rate) induce increased saving and a reduction of current aggregate demand.
- The *AS equation* establishes the interaction of aggregate supply and inflation in terms of a New Keynesian Phillips curve. Current inflation is determined by expected inflation and the current output gap. The latter results from profit maximisation of price-setting enterprises under monopolistic competition. If energy prices or nominal interest rates unexpectedly rise or if other shocks occur, a number of firms will prefer to reduce supply rather than increasing prices.
- The *MR equation* describes the reaction function of monetary policy makers in terms of a Taylor rule: Short-term nominal interest rates are set by the central

[4] See Woodford (2003: ch. 4). For a less demanding and more graphically oriented description, see the textbook by Carlin and Soskice (2006). An introduction to a similar kind of modelling in German language is given by Spahn (2006: ch. 4).

bank in such a way that they positively fluctuate (with specific weights) with the deviations of inflation and the output gap from their target value. If current inflation exceeds the target value, nominal interest rates are raised, according to the Taylor principle even overproportionally, in order to reduce inflation.

Combining intertemporal optimisation, monopolistic competition and price rigidities, the IS-AS-MR model embodies a synthesis of New Classical and New Keynesian approaches. Woodford's approach, however, refers further back in history labelling his version of the IS-AS-MR models as "Neo-Wicksellian". It refers to Knut Wicksell's (1898) work on interest and prices, which can, for good reasons, be considered as a stepping stone in the development of both Neoclassical and Keynesian macroeconomics. Woodford's output-gap concept in the IS equation refers to a "natural rate of output" that corresponds to the "natural rate of interest" – a term coined by Wicksell (1898). Furthermore, Woodford's "welfare-analytical foundation" of monetary policy (2003: ch. 6-8) refers to Wicksell's simple rule of interest: According to that rule, changes in the price level of goods need to be answered only with parallel changes of money interest rates until the changes in the price level come to a standstill since the money rate of interest coincides with the natural rate (which is not directly observable).

Woodford's benchmark variable in terms of natural output is the notional output level in an environment of monopolistic competition and perfectly flexible prices. In this case there would be welfare losses due to monopolistic price-setting that, compared to perfect competition on the supply side, reduce demand. However, there would be no additional welfare losses resulting from price rigidities that reduce supply and distort the price structure. Since it should not be expected that prices are perfectly flexible under monopolistic competition, output gaps are best reduced by ensuring that the price level remains largely stable and price rigidities cannot take effect. As a typical "second best" solution to the welfare theoretical problem of optimisation (as opposed to the utopia of perfect competition), the Taylor rule, thus, forms a modern version of Wicksell's rule for monetary policy.

Woodford's approach and further developments of the New Neoclassical Synthesis lead to criticism concerning the two standard methods for calculating potential output, namely trend-filtering and estimations of production functions (e.g. Andrés, López-Salido, & Nelson, 2005). Statistical methods that extrapolate potential output as a growth trend based on past output developments generate results that coincide with analytically determined values by accident at best. Trend-oriented methods project past developments without considering the influence of future expectations on potential output. On the other hand, methods solely based on production functions or Phillips curve equations and embedded NAIRU estimations bring about logical short-circuits as potential output is identified on the basis of the unemployment rate that is consistent with stable inflation. According to the logic of the New Keynesian Phillips curve (the above-mentioned AS equation), however, low inflation can, in the case of nominal rigidities, be associated with inefficiently high unemployment rates due to output adjustments. Secondly, stable inflation is achieved only as a result of monetary policy, which in turn requires that potential output is determined independently. Within the framework of New

Neoclassical Synthesis, the conclusion that minimising inflation by means of monetary policy keeps current output close to potential output strictly holds only if purely nominal rigidities exist. As Woodford (2003) and Blanchard and Galí (2005) show for the case of real rigidities (when prices and nominal wages are both inflexible or shift at the same rate), supply shocks (e.g., rising energy prices) can revive the classical Phillips curve trade-off. In this case, strict inflation control is bound to generate output gaps and involuntary unemployment in the sense of Keynes (1936), at least in the short run. If the model is extended to include investment (Woodford, 2003: ch. 5.3), potential output might even be permanently reduced. The framework of the New Neoclassical Synthesis, thus, opens avenues to the explanation of long-term real effects of monetary policy.

One need not agree with all of the current criticism concerning the standard methods of estimating potential output. The new synthesis itself creates problems by defining the benchmark variable as output in an environment of monopolistic competition and perfectly flexible prices. This does not only carry the usual problems of dealing with unobservable quantities. It is also theoretically dubious: If enterprises are able to set prices and, faced with the choice of either adjusting prices or quantities, opt for the latter, one cannot assume that price adjustments would "actually" be the optimal solution. At least it cannot be claimed that this version of macroeconomic theory has micro-foundations superior to traditional IS/LM analysis. The discrepancy between individually and macroeconomically optimal behaviour is explained *ad hoc* by introducing specific assumptions concerning sticky prices rather than deriving it from the model. The new synthesis has, nevertheless, made progress over the old with respect to its dynamic analysis of inflation, output gaps and interest rate policy. Exactly in these features, however, the new synthesis refers to approaches that shaped macroeconomic theory before Okun's (1962) contribution and are associated with Knut Wicksell and John Maynard Keynes.[5] The following section outlines those early Wicksell and Keynes connections of modern macroeconomics.

[5] There are, however, fundamental differences between the new synthesis and Keynes' and Wicksell's theories, especially with respect to coordination failures of the interest rate mechanism. In the new synthesis coordination failures are disregarded due to the assumption implicit in the *IS equation* that investment invariably equals the intertemporal optimum of the representative consumer. For differences between Wicksell and current approaches, see Boianovsky and Trautwein (2006a) and the response by Woodford (2006); concerning Keynes, see van der Ploeg (2005).

2.4 Wicksell and Keynes Connections

2.4.1 Interest Rate Gaps and Inflation

Wicksell (1898) developed a theory of inflation based on the gap between the money rate of interest and the "natural rate of interest". The natural rate of interest is the rate of return on capital that equalises savings supply and planned entrepreneurial investments – irrespectively of influences stemming from the loan supply of commercial banks and the monetary policy of the central bank. The most important forces affecting this equilibrium rate include technical progress and demographic change but also institutional changes, natural disasters and war. Because of these various and continuously varying influences on aggregate saving and investment, the "natural interest rate" is highly variable. By contrast, the money rate of interest that commercial banks demand from their customers – and that Wicksell defined as the representative market rate of interest – is sticky in the short run and adjusts only laggingly to changes in the market conditions. The main reasons for this lack of flexibility are contract obligations, conventions and other aspects of tending to customer relationships. If the profit expectations of entrepreneurs suddenly improve substantially, for instance, due to the opening-up of new markets by way of innovations or reforms, the natural rate of interest rises to exceed the market rate. The demand for loans increases and is normally met by commercial banks, owing to their own interests in increasing revenues.[6] As a consequence of the credit expansion, aggregate demand begins, sooner or later, to exceed available output. Excess demand leads to a rise in the general price level, which continues in a cumulative inflationary process for as long as the gap between the natural rate of interest and the money rate prevails.[7]

In Wicksell's view, market forces cause the money rate of interest sooner or later to adjust to the natural interest, thus, restoring the original equilibrium state of the economy.[8] While the interest rate structure is stable in this sense, there are no market forces that would automatically return the price level to its original position. The price level is meta-stable, i.e. its index value at the end of the cumulative process differs from the initial value. The interaction of stable and meta-stable movements in a system of interdependent markets is the trademark of all macroeconomic theories that developed from Wicksell's monetary theory: The failure of

[6] It is presupposed that sufficient collateral is provided. However, the value of the collateralised assets is itself indirectly dependent on the level and growth of the aggregate loan supply.

[7] In Wicksell (1898), the same logic applies to the process of disinflation that starts whenever the natural rate of interest falls short of the money rate.

[8] However, Wicksell's hypothesis that the money rate adjusts to the natural rate of interest cannot be conclusively deduced in a modern credit economy that is not restricted by a gold standard, an assumption that Wicksell himself made in terms of the "pure credit economy" in his theory of cumulative processes; see Trautwein (1996).

the interest rate mechanism to coordinate savings and investments in the capital market forces prices – and sometimes also quantities – in other markets (in this case, the goods market) to adjust as well. Temporary coordination failures of the interest rate mechanism can, thus, induce permanent changes of prices (and quantities) in other markets.

Wicksell considered inflation to be a social grievance, as it gives rise to distributional conflicts and particularly puts recipients of nominally fixed incomes, who have little bargaining power, at a disadvantage. This way it undermines social peace. However, inflation can be avoided quite easily, if the central bank reacts quickly to price-level increases by raising interest rates until price-level stability is regained.[9]

Wicksell's interest-rate gap theory of inflation contains the core of a theory of potential output and output gaps. Wicksell himself, however, was merely looking for an explanation of inflation. He proceeded on the assumption that the economy is in a state of full employment and full utilisation of capacities at all times. Although he conceded at times the possibility that inflation and disinflation, through distributional effects, may cause investment and output capacities to change (e.g., 1898), he dismissed these effects as non-cumulative and hence insignificant. It was not until the 1920s and 1930s that Wicksell's interest gap theory was systematically extended by economists in various places who endeavoured to develop business cycle theories and models of macroeconomic dynamics. Particularly noteworthy are the contributions by Cambridge economists Dennis Robertson (1926) and John Maynard Keynes (1930), by Friedrich August von Hayek, Vienna/London (1929, 1931), and by the Stockholm School, led by Erik Lindahl (1930) and Gunnar Myrdal (1931). The contributions by Johan Åkerman, Lund (1928) and Ragnar Frisch, Oslo (1933), who were both inspired by Wicksell's (separate) theory of the business cycle, are also of relevance with regard to the relationship between growth trends and cyclical fluctuations. In the following, the focus is set on approaches that formed the base for subsequent discussions on potential output and, at the same time, provided valuable insights nowadays neglected.[10]

2.4.2 Impulse Propagation Mechanisms

As noted above, Wicksell considered his interest-rate gap model to be a theory of inflation rather than an explanation of business cycles. In his view cyclical fluctuations are caused solely by changes in the natural rate of interest, not by deviations of the market rate.[11] He explained the variability of the natural rate of interest

---

[9] Wicksell's simple rule of interest in the combat of inflation constitutes the core of the Taylor rule in the MR-equation described in Section 2.3.

[10] We present only a rough outline of a selection of evolutionary strands. Some of these contributions are addressed in more detail in chapter 3.

[11] In Wickell's view, interest rate gaps are at best a reinforcing element in the progression of prices, and while they might aggravate speculative hyperboles and crisis, they cannot

as a result of asynchronous changes in the economy's set of fundamental data: While labour supply and the demand for consumption goods grow more or less steadily, technical progress in the form of new products and production processes occurs irregularly and by leaps and bounds. The corresponding increases in productivity raise the returns on investment projects and, thereby, the equilibrium rate of interest because saving does not adjust immediately, given that income and the demand for consumption goods change more slowly. Once the peak in investment activity that was caused by the leap in technology has been passed, output falls until the investment goods acquired at those peak times need to be replaced. Output oscillates until the systems returns to its equilibrium state or further technological progress occurs. Wicksell (1918) compared the business cycle mechanism to a rocking horse that pushed by means of a stick, starts to sway strongly. If the horse is built solidly, it will gradually return from vigorous rocking to a state of rest unless it is pushed again. The push is the external impulse that sets the horse off, but the horse's movements are independent of the shape and further movement of the stick. They are solely determined by the strength of the impulse and the shape of the horse.

Wicksell's rocking horse metaphor gave rise to the famous dichotomy of impulse propagation mechanisms that characterises macroeconomic and econometric thought in various areas.[12] Fluctuations of real economic activity and other processes are, thus, defined as adjustments of the system in question to changes in exogenous variables. Like waves, external impulses diffuse across the system according to its laws of motion. The dissemination of this idea was promoted especially by Åkerman (1928) and Frisch (1933).

Åkerman (1928) attempted to reconcile the observation of seemingly irregular fluctuations in crude steel production and other business cycle indicators with general equilibrium theory by developing a method for empirical analysis of the cycle.[13] He proceeded from Fourier's theorem, which states that any curve, no matter how irregular its appearance, can be decomposed into a specific number of mutually overlapping sinus curves. Accordingly, Åkerman developed a hydrodynamic model of the economy based on the idea of a normal output capacity in the hypothetical equilibrium state. The normal capacity forms the motionless water surface at "sea level". Changes in productivity, due to technical progress and population growth, occur sometimes more and sometimes less intensively and give rise to "long waves", causing the normal capacity to fluctuate over decades. The interaction between long-term, short-term and very short-term waves induced by techni-

generate business cycles. Concerning Wicksell's distinction between business cycles, crises and cumulative processes, see Boianovsky (1995) and Boianovsky and Trautwein (2001).

[12] Changes in GDP growth, inflation rates and other variables are routinely analysed as sequences of "shocks" in terms of comparative statics as well as dynamics. The effects of policy measures and other "shocks" are frequently represented using impulse response functions in structural vector autoregressive models (SVAR); see also section 2.6.2.

[13] Consistent time series of changes in national income were not available at the time; see section 2.6.1.

cal innovation cycles as well as by psychological and seasonal fluctuations in the degree of utilisation creates regular economic cycles lasting three and a half to six years depending on their position within the long wave. By treating business cycle impulses as the result of overlapping effects of various exogenous but more or less regularly occurring factors, Åkerman attempted to endogenise the timing of the occurrence of impulses and to render it accessible for business cycle forecasting.

Frisch (1933) developed Wicksell's rocking horse metaphor into models of impulse propagation mechanisms, drafting a system of difference and differential equations that describe the aggregate production of capital and consumption goods. By means of modelling a mechanism of acceleration (overproportional reactions of investment in response to changes in consumption) that works in the presence of liquidity constraints for consumption, Frisch was able to explicitly describe and consistently quantify the dynamics of investment and consumption activities as well as to make rigorous distinctions between competing business cycle theories on the basis of differences in their functional design and parameter magnitudes. Unlike Åkerman's spectral analytical approach, however, in Frisch's model impulses do not lead to permanent fluctuations, owing to their irregular nature. After a time, their effects peter out because the system's fluctuations are dampened by frictions (mainly inelasticities of demand and supply). In the absence of impulses (in modern terms: "shocks"), no difference between potential and current production exists.

2.4.3 Monetary Policy and the Formation of Expectations and Capital

All over Europe the early 1920s were marked by discussions on whether and under what circumstances the gold standard prevailing before World War I could be revived. When, in 1925 and after, the gold convertibility of most currencies was re-established but shortly afterwards called into question by the onslaught of the Great Depression (1929-33), the issue of manipulating aggregate output by means of interest rate policy came to the fore. During this period, it seemed consequent to extend Wicksell's interest rate gap theory of inflation to construct monetary theories of the business cycle and macroeconomic theories of economic policy. With regard to systematic investigations of the relationship between potential output and monetary policy, the approaches developed by the Stockholm School are particularly noteworthy. Path-breaking contributions were made by Lindahl (1930) and Myrdal (1931).

Lindahl (1930) as well as Myrdal (1931) subjected Wicksell's concept of the natural rate of interest to critical examination. Both of them demonstrated that in a modern monetary economy with a multitude of products no equilibrium interest rate can be conceptualised independently of the money rate of interest and monetary policy (see also Trautwein, 2005; Boianovsky & Trautwein, 2006b). They redefined the equilibrium rate of interest as the expected rate of return on real investment (purchases of durable means of production) that equals the planned savings of households and enterprises. For these definitions of the "real interest rate", expectations concerning the future development of the value of investment goods are of crucial importance. Similar to modern rentability concepts that proceed from the present value of an investment project, Lindahl (1930: 248) and Myrdal (1931: 32) considered the real interest rate to be the "relation between the expected future value of output (net of fair risk-premium)" and "current invested values". These current invested values depend on investment demand, which in turn is affected by lending rates and, hence, in the end, by the central bank's monetary policy.

Lindahl (1930: 167 and 249) and Myrdal (1931: 164), thus, concluded that the real interest rate tends to adapt to the current money rate rather than the reverse. Lindahl (1930: ch. II) substantiated this conclusion by constructing various scenarios of cumulative processes that emerge in response to a cut of nominal interest rates by the central bank. For this he varied certain assumptions in the basic model, such as the degrees of capacity utilisation and employment, the intersectoral mobility of capital goods and labour, as well as incomplete foresight with regard to changes in the price level. He showed that, in an environment of underutilisation and unemployment, the decrease in the central money rate of interest (in those days: the discount rate) brings about an expansion of output until potential output is completely utilised. However, under certain conditions the decrease in interest rates may serve to expand potential output itself: if, due to interest rate cuts, aggregate demand exceeds supply while the emerging inflation is not perfectly anticipated by lenders and jobholders, enterprises earn so-called "windfall profits". They gain returns that result solely from the redistribution of purchasing power away from consumers with comparatively fixed incomes. Since the entrepreneurial propensity to reinvest retained earnings is normally higher than the households' propensity to save, it is safe to assume that the extra profits caused by inflation enhance entrepreneurial investment activity. With the extension of productive capacities potential output grows, and, open competition provided, inflation decreases as supply adapts to demand.

In this scenario as well as in the multitude of other designs of cumulative processes that abound in the key works of the Stockholm School (especially Lindahl, 1930; Myrdal, 1931, & Lundberg, 1937), disequilibria of aggregate supply and demand that give rise to inflation or disinflation are explained by deficiencies in the coordination of planned investments and planned savings by way of the interest rate mechanism. When discussing these kinds of coordination failures, the Swedish tradition particularly emphasised the formation of expectations in an environment of imperfect foresight. *Ex ante* disequilibria in the sense of incompatible plans bring about adjustments of prices and quantities that result, *ex post,* in equilibrium states of investments and savings, which differ from the original full-employment equilibrium.[14] In the above-mentioned scenario of inflation-driven growth aggregate saving deviates from the level that was originally planned, adjusting to entrepreneurial investments. Eventually, the real interest rate coincides with the decreased money rate since the formation of extra capital tends to in-

[14] The famous distinction between *ex ante* and *ex post* values in macroeconomics originates in Myrdal (1933).

crease productivity and thereby lower prices such that aggregate real income may increase.

Lindahl (1930 and 1961) was nevertheless quite sceptical with respect to efforts of fostering economic growth by means of reducing interest rates (under conditions of full employment). He assumed that, sooner or later, inflation expectations adapt to actual inflation and eventually accelerate the inflationary process by inducing interest rate-price and wage-price spirals. In the course of these processes, the income rigidities that produce windfall profits are dissolved. Furthermore, social conflicts may develop as well as a decline in saving. For both reasons, the central bank may be forced to increase interest rates in order to dampen inflation without enterprises, lenders, and jobholders being prepared for this. In any case, not only a decrease in current output but also a decline of capital stocks and, thus, potential output is imminent. Like Wicksell, Lindahl, therefore, advocated a rule-bound interest rate policy. He argued that, by stabilising expectations on inflation, the central bank should be able and obliged to stabilise capital formation as well.[15]

Lindahl and Myrdal were aware of the fundamental problem associated with a consistent definition of the equilibrium "real" interest rate – and, therewith, implicitly of the "normal" capital stock and potential output. To serve as a benchmark for evaluating measures of monetary policy, the equilibrium interest rate has to be determined independently of the impact of monetary policy. The only solution to this problem is to define the equilibrium interest rate as a path-dependent variable: Past influences of monetary policy are co-determinants of the current equilibrium interest rate.

2.4.4 The Term Structure of Interest Rates and the Business Cycle

It is considered a "stylised fact" that the central bank's monetary policy is capable of directly influencing the short-term interest rate in the money market. However, entrepreneurial investment activity – and thus the formation of capital that is decisive for potential output – primarily depends on the long-term interest rate in the capital market. How are short-term and long-term interest rates connected? Is the central bank in a position to influence the term structure of interest rates? Is it possible to extrapolate from the term structure to future potential output?

The first building blocks for answering these questions were provided by US economists Irving Fisher (1896) and Wesley Mitchell (1913). Mitchell promoted the concept of the yield curve as a representation of interest rate term structures. He observed that the yield curve is normally sloped upwards, the long-term interest rates being higher than the short-term interest rates. By contrast, in the case of

[15] Lindahl went even further and in a separate book on the rules of monetary policy (Lindahl, 1929) advocated the rule of targeting a nominally constant national product, i.e. the price level should be allowed to decline if labour productivity rises and vice versa. Given the relative rigidity of nominal wages, risks for profits and employment are evenly distributed evenly between employers and employees. For Lindahl's views on various rules for monetary policy, see Boianovsky and Trautwein (2006b).

imminent recession the yield curve is frequently inverse, the short-term interest rates being higher than the long-term interest rates. In his subsequent contributions (e.g., Burns & Mitchell, 1946), Mitchell concluded that the yield curve might be employed as a leading indicator for the course of the business cycle.[16]

Fisher (1896) postulated that it is possible to decompose the long-term interest rate observable as a nominal quantity into the expected real interest rate and the expected rate of inflation (at the time of payment). Given a constant real interest rate, if inflation expectations change, the nominal interest rate is adapted. If, however, a credible monetary policy manages to keep inflation expectations stable (or otherwise known), this hypothesis known as the "Fisher effect" can be employed for forecasting economic progression.

However, concerning the deduced changes of the real interest rate, there is scope for interpretation with respect to the progression of potential output. For instance, increases in real interest rates may be caused by improved revenue expectations on the part of enterprises and, thus, signalise an expansion of potential output, but they may also be due to a declining capital supply and, thus, imply at least stagnating potential output. Powerful forecasts based on the yield curve, therefore, require additional "identifying" information.

The difference between nominal and real interest rates in terms of the Fisher effect needs to be distinguished from the difference between the monetary and real interest rates in Wicksellian theories of interest rate gaps. Fisher's "real interest rate" denotes Wicksell's "money rate of interest" in terms of a rate of return on financial assets in the capital market – as opposed to the expected rate of return to real investments, as understood by Lindahl and others (see section 2.4.3). Fisher's real interest rate is an *inflation-adjusted* money rate. The actual real interest rate may differ from the "natural" or equilibrium interest rate. A general connection between interest rate theories in the style of Fisher and Wicksell is that intertemporal equilibrium prevails if the nominal rate of interest equals the real interest rate plus the inflation expectations of both lenders and borrowers. A fundamental difference between them is the notion that, according to the Fisher effect, intertemporal equilibrium is, in principle, consistent with any rate of inflation. By contrast, in Wicksell's view intertemporal equilibrium is characterised by zero inflation (price level stability).[17] From the viewpoint of more recent macroeconom-

[16] With respect to this and similar recommendations, mockers like to annotate that financial markets have predicted eleven of the last seven recessions. Concerning the forecasting power of the term structure of interest rates see, however, chapter 7 of the present study.

[17] However, Lindahl (1930), von Hayek (1931), and Myrdal (1931) criticised Wicksell's fixation on price level stability as an equilibrium condition; see Trautwein (2005). As pointed out by Hayek and Myrdal, disequilibria may prevail even with zero inflation. Lindahl demonstrated that high and accelerating inflation can be reconcilable with intertemporal equilibrium, provided that it is foreseen. In his examination of the relationship between interest and prices (1930), he took account of both Wicksell's and Fisher's interest rate theories.

ics following Woodford (2003), "quasi-zero inflation" is required for maximum convergence of current output to potential output.[18]

Theories inspired by Wicksell (including Woodford, 2003) assume – more or less simplifying – that the central bank is in a position to control the money market rate of interest and, thereby, also affect the long-term interest rates. Thus, the existence of an interest rate term structure does not change the reasoning put forward in the previous sections. The influence of monetary policy on capital market interest rates was analytically substantiated by Keynes (1930, ch. 37) and Lindahl (1930, ch. III). Both lines of argument were fully developed by Hicks (1939, ch. XI) to form the now well-known theory of expectations of the term structure. Keynes and Lindahl demonstrated the possibility that measures of open market policy (purchases and sales of long-term loans) by the central bank might directly affect interest rates in the capital market. But both they and Hicks put even more emphasis on the significance of the so-called "expectations channel" of transmission. They reasoned that long-term interest rates ought to be primarily considered as the average value of current interest rates and expected short-term interest rates over the relevant time horizon (see, e.g., Hicks, 1939: 145). Due to the existence of a risk premium, which takes account of the probability of illiquidity and credit default, the yield curve is sloped upwards. However, if future short-term interest rates are expected to be lower, current long-term interest rates decrease – perhaps even below the current short-term interest rates. In such periods the yield curve's shape is inverse.

Various causes may give rise to an inverse interest rate structure. Lindahl (1930: 190-194), however, stressed the importance of monetary policy for the formation of expectations and the yield curve. By means of a thought experiment he demonstrated the central bank's potential to influence the time path of inflation by affecting the term structure of interest rates. According to that, the announcement of a temporary rise in the discount rate and subsequent decrease below the current level gives rise to a distinct inversion of the yield curve. As short-term investments are now discounted by a higher interest rate while long-term investments have become more profitable due to a lower interest rate, reallocations of credits and resources (fixed capital, labour, stocks of inventory) to longer-term projects occur. In the real world, smooth reallocations of resources from one sector of the economy to another cannot be expected. Therefore, prices for inputs in short-term investments deteriorate initially leading to deflation. Then, due to the increase in the demand for inputs in long-term investments, the price level rises albeit not steadily. At the point of completion of those investment projects to which the same interest rate applies as at the original point on the inverse yield curve, the increase of the price index subsides. Thereafter, due to the excess demand for inputs in long-term investments inflation starts to accelerate.

---

[18] "Quasi-zero inflation" means that the New Neoclassical Synthesis does not consider perfect price stability as optimal in all events. Especially in the aftermath of supply shocks, tolerating a temporary minor price drift may be a superior solution from a welfare-theoretical perspective.

Purely hypothetically, by announcing changes in refinancing terms, the central bank would be able to affect not only the term structure of interest rates and investment activity but also the progression of inflation and (in the case of frictions in the reallocation process) of macroeconomic output. The central bank would, thus, be in a position to generate business cycle fluctuations by means of term structure policies. Since such policies would have destabilising effects, Lindahl (1930: ch. IV) advocates a rule-bound monetary policy that averts inflation by stabilising the market participants' formation of expectations (see section 2.4.3). The nowadays-common argument that the combat of inflation may require an inversion of the term structure by means of monetary policy was part of Lindahl's argument. Unlike his thought experiment of inversion, the general idea does not refer to announcements of a specific interest rate cut at a certain point in time but on making interest rate reductions dependent on the progression of the rate of inflation.

2.4.5 Effective Demand and Unemployment

The publication of *A General Theory of Employment, Interest and Money* by John Maynard Keynes (1936) changed the perspective of macroeconomic thinking considerably, although Keynes tied in with the Wicksellian tradition in many ways. In his *Treatise on Money* (1930), Keynes had, similar to many other economists, attempted to construct a monetary theory of the business cycle using his specific version of Wicksell's interest rate gap theory. Like Wicksell, he set the focus on cumulative processes of inflation but even more of deflation. Like Wicksell, he explained cumulative processes as results of coordination failures of the interest rate mechanism and associated disequilibria in the product market. Faced with the Great Depression, Keynes (1936) altered his perspective in many regards. Emphasis now lay on equilibrium constellations in goods markets and financial markets which, given constant prices, emerge from cumulative processes of *quantities* and result in involuntary mass unemployment. The focus, thus, changed from price adjustments to quantity adjustments and from dynamic analysis of disequilibria to comparative-static analysis of equilibria characterised by full- and underemployment. This change of perspective was reinforced by Hicks' (1937) attempt at reconciling the static core of Keynes' theory with the "classical" views held by Arthur Cecil Pigou and others. IS/LM analysis as developed by Hicks (1937) has significantly promoted the popularity of Keynes' theory. It forms the core of the traditional Neoclassical Synthesis, which is still part of most macroeconomic textbooks and, despite all criticism, has survived in some realms of political advisory.

Keynes (1936: ch. 3) emphasised the principle of effective demand, which states that aggregate demand may fall short of potential output. Keynes (1936: ch. 5-10) considered the general reason for this gap to be the interest rate mechanism's failure to coordinate investments and savings, causing it to be replaced by a mechanism of aggregate income adjustments. In Keynes' view, the capital-market equilibrium of investments and savings is not generated by adjustments of interest rates that would reconcile the planned investments of the firms with the intertemporal consumption plans of the households. Rather, autonomous changes of aggregate investment via multiplier processes give rise to cumulative changes in national income and consumption expenditures. With income and consumption, the volume of savings also adapts.

The hypothetical starting point of a typical multiplier processes according to Keynes is a full employment equilibrium with aggregate saving equalling aggregate investment and current output coinciding with potential output.[19] A decline of the demand for investment goods, thus, gives rise to a loss of national income that adds up to a multiple of the investment decrease because the corresponding employment reduction goes with a cut of the demand for consumption goods. Even though this cut is underproportional, it results in additional income losses. Due to the cumulative income losses the volume of saving also decreases until it equals investments once again. The corresponding income level is associated with a new equilibrium in the markets for investment and consumption goods while excess supply prevails in the labour market. In its simplest form the investment multiplier can be written as follows:

$$1/s = \Delta Y/\Delta I \qquad \text{and} \qquad \Delta Y = (1/s)\Delta I, \tag{2.1}$$

s being the marginal savings rate ($s < 1$), ΔY the change in aggregate income and ΔI the change in investment between the initial and the final equilibrium state.

Ever since Hicks (1937), Keynes' theory is usually presented in a simplified version that explains decreases of investment that lead to underemployment by referring to "investment traps" or "liquidity traps".[20] Investment traps are constellations in the product market where enterprises expect their net revenues to be that small that the investment activity required for full employment could be achieved only if interest rates in the capital market were distinctly *negative* – and, thus, it cannot be achieved at all. Liquidity traps are constellations in the financial market where most asset holders speculate for an increase in interest rates and, because of the associated fall in asset prices, substitute circulating bonds or shares with highly liquid assets or money. Due to liquidity preference and low demand for less liquid assets, the level of interest rates in the capital market will indeed remain high and cause investment activity to fall short of the volume required for full employment. In both cases, measures of monetary policy take no effect whatsoever on the funding of investments because the demand for investments is inelastic or the demand for money is perfectly elastic with regard to the interest rate, respectively. According to Keynes (1936: ch. 19), wage cuts do just as little to fix the misery because they curtail effective demand and negatively affect macroeconomic revenue expectations. Thus, as a last resort for stabilising national income

[19] Keynes (1936: ch. 10) basically adopted the concept of the investment multiplier from Kahn (1931).

[20] Whether this canonical interpretation does justice to Keynes' (1936) intentions need not be gone into. The case of "sticky wages" mentioned in textbooks as the third cause of underemployment equilibria in Keynes (1936) plays a far less important part compared to explanations referring to pessimistic entrepreneurial revenue expectations and liquidity preference on the part of wealth owners.

and employment, from a (traditional) Keynesian viewpoint only effective demand management by means of fiscal policy remains.[21]

Keynes' theory and its Keynesian standard interpretation in terms of IS/LM analysis have come under much criticism during the course of time. In the context of the present study, however, the bottom line is that Keynes (1936) has substantially contributed to the idea that market processes do not automatically ensure a national income level measuring up to potential output. Keynes considered sub-optimal curtailments of production and employment by effective demand as the normal case and, thus, saw a chronic need for action on the part of stabilisation policy. With decreases of investment activity, involuntary unemployment emerges. In such underemployment equilibria the unemployment rate is consistent with stable inflation (or rather with stable deflation). In the course of the multiplier process quantities react prior to prices. Due to adjustments of aggregate supply to the decrease in aggregate demand, price adjustments may not occur at all. However, Keynes only analysed the impacts of investment changes on national income and treated adjustments of aggregate supply in the course of the multiplier process essentially as unplanned reductions of inventory stocks (negative investments). Effects of investment changes on the capital stock were mostly disregarded in his primarily short-term-oriented theory. They were not investigated until the business cycle theories of the 1930s were further developed into growth theories.

2.4.6 Business Cycles and Economic Growth

Apart from Wicksellian cumulative processes and Keynesian multiplier analysis, the accelerator principle played an important part in business cycle theories of the interwar period.[22] According to this principle, investment demand overproportionally responds to a change in the demand for consumption goods and thus, by means of "accelerating" aggregate demand, generates corresponding fluctuations in macroeconomic production. Roy Harrod (1936) and Erik Lundberg (1937) almost synchronously discovered that a dynamic theory of the business cycle could be designed by combining the accelerator and the Keynesian investment multiplier. Lundberg (1937) developed formal models of sequences that couple both mechanisms by means of lags and, thus, generate a unique time structure.[23] In various scenarios he reconsidered Wicksellian and Keynesian models of economic

[21] Again, there are discrepancies between the positions of Keynes (1936) and the Keynesian standard interpretation known as the Neoclassical Synthesis during the post-war period. As pointed out by Laidler (1999), during the inter-war period advocating expansive fiscal policy to combat depression and unemployment was not a unique selling point that singled out Keynes and his supporters.

[22] See, e.g., the classic survey by Haberler (1937: ch. 3) as well as Boianovsky and Trautwein (2006c) for a documentation of contemporary discussions of the accelerator principle.

[23] For example, the well-known *Lundberg lag* characterises the time required for production to adjust to changes of effective demand.

upswings that, due to accelerator effects or measures of interest rate policy, may be reverted into a downswing but under certain conditions may also result in a new equilibrium state. That way, Lundberg (1937) designed a self-contained synthesis of macroeconomic theories that, unlike the contemporary and now "classical" approaches by Haberler (1937) and Hicks (1937), was strictly based on dynamic modelling.

However, Lundberg's modelling was so complex that it initially attracted little attention. Paul Samuelson (1939) employed its basic elements for a simpler and more general discussion about the dynamic stability of a multiplier-accelerator model of national income fluctuations. At the same time he followed Frisch's approach, in which an impulse causes fluctuations of the system that peter out in the course of time (see section 2.4.2). Samuelson demonstrated that multiplier-accelerator models are dynamically stable under plausible conditions. Samuelson's model became pathbreaking for the further advancement of business cycle theories.

However, Lundberg's *Studies in the Theory of Economic Expansion* (1937) are interesting not only as a synthesis of theories of the business cycle but also as a point of origin for modern growth theories. Unlike Keynes (1936) and other contemporaries, Lundberg employed multiplier analysis not primarily for the investigation of contractive processes but was chiefly interested in expansion. In a simple model of the circular flow of income and expenditures, the investment multiplier in eq. (2.1) can also be defined as the ratio of investment to macroeconomic output in a goods-market equilibrium:

$$Y = (1/s)\, I, \tag{2.1a}$$

where Y denotes aggregate demand, which in equilibrium must equal aggregate supply – and, hence, under the usual simplifying assumptions, represents national income as well. Erik Lundberg (1937), and after him Roy Harrod (1939) and Evsey Domar (1946), established that, via multiplier processes, investment has an effect not only on income but also on production capacities. It increases potential output and, hereby, alters the equilibrium position in the goods market.

Following Cassel's (1918) conception of the economy in a progressive state, Lundberg (1937: 183f. and 240f.) devised the conditions for a dynamic growth equilibrium (*steady state* growth equilibrium) that later became known as the Harrod-Domar model. The pivotal condition requires that aggregate demand grow at the same rate as productive capacity. This connection is illustrated by a few simple extensions of eq. (2.1a):

- The relationship between investment and national income, I/Y, can be expanded to $(I/K)(K/Y)$, where I/K denotes the capital stock (K) increment with $I = \Delta K$. This rate is also the growth rate of potential output, in the literature mostly written as "g". K/Y or "v", respectively, denotes the capital coefficient, i.e. the amount of capital required for the production of a specific national income level. From this it follows:

$$I/Y = gv. \tag{2.2}$$

- The multiplier term in the goods market equilibrium condition (2.1a) can be rewritten as $I/Y = s$. If g is understood as the capacity growth rate that sets the pace for employment (and, thus, labour demand as derived from demand for goods), inserting s into (2.2) and solving the equation for g yields the condition for *steady state* growth going with full employment:

$$g = s/v. \tag{2.3}$$

  g here is the desired growth rate since at this rate the income effect of investments on the demand side exactly matches their capacity effect on the supply side.[24]

The important part of this reasoning is that the progression of potential output is not independent of current demand. Changes in the volume of investments affect aggregate demand as well as aggregate supply. Discrepancies between current potential output and current demand, via their feedback effects on investment activity, also affect future potential output.

Harrod (1939) and Domar (1946) regarded the savings rate and the capital coefficient as institutionally given constants. The latter assumption, in particular, led to a shift of the discussion about the capacity effects of investments towards a debate about "unacceptable" dynamic instabilities of the *steady state* equilibrium. For any deviation of the current growth rate g gives rise to self-reinforcing capacity excesses or shortages, and any discrepancy between g and the "natural growth rate" (population growth plus increase in productivity) brings about incessantly rising under- or overemployment. The treatment of economic growth as a *razor edge equilibrium*, that is achieved coincidentally at best and results in the system's complete instability if the equilibrium conditions are not met, did not seem plausible (Solow, 1988). It prompted the design of models characterised by a stable *steady state*, brought about by endogenous changes of the capital coefficient.

Models of this type were developed by Robert Solow (1956) and Trevor Swan (1956) on the basis of a macroeconomic production function that exhibits positive but diminishing marginal returns at all points. Due to these and other features the Solow-Swan theory is labelled "Neoclassical Growth Theory" and is contrasted with the "post Keynesian growth theories" à la Harrod and Domar. Its vital attribute is the convergence of the equilibrium path of capital formation towards the long-term *steady state*, which is exogenously determined by the growth rates of population and productivity (as well as implicitly by consumer preferences and the state of technology). Since the Solow-Swan theory also presumes continuously cleared labour and capital markets, any discrepancy between current and potential

---

[24] This is a slightly modified version of Harrod's (1939) simple equation. Lundberg (1937: 185), by contrast, deduced the equilibrium growth equation by using a dynamic model and denoted the time path of income as: $Y(t) = c\, e^{t(s/v)}$. His advanced pioneer version was probably less noticed than Harrod's because it was stashed in a footnote in the context of a complex analysis of growth sequences (another reason might be that it did not stem from Oxbridge).

output as well as between the current and the desired growth rate are ignored.[25] Any potential effects such differences may exert on the progression of potential output are naturally disregarded as well. Potential output is determined solely by effective factor supply, adjusted for the effects of technical progress.

Nevertheless, the development of Neoclassical growth theory significantly influenced the development of methods for estimating potential output. Based on a Cobb-Douglas production function, Solow (1956) decomposed empirically observed growth rates into the contributions of labour, capital and technical progress (total factor productivity) by means of *growth accounting*. This procedure forms the basis of most "economic" estimations of potential output that are presently employed in political advisory (see section 2.6.2).

Even though in *mainstream* economics Neoclassical growth theory quickly prevailed over post-Keynesian theory, with Okun's law a reminiscence of the latter emerged. Okun (1962) demonstrated that the current growth rate of national income needs to equal or exceed the natural growth rate (the growth rate of population and productivity) in order to prevent an increase in unemployment. From an empirical point of view this only happens by way of an exception; the time series show a frequent occurrence of employment gaps that in the course of the business cycle are not automatically dismantled.

2.4.7 Inflationary Gaps and Output Gaps

Okun (1962) defined potential output as the macroeconomic output level associated with neither inflationary pressure nor unemployment (see section 2.2). Thus, it suggests itself to treat deviations of current demand from potential output directly as gaps: If demand exceeds potential output, in the very short run a (positive) *output gap* emerges. However, the overutilisation of productive capacities is accompanied by supply shortfalls and sooner or later gives rise to price pressures and an inflationary gap. Conversely, if demand falls short of potential output, a (negative) *output gap* arises. Since Wicksell (1898), the interest rate gap concept had served as an explanation for inflation, and since the early 1930s it had also been employed for explaining underutilisation and unemployment. The first formalised concepts of inflationary gaps and output gaps, however, emerged only after Keynes' *General Theory* (1936) had been published and were only indirectly related to it. Nevertheless, John Maynard Keynes and Erik Lindahl were key figures in the development of gap concepts that paved the way for Okun (1962).

The development of the inflationary gap concept is commonly accredited to Keynes (1940). In his collection of essays *How to Pay for the War* Keynes discussed the drastic increase in living costs that began to show in Great Britain at

[25] In the Solow-Swan model, the dynamic stability of the *steady state* is ensured only with respect to the coincidence of the desired with the natural growth rate, not with respect to the relationship between the current and the desired growth rate; see Hahn (1960). The problems associated with the use of a macroeconomic production function in Neoclassical growth theory are addressed in section 3.2.

the beginning of World War II. As Keynes (1940: 4 and 17) emphasised, this development constituted a reversal of the pre-war situation when the level of production constantly fell short of its potential capacity. In wartimes, capacities available for private consumption are drastically reduced and the nominal excess demand for obtainable consumption goods is bound to cause inflation (which could be subdued by means of price controls but not fully averted). Keynes proposed to prevent inflation by introducing a system of forced savings that accredits claims for higher income in the post-war period for the general public. Noteworthy is his attempt to determine potential output and the demand gap propelling inflation on the basis of data on productive capacity, national income and demand components (Keynes 1940: ch. III, IX and App. I). Bringing Keynes' (1936 and 1940) lines of reasoning together, the systematic relationships of potential and gaps can be represented by the "Keynesian cross", which is well-known from introductory macroeconomic textbooks (see Figure 1).[26]

The case of the output gap (or deflationary gap) is the typical case described by the simple investment multiplier according to Keynes (1936). In this model, aggregate demand (Y^d) and aggregate supply (Y^s) are presented as real quantities, and Y_1 is the aggregate supply in full-employment equilibrium, thus, equalling potential output. In the typical case the impulse for the emergence of an output gap is an autonomous decrease of investment ($I_0 < I_1$). This, via its impact on employment, income and consumption, leads to a fall of aggregate demand until underemployment equilibrium is achieved at the income level Y_0 ($Y^d = Y^s$ is below the level required for full employment). In the Keynesian model, quantities react prior to prices, and in the course of the multiplier process effective supply adjusts to aggregate demand after a time lag. Thus, there are no discrepancies between nominal and real variables, i.e. the inflation rate is zero. Effective supply decreases from Y_1 to Y_0. But given unchanged prices, the capital stock and labour supply in the short run have not been reduced, and potential output remains at the level Y_1. Therefore, the output gap can be written as the difference $Y_0 - Y_1$ and, provided data for the marginal rate of consumption and relevant aggregates are available, can also be quantified.

In the case of an inflationary gap, Y_0 forms the starting point of the consideration; Y^d and Y^s are nominal variables. The economy is in a state of full-employment equilibrium where current output matches potential output. If effective demand now rises – for instance, due to an increase in public spending ($G_1 > G_0$), as observed by Keynes (1940) on account of the war – aggregate supply cannot adjust in the short run due to shortages. A rise in prices sets in, which gradually increases nominal national income to the level Y_1 while its real (inflation-adjusted) value remains at Y_0. The difference $Y_1 - Y_0$ represents the inflationary gap.

[26] The Keynesian Cross has shaped didactics concerning circuit- and multiplier analysis since the first edition of Paul Samuelson's classic textbook (Samuelson, 1948).

Fig. 1. The Keynesian Cross

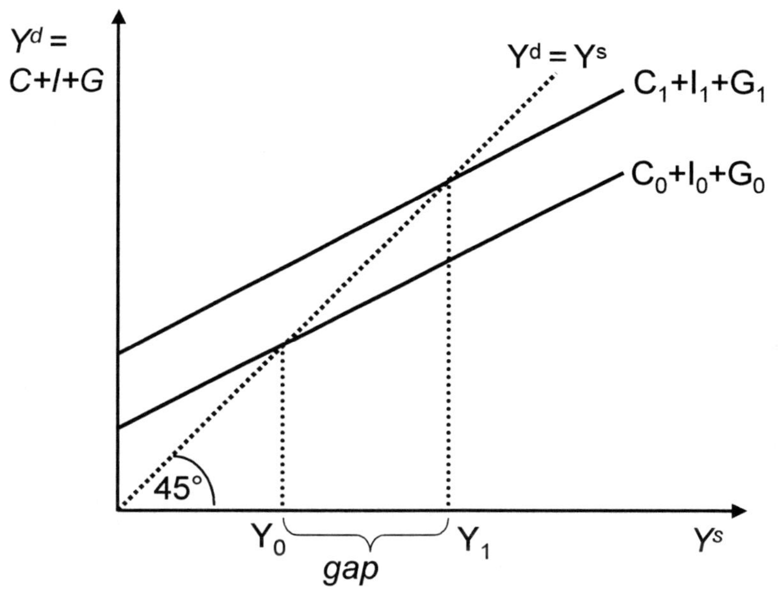

This simple representation of possible deviations from potential output is based on comparative-static equilibrium theory. In the 1940s and 1950s it was widely used in political advisory as well, especially in the U.S. and Great Britain. However, it did also meet criticism (e.g., by Friedman, 1942). Lundberg (1937: 196f.) in his dynamic periodic analysis investigated a sequence featuring inelastic factor supply and flexible prices, and using a numerical example he calculated the magnitude of an inflationary gap – even before Keynes made a similar attempt in 1940. Under the direction of Lundberg, the Swedish National Institute of Economic Research regularly calculated inflationary gaps from 1943 onward (Ohlsson, 1987; Berg, 1987). It was an attempt to determine both the actual inflation and the inflation suppressed by means of price control, which was caused by deviations of demand from potential output.

However, Lundberg and his colleagues were not quite convinced by their own endeavours. Apart from shortcomings in the data basis, the more fundamental problem of static analysis that potential output is an unobservable variable, which results from plans of both suppliers and buyers in goods and factor markets, forced them to make oversimplifying assumptions. Even if planned quantities and prices could be assessed by means of surveys, the effective potential output may deviate from the aggregate planned variables since plans need not necessarily be compatible. Adjustment processes of planned *(ex ante)* variables towards observed *(ex post)* results of the market process have to be explicitly modelled in order to distinguish price and quantity effects and to determine inflationary pressure.

In the tradition of the Stockholm School (see section 2.4.2), Turvey (1949), Hansen (1951), and Lundberg (1953) emphasised the importance of disequilibria between savings and investments but also between labour demand and supply. They demonstrated that consumption and investment functions are by no means as unalterable during the course of inflation as presumed in simple Keynesian approaches. Same as in the analyses by Lindahl and Myrdal, the formation of expectations concerning the progression of inflation played a vital part for Hansen and Lundberg. Expectations determine the answer to the questions whether inflationary pressure generates market forces that lead to a new equilibrium state with consistent plans and whether the new equilibrium state is different from the initial state in real terms. Moreover, similarly to Lindahl (1930) they discuss various cases where deviations of *ex post* from *ex ante* variables give rise to changes in budget constraints and revisions of plans in future periods. That way, adjustment processes in disequilibrium generate changes of the system's real equilibrium positions including potential output.[27]

2.4.8 Interim Conclusion

It is safe to say that for a complete *tour d'horizon* of the historical background of potential output analysis a number of other approaches could have been included in the story. However, the gap-theoretical approaches and their Wicksell and Keynes connections presented in this section contain the essential foundations of potential output analysis that were developed prior to Okun (1962). The arguments and characteristics can be summarized as follows:

- In a modern monetary economy, market rates of interest tend to deviate continuously from the level associated with zero inflation, full employment and full utilisation of productive capacities. The interest rate gaps give rise to divergences of aggregate demand and aggregate supply, which cause inflation and output gaps.
- Expectations on future monetary policy, inflation and real returns on investment play a pivotal part in the formation of both cumulative inflationary and deflationary processes (in Wicksellian approaches) and underemployment equilibria (in Keynesian approaches). The significance of the interaction between expectation formation and monetary policy is expressed, amongst other things, in the term structure of interest rates and has led, in the early 1930s, to propos-

[27] This primarily concerned the discussion of negative output gaps (or "deflationary gaps"). However, the existence of positive output gaps due to overutilisation of productive capacities and overemployment was not ignored. It was treated either as a concomitant of "suppressed inflation" (because of price regulations and the like), causing premature wearout of productive resources and bottlenecks, or as a short-lived pre-stage of inflation.

als of a rule-bound monetary policy aiming at the closure of the interest rate gaps.

- Investment is a key variable that affects both aggregate demand and aggregate supply. A joint characteristic of Wicksellian and Keynesian theory, which clearly distinguishes them from most Classical and Neoclassical approaches, is the treatment of the progression of potential output as **not** being independent of current demand.[28] Via their feedback effects on revenue expectations and investment, gaps between potential and currently demanded production affect future potential output as well.
- Potential output is not independent of monetary policy. Even though it is (explicitly or implicitly) used as a benchmark for current monetary policy, it is affected by the monetary policy of the past. Current monetary policy, thus, influences future potential output. This is also expressed in the term structure of interest rates.
- One major difference between Wicksellian and Keynesian theories concerns their methodological perspective: The former put emphasis on a dynamic analysis of disequilibria with a discrepancy of initial and final equilibrium states. The latter initially focussed on a comparative-static analysis of full-employment and underemployment equilibria and later on the analysis of growth equilibria.
- Even though literature at the time of the Great Depression and especially Keynes (1936) gave priority to the phenomenon of mass unemployment, macroeconomics in the first part of the 20th century primarily focussed on the analysis of interactions between goods markets and capital markets.

When Okun's conception entered stability and growth politics in the 1960s, the terms of debate about inflationary and output gaps had changed. The gaps became pitfalls in controversies about the existence of a stable long-term Phillips curve and the notion of a "natural rate of unemployment".

2.5 Phillips Curve Debates

2.5.1 Full Employment and Monetary Stability – A Trade-off?

Given the discussions about the danger of inflation in a state of full employment that seemed to be imminent in Europe as a result of the Korea boom and the reconstruction after the war, in the 1950s the counter question, how much unemployment is compatible with price-level stability, was already familiar.[29] But the notion of the non-inflationary unemployment rate, which today is known as the

[28] Wicksell (1898) himself, however, disregarded this aspect and focussed solely on the explanation of "secular inflation."

[29] See, e.g., Turvey (1952), Hague (1958, 1962), and Boianovsky and Trautwein (2006b).

NAIRU and seen in close connection with the concept of potential output, became the pivotal concept for defining potential output only when Friedman (1968) equated it with the "natural rate of unemployment" in the course of debates that centred on the Phillips curve. Consequently, in the following we outline those aspects of the Phillips curve controversies that are particularly important for the discussion of concepts of potential output.[30]

Fig. 2. Phillips curve and AD/AS model

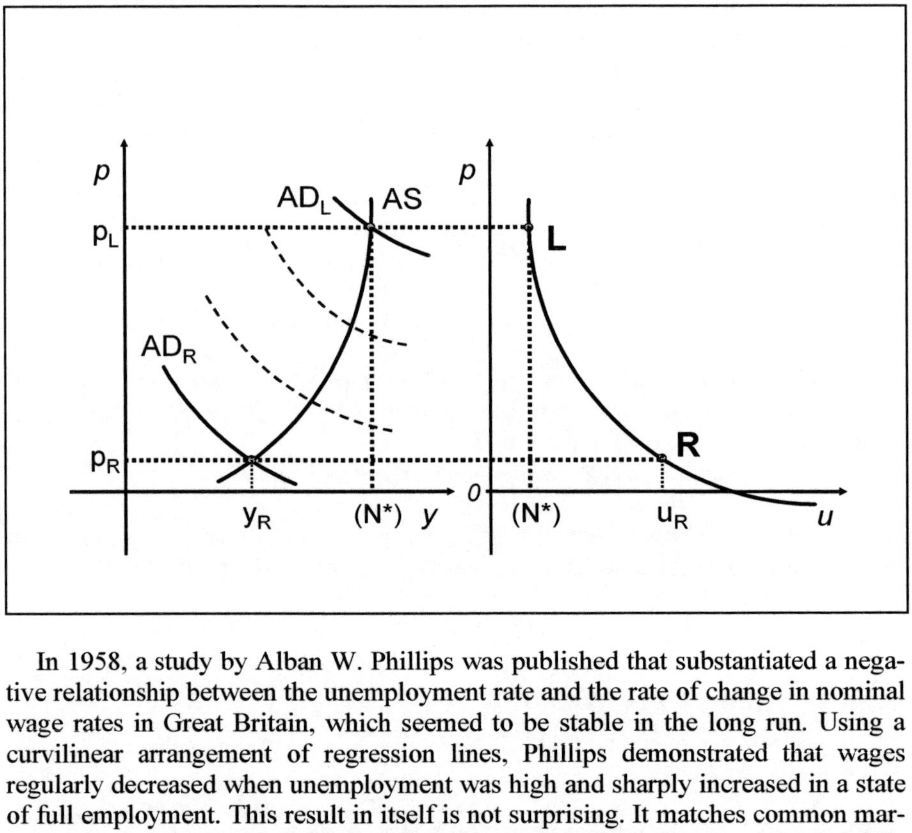

In 1958, a study by Alban W. Phillips was published that substantiated a negative relationship between the unemployment rate and the rate of change in nominal wage rates in Great Britain, which seemed to be stable in the long run. Using a curvilinear arrangement of regression lines, Phillips demonstrated that wages regularly decreased when unemployment was high and sharply increased in a state of full employment. This result in itself is not surprising. It matches common market logic that the price of labour rises when labour is in short supply and falls when there is an excess supply of labour. Two years later, however, the essay obtained brisance for economic policy debates, as Paul Samuelson and Robert Solow substituted the change rate of nominal wages by the rate of inflation based on some assumptions on the increase in productivity and profit mark-ups.

Samuelson and Solow (1960) proceeded on the assumption that a stable trade-off between inflation and unemployment prevails (p and u, respectively, in the right-hand side quadrant in Figure 2). Consequently, a goal conflict between monetary stability and full employment exists that obliges decision makers in eco-

30 For an overview, see Santomero and Seater (1978) and the contributions in Cross (1995).

nomic policy to choose between two "menus": either low inflation coupled with high unemployment or full employment coupled with high inflation. A government of the "left", which primarily represents the concerns of workers, chooses the latter combination (point *L* in Figure 2); a government of the "right", mainly representing the concerns of holders of financial wealth, chooses the former (point *R* in Figure 2). The trade-off illustrated by the Phillips curve gained plausibility because it was possible to deduce it from the AD/AS extension of the IS/LM model with the aid of Okun's law (section 2.2).[31] The usage of Okun's law as a link is intuitive because high economic growth as a rule implies full employment. In a state of low economic growth the number of unemployed rises. Also, in a state of strong economic growth, due to full utilisation of capacities, a tendency towards increasing prices exists. In general, boosts of growth are caused by increases in private investment activity and/or public spending that trigger multiplier processes. Consequently, they are treated as an outward shift of the AD curve. Proceeding on the plausible assumption that *nominal* wages are not entirely flexible, a relationship between the Phillips curve and the AD/AS model of the (traditional) Neoclassical Synthesis can be established.[32]

2.5.2 Inefficiency of Expansive Stabilisation Policy

The proposition that full employment can only be possible at the cost of inflation did not go unobjected for long. Edmund Phelps (1967) and Milton Friedman (1968) considered the concept of a Phillips curve that is stable in the long run as incompatible with rational economic behaviour. What matters for employees is what their money wages can buy, i.e. the *real* wage. Thus, an unambiguous relationship between unemployment and inflation does not exist. The level of employment in a state of labour-market equilibrium is compatible with any rate of inflation as long as nominal wages change in step. Following Wicksell's "natural rate of interest", Friedman coined the term "natural rate of unemployment" for the

---

[31] The AS/AD extension is a combination of the IS/LM analysis of product and financial markets and a Neoclassical labour market diagram. The linkage is established by means of a macroeconomic production function representing aggregate supply (AS) in the case of sticky real wages and/or of full employment. The aggregate demand curve (AD) represents the sequence of IS/LM equilibria given different price levels.

[32] Figure 2 illustrates this relationship in a simplified form that replaces the level of national income *(Y)* and the price level *(P)* by their rates of change, i.e. the economic growth rate *(y)* and the rate of inflation *(p)*: AD_R corresponds to a restrictive monetary and fiscal policy; if monetary and fiscal policy is expansive, the AD curve shifts upwards (AD_L). The intersection points of AD and AS (which is upward sloped and not vertical due to wage rigidities) represent macroeconomic equilibria. Higher growth and inflation rates are associated with higher employment as the real wages fall when nominal wages are sticky. Labour demand increases and labour supply declines until the theoretical full-employment point *(N*)* is reached. More employment means less unemployment and, thus, the Phillips curve mirrors the under- and full-employment equilibria in an economy with sticky wages.

level of unemployment that corresponds to theoretical full employment.[33] He defined the natural rate of unemployment as the result of rational choice acts determined by real economic factors (especially the fundamental data of technology and tastes, i.e. consumer preferences) but not by monetary policy.

Nevertheless, Friedman (1968) conceded that boosts of inflation might lower statistical unemployment in the short run. This can happen if employers have information about the progression of prices in advance of their employees. Such information asymmetries can prevail if workers and their representatives confound nominal wage increases in phases of expansion with corresponding increases in purchasing power and accordingly raise labour supply (step 1 in Figure 3). Due to this "money illusion", expansionary stabilisation policy can generate inflation that is underestimated. Sooner or later, however, workers will learn from their mistakes and correct their expectations on future inflation according to the observed rise of inflation. Friedman used the hypothesis of adaptive expectations – i.e. past expectational errors are taken into account in the formation of expectations concerning future time periods. In Friedman's view, deviations of unemployment from the "natural rate" are short-dated because of adaptive expectations. If workers succeed to negotiate wage increases that compensate their (earlier and) expected losses from inflation (when compared to expected real wage increases), labour demand falls since full employment is not profitable; if, however, these wage increases fail to occur, labour supply is reduced (step 2 in Figure 3).

Thus, according to Friedman (1968) and Phelps (1967), an inverse relationship between inflation and unemployment can only prevail in the short run. If, after the return to the natural rate of unemployment, expansionary monetary and fiscal policy tries to reduce unemployment anew (for example to the level u_p), the adaptation of expectations will push the next Phillips curve to a higher inflation rate and that Phillips curve will have a steeper slope (step 3 in Figure 3). This way, a host of short-term Phillips curves can be designed that, with increasing acceleration of inflation and inefficiency of expansionary policy, converges onto a vertical line.

The long-term Phillips curve is independent of inflation and will have an intersection at the point of observed unemployment and stability of the price level, i.e. at unemployment rate u_n (see Figure 3).

[33] The theoretical definition of full employment deviates from the statistical one as the latter also includes those who are registered as unemployed but who are not prepared to work at the equilibrium wage rate. However, Friedman (1968: 8) in his definition of full employment as "natural rate of unemployment" also included "frictional unemployment", which emerges due to structural imperfections in the labour market, for example, lacking information about job opportunities, mobility costs and stochastic changes of supply and demand.

Fig. 3. Accelerating Inflation

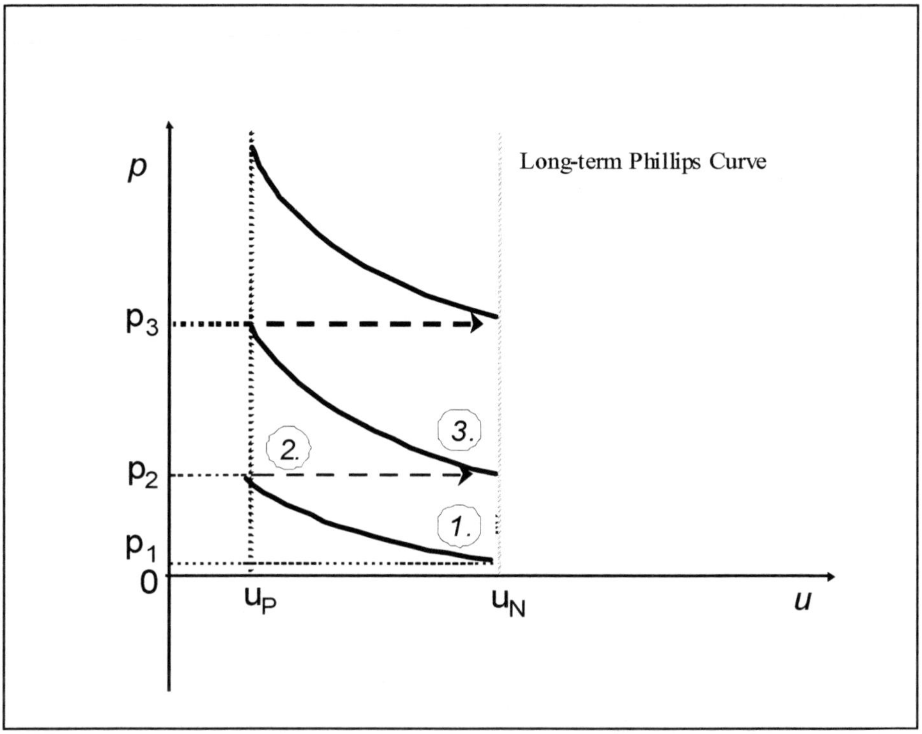

This implies that, with respect to real economic variables, monetary policy is neutral in the long run. Based on the long term Phillips curve, most mainstream economists directly equate the natural rate of unemployment with non-inflationary unemployment or the NAIRU.

Following from Friedman's (1968) concept of the natural rate of unemployment, the concept of potential output is implicitly defined as the level of national income compatible with the natural rate of unemployment. This leads to the conclusion that any stabilisation policy that aims at displacing the unemployment rate from its natural location causes only inflation gaps in the long run and not an increase in employment. It is, thus, inefficient as inflation causes adjustment costs and absorbs economic resources. Friedman and other Monetarists accordingly advocated a rule-bound monetary policy that prevents the emergence of money illusion and inflationary expectations by obliging the central bank to target a growth rate of the money supply that stabilises the value of money in terms of the (inverse of the) price level.

Criticism at the hypothesis of a stable Phillips curve trade-off was radicalised by Lucas (1972) and Sargent (1973). They considered the Monetarist hypothesis of adaptive expectations as irreconcilable with the basic principles of rational economic behaviour. Since it merely considers information related to the past, and, thus, constantly underestimates unidirectional changes in the rate of inflation, it allows for systematic errors in expectations and associated losses of real income. Lucas and Sargent replaced adaptive expectations with (Muth-)rational expectations. This hypothesis eliminates systematic expectation errors in all market activities; consequently the plans of the agents in the system are compatible.[34] Basically, expectations would be self-fulfilling in the absence of shocks – i.e. unpredictable events leading to deviations of reality from expectations.[35] Furthermore, Lucas and Sargent assumed completely flexible prices and continuous clearing of markets. Consequently, they concluded that measures of monetary and fiscal policy cannot shift the level of output and employment from their "natural" positions even in the short run. This could only be achieved by means of erratic, unpredictable economic policy, which cannot be any government's serious and lasting intention.

As demonstrated by Barro (1974), the Ricardian theorem of equivalence holds under the above-mentioned assumptions: Concepts of demand management by means of *deficit spending* are bound to fail as the private sector rationally expects present public spending to be funded by tax increases in the future. Since savings increase accordingly, the investment multiplier cannot take effect, and aggregate demand cannot affect potential output. The same assumptions were invoked by Sargent und Wallace (1975) in order to demonstrate that not only Keynesian measures of macroeconomic demand management but also Wicksellian prevention of inflation by means of interest rate management are bound to be ineffective because neither real aggregate demand nor the price level can be controlled by economic policy.

2.5.3 Time Inconsistency of Stabilisation Policy

The combined assumptions of rational expectations, flexible prices and continuous market clearing signified a "New Classical" revolution of macroeconomic thought in mainstream economics. From then on, any modelling of output fluctuations, unemployment and other macroeconomic phenomena were put under the categorical imperative of micro-theoretical foundations. This, in turn, was equated with the development of stochastic-dynamic versions of Walrasian general equilibrium theory. Until then, as outlined in section 2.4 with respect to gap theories, cyclical output fluctuations had generally been treated as deviations from the equilibrium potential output and growth trend; they were considered as disequilibria of aggregate demand and aggregate supply. Within the analytical framework of New Clas-

---

[34] Since models following the tradition of Lucas und Sargent are mostly confined to discussing the optimisation problem of a single "representative agent", compatibility of plans in the private sector is assumed rather than established; see, for example, Hoover (1988: ch. 9). Concerning the problems of learning behaviour and the convergence towards rational expectations, an extensive literature has developed, with Howitt (1992) and Evans and Honkapohja (2001) as outstanding contributions.

[35] Formally, shocks are stochastic events with an objective expected value of zero, i.e. "white noise". The hypothesis of rational expectations as used in mainstream theory dates back to Muth (1961).

sical economics, short-term output fluctuations had to be representable as continuous equilibria. Deviations of current GDP growth rates and unemployment rates from their "natural" levels were explicable as the result of inefficient economic policy at best. Both lines of argument (policy errors and equilibrium business cycles) were further advanced by Edward Prescott and Finn Kydland.

Fig. 4. Time Inconsistency of Monetary Policy

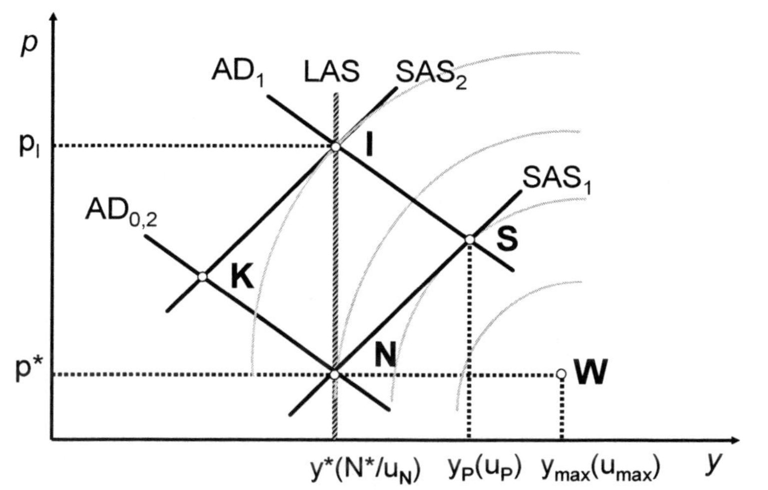

The first advancement of New Classical economics with respect to potential output concerned the demonstration that rule-bound stabilisation policy is economically optimal. As argued by Kydland and Prescott (1977) as well as Barro and Gordon (1983), discretionary policy would not be credible, even if it were explicitly aiming at monetary stability.[36] If this goal (N at the inflation rate p^* in Figure 4) were actually achieved, it would offer an incentive for the government to promote growth and employment by means of low interest rates and a high level of public spending ($AD_0 \rightarrow AD_1$). This way, tax revenues and the chances of a re-

[36] The term "discretionary" describes a policy that determines the optimal reaction as necessity arises. The favoured price level in Figure 4, defined as a low inflation rate (p^*) rather than zero inflation, is in accordance with the standard target definitions concerning inflation, which take account of measurement errors and similar problems.

election could be increased.[37] The resulting inflationary push is the prerequisite for the intended positive output gap to emerge (y^*-y_p) at the equilibrium point *S*. The private sector would have to underestimate inflation to the extent that the long-term, "natural" supply position *(LAS)* is displaced by a higher growth equilibrium *(SAS_1)* in the short run. Since the agents in the market realise the incentives for this kind of "surprise inflation" *(S)* once it has happened, the expansionary effects of such measures quickly vanish. With rational expectations, the private sector will accommodate its plans such that higher inflation rates result but no gain in real growth *($SAS_1 \rightarrow SAS_2$)*. The economy will settle in the inflation-bias equilibrium *I*.

Announcing a policy of inflation prevention is understood as a game between the government and the private sector in which the government's position is dynamically inconsistent and, thus, not credible. Even if the government does not have "surprise inflation" in mind, an inflation bias arises from time inconsistency. This constantly causes adjustment costs and runs counter to both the government's intentions and the private sector's interests.[38] If political decision makers try to break inflationary expectations by means of high interest rates *($AD_1 \rightarrow AD_2$)*, a negative output gap emerges and – according to Okun's law – a substantial increase in unemployment results.[39] Literature initiated by Kydland and Prescott (1977) and Barro and Gordon (1983) concluded that credibility could only be achieved by a stabilisation policy that restricts itself to clear rules with respect to combating inflation. Strict adherence to a rule of monetary policy that retains the system at the equilibrium point *N* prevents the emergence of positive and negative output gaps from the outset and ensures that current GNP and potential output coincide.

In the 1980s and 1990s, the relationship between time inconsistency and binding rules in monetary and fiscal policy gained much attention and promoted a vast amount of literature. This can be explained in part by the incipient popularity of game-theoretical models that were readily applied in this field, in part by preliminary considerations concerning the design of the European Monetary Union. In textbook literature and political discussion, time inconsistency is still invoked to advocate rule binding of monetary and fiscal policy. However, in the light of

---

[37] Policy calculus can be represented by means of a social welfare function or utility maximisation on the part of political decision makers (following the theory of political business cycles by Nordhaus, 1975). The point *W* in Figure 4 thus represents either maximum social welfare or maximum votes. The concentric indifference curves describe, in the manner of topographic lines, declining levels of welfare or utility towards the upper left side.

[38] While in cases of discretionary policy *N* and *S* denote unstable equilibria, *I* represents a stable inflation equilibrium associated with a lower welfare level (or politician utility level) than in the original equilibrium state *N*.

[39] The equilibrium AD_2/SAS_2 in Figure 4 corresponds to the constellation AD_R/AS in Figure 2. However, as opposed to the Phillips curve in the Samuelson/Solow version, this situation is unstable as it is based on a disinflationary shock and erroneous expectations of product suppliers.

common evidence concerning measures of monetary and fiscal policy and their well-known lagged effects, the idea of a surprise inflation and inflation propensity is hardly plausible, especially if rational expectations are assumed.[40]

2.5.4 Equilibrium Business Cycles

Real business cycle theory (RBC) constitutes the second advancement of New Classical economics with respect to potential output. Prior to New Classical economics, business cycles were commonly considered as disequilibria of aggregate demand and aggregate supply. Following Lucas (1972), the first wave of New Classical economics explained business cycle fluctuations as phenomena of equilibria under incomplete information concerning monetary policy, i.e. as unexpected shifts of aggregate demand that trigger responses from aggregate supply. Kydland's and Prescott's (1982) approach went even further: It attempted at explaining stylised facts of business cycle theory[41] entirely as optimal responses to real shocks that solely emerge on the supply side.

RBC theory is radical in its negation of the business cycle as an independent phenomenon discernable from growth. Any fluctuations of macroeconomic activity are treated as consequences of changes in the reference data of general equilibrium theory. Monetary impulses and other factors that, according to prior theories, affect the business cycle are disregarded in order to exhaust the explanatory potential of general equilibrium theory. The RBC approach consists in constructing "stylised" dynamical models of stochastic growth processes in an Arrow-Debreu framework. In general, these models are limited to the decision problem of a representative household (or social planner) that over an infinite time horizon optimises consumption and leisure time, and they exclude any problems caused by heterogeneity, incomplete information and other frictions.[42]

According to Frisch's impulse propagation scheme (see section 2.4.2), technological shocks are the most important exogenous impulses that, by being processed within the intertemporal optimisation system of consumption and leisure time, are transmitted to investment, employment and output. Assuming that households aspire to smooth their consumption over their life cycle, it is demon-

---

[40] See Spahn (2006: 230f.) and the critique in Section 2.5.5 of the present report.

[41] According to a long tradition following Mitchell (1913), Haberler (1937), and Lucas (1977), stylised facts confirmed by a multitude of empirical studies and explicable by any business-cycle theory are said to be:
- cyclical variability of the main macroeconomic aggregates;
- positive correlation (pro-cyclical progression) of fluctuations of GDP, productivity, prices, profits, investment and consumption;
- the accelerator principle (investment fluctuates more forcefully than consumption).

[42] As stated by Lucke (2002: 3), under these drastically simplifying assumptions there remains an economy reduced to its bare essentials – a caricature of an economy. RBC theory maintains that this caricature exhibits the true nature of mid-term fluctuations more clearly than the multitude of existing portraits.

strated that positive technological shocks bring about increasing systems activity and, thus, resemble a boom in the business cycle: If, due to product and process innovations, productivity rises, current attainable real income increases. This causes a substitution of present leisure and consumption for future leisure and consumption as well as an increase in current employment, production and investment. The latter gives rise to a corresponding change of the capital stock, thereby making the productivity shocks' effect persistent.[43] By the same logic, negative productivity shocks diminish real activities manifesting as recessions.[44]

In RBC theory, the trend around which the observed variables of real activities fluctuate corresponds to equilibrium positions of the system in the absence of shocks. However, these shocks are considered as random, and their effects are not readily reconcilable with the stylised fact of cyclical variability of macroeconomic aggregates. Cyclical variability implies certain regularities and a systematic relationship of positive and negative deviations from the trend. In RBC theory, endogenous regular fluctuations are excluded, but internal feedbacks as a temporary phenomenon (decreasing fluctuations) can be generated by choosing appropriate types of equations (e.g., second order difference equations). Conformance of RBC models with stylised facts is normally achieved by calibrating model parameters, conducting model simulations on this basis and comparing the simulation results with statistical time series. Due to various restrictions, RBC models are not suitable for forecasting business cycles but – again based on their restrictions – are employed for identifying macroeconomic shocks in structural vector autoregressive (SVAR) models.[45]

Within the framework of RBC theory, the ideas of a "growth trend" and "current output" have nothing to do with the distinction between potential output and output gaps. As any fluctuations of macroeconomic output are treated as optimal responses to shocks, current output is considered to be pareto-efficient and equivalent to potential output. Thus, there is no need for political action with respect to stabilising output to match the growth trend – on the contrary: Such kinds of interventions would cause welfare losses because of their implicit tax burdens. Accordingly, in RBC theory, output gaps are representable as a result of government failure at best. In this respect, RBC theory is related to the Monetarist and monetary New Classical criticism of the idea of a stable long-term Phillips curve (sections 2.5.2 and 2.5.3).[46]

RBC theory is a research programme rather than a specific theory of the business cycle, and nowadays the choice of shocks causing fluctuations is made in a less dogmatic manner. The original modelling strategy showed fundamental weaknesses, especially with respect to the explanation of fluctuations of consump-

---

[43] In some RBC models this persistence co-determines the growth trend, but in general the trend is treated as independent.

[44] Negative productivity shocks include all events that increase unit costs of production – for example, massive increases in energy prices, costly charges or climatic and political catastrophes (like droughts, storms and war).

[45] See Lucke (2002). Some of these restrictions are discussed in sections 2.6.2 and 3.3.

[46] A similar argument is put forward by Lucas (1995 and 2003).

tion and employment.[47] Thus, outside the "strictly New Classical core", experiments with different types of real as well as monetary shocks are conducted, and the mechanisms of transmission are modified by integrating "frictions". The approach is now more aptly labelled as DSGE approach *(Dynamic Stochastic General Equilibrium)*. The New Neoclassical Synthesis outlined in section 2.3 is based on the DSGE approach enhanced to encompass inertia and inflexibility of prices and other nominal variables. In the framework of the new synthesis, the original RBC theory is but an indirect reference core for determining output gaps. Each RBC equilibrium represents the purely hypothetical potential output in an environment of perfect competition; it is the reference equilibrium for the "actual" potential output under monopolistic competition *and* price flexibility (see, e.g., Woodford 2003: ch. 3-4). As such, it provides the basis for determining welfare losses caused by monopolistic pricing power (*deadweight losses)*. These welfare losses need to be distinguished from welfare losses due to price inflexibilities *(output gaps)*, which are caused by a deviation of current production from potential output under monopolistic competition.

2.5.5 Persistent Unemployment

While New Classical thoughts became established in academic macroeconomics during the 1980s, Monetarist and Keynesian ideas remained dominant in the realms of stabilisation policy and the media. The concept of a non-inflationary unemployment rate (NAIRU) gained more and more importance as a reference variable for stabilisation policy. If the NAIRU is considered as the natural rate of unemployment encompassing only "structural" unemployment, which is not susceptible to influences by monetary policy and with respect to labour input conforms to potential output, it provides a simple rule for action for monetary policy, similar to Wicksell's rule of interest (section 2.4.1):

- If current unemployment is lower than the NAIRU, interest rates must be raised in order to reduce inflationary pressure.
- If current unemployment is higher than the NAIRU, interest rates must be cut in order to close the output gap.

As the combined time path of inflation and unemployment between the early 1970s and the early 1990s in the U.S. was consistent with the idea of a vertical Phillips curve and a NAIRU of about 6%, the interest rate policy of the Federal Reserve System seemed to be fairly predictable by the above-mentioned procedure.

In Europe, however, and especially in the core countries of the European Monetary Union, the NAIRU left, from the 1980s onwards, the impression of a highly unsteady variable showing substantial increases from one period of high in-

[47] A well-known weak point is the explanation of mass unemployment during the Great Depression. As no evidence for sufficiently negative productivity shocks could be found, the less than plausible hypothesis of a sudden outbreak of contagious sloth (increased preferences for leisure) was all that remained.

terest rates to the next. Consequently, the convention of equating the NAIRU with "natural unemployment", which is independent of monetary policy and basically of voluntary character, was called into question. Attempts were made to systematically analyse the structural causes of persistent mass unemployment within the framework of both a micro- and macroeconomically founded theory of the labour market. These efforts are particularly relevant for forecasting the growth of potential output as estimations of the NAIRU are frequently employed in structural and semi-structural methods of forecasting. The literature dealing with the identification of the NAIRU and persistent unemployment is diverse and extensive. For an overview, see Bean (1994) and Wyplosz (1994). With respect to potential output, two concepts are particularly important: the quasi-equilibrium rate of unemployment (QUERU) and hysteresis.

Unlike (Neo-)Classical analysis, modern labour market theories do not proceed on the assumption of perfect competition.[48] With reference to real world behaviour, the presumption is that, due to market power and negotiation authority, wages and prices are ordinarily set by suppliers or buyers. Individual labour supply of employees (N^s in Figure 5) is not disregarded. However, it solely provides a point of reference that is represented as the usual intertemporal substitution calculus concerning consumption and leisure (w/P denoting the real wage). Based on empirical studies, a low elasticity of wages and a lower bound at the level of the reservation wage (w_R/P) are assumed.[49] Presuming a Neoclassical labour demand curve (N^d) with marginal costs of labour corresponding to (decreasing) marginal productivity, the Neoclassical labour-market equilibrium with purely voluntary unemployment is reached at N^*_{hyp}. Thus, the difference between the maximum potential labour supply L and labour supply at the market wage in N^*_{hyp} represents "natural unemployment" (u_N).

However, market-clearing equilibrium is purely hypothetical if wages in the labour market do not result from individual labour supply but from wage setting behaviour on the part of unions and employers (*WS* curve in Figure 5). Recent labour market theories explain this kind of wage setting behaviour for the most part by means of the *insider-outsider* approach[50] or efficiency wage theory.[51] Both ap-

[48] The development of modern labour-market economics is, for example, surveyed by Layard, Nickell, and Jackman (1991), Franz (1996), and Carlin and Soskice (2006: ch. 4 and 18).

[49] The reservation wage corresponds to the opportunity costs of taking up work, for example, the magnitude of social transfers received in the case of unemployment.

[50] The insider-outsider approach rests on the assumption that in wage bargaining trade unions, which mainly represent employees *(insiders)*, make use of the cost disadvantages that employers face if they hire competing unemployed *(outsiders)* due to the required transfer of knowledge specific to the enterprise, prevention of conflicts etc. This generates a real wage level that renders the recruitment of *outsiders* unprofitable.

[51] According to efficiency wage theory, the wage rate is not an absolute cost factor to be minimised (as on the N^d curve in Figure 5) but is also invoked as a performance incentive in the presence of asymmetrical information about work performance. The higher the state of employment, the more enterprises make use of fringe benefits in order to ensure the commitment of well-skilled employees. When optimising their price and wage

proaches may also be combined. Due to wage setting on the *WS* curve, labour-market equilibrium is attained at a market wage higher than in N^*_{hyp}. At this real wage *(w/P*)*, effective labour demand matches the labour supply that is effective for employees because of cost concerns. The effective labour-market equilibrium N^* is not a market-clearing but a rationing equilibrium.

Fig. 5. Quasi-Equilibrium Unemployment

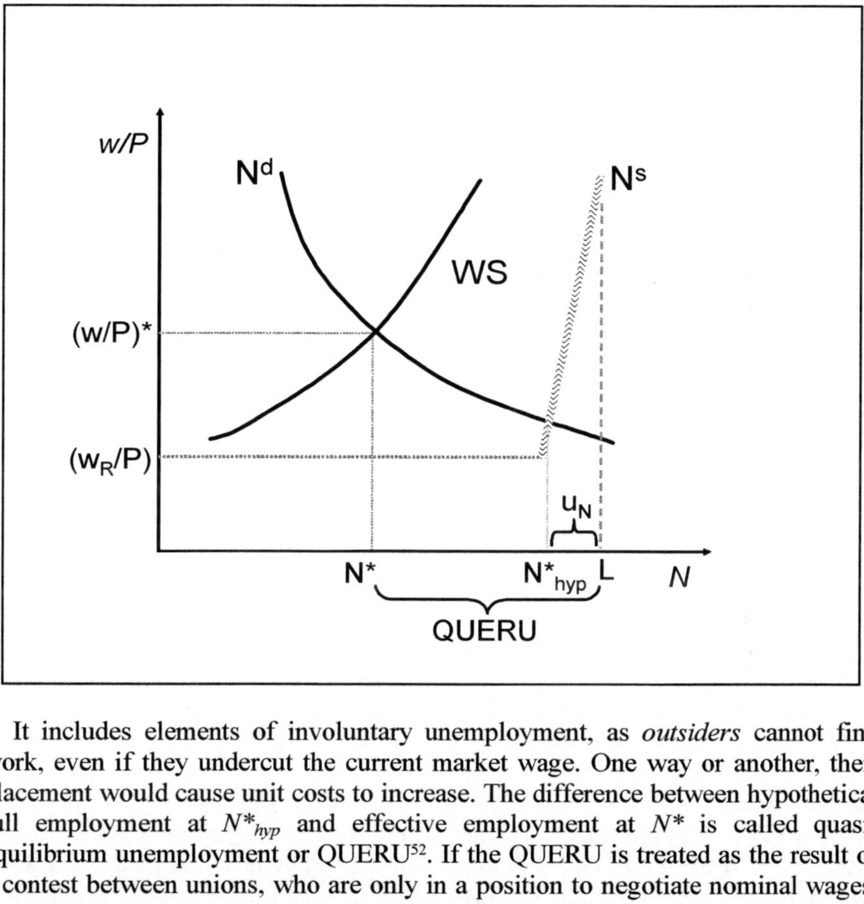

It includes elements of involuntary unemployment, as *outsiders* cannot find work, even if they undercut the current market wage. One way or another, their placement would cause unit costs to increase. The difference between hypothetical full employment at N^*_{hyp} and effective employment at N^* is called quasi-equilibrium unemployment or QUERU[52]. If the QUERU is treated as the result of a contest between unions, who are only in a position to negotiate nominal wages, and price-setting employers, wage-price spirals may emerge *(battles over mark-ups)*. This amounts to an upward movement along the long-term vertical Phillips curve, provided that the relationship between nominal wages and prices remains stable with differing rates of inflation. If, however, the rates of increase of inflation and wages can be driven down to approach zero, the QUERU matches the

settings (the N^d curve being interpreted as price setting curve including a profit mark-up), enterprises set the real wage (at N^*) above the market-clearing level (at N^*_{hyp}).

52 QUERU stands for "quasi-equilibrium rate of unemployment".

NAIRU. It exceeds, nevertheless, the "natural rate of unemployment" in the sense of a market-clearing equilibrium (by the difference of $QUERU - u_N$ in Figure 5).

In the formation phase of a QUERU, its difference to the natural rate of unemployment could be considered as a negative output gap as in this situation potential output exceeds current output. However, the separation of *insiders* and *outsiders* may consolidate quite rapidly after the increase of unemployment. Along with their job, displaced workers lose part of their qualification whilst others are not in a position to acquire the specific human capital of *insiders* in the first place. Thus, a lasting rise of the QUERU connotes a decline of potential output as *outsiders* are no longer considered as efficient labour suppliers by potential employers. Temporary increases in real wages can therefore give rise to persistent unemployment since the displaced workers, owing to the cost increase, after a short time no longer match up to the job requirements. Underemployment does not even vanish if subsequently real wages fall to their original level (e.g., due to increases in consumer prices or longer labour time without compensatory wage increases). In economic literature this continuance of effects after their causes have vanished is commonly termed "hysteresis" or (in the case of gradual abatement) "persistence".[53]

Recent labour market theories can, thus, explain the existence of persistent involuntary underemployment and corresponding decreases in potential output by invoking assumptions about imperfect competition, asymmetrical information and other types of "frictions". In the simplest case of *insider-outsider* theory, both the triggering shocks (excessive wage claims) and the propagation mechanisms (downward rigid wages, costs of conflicts, devaluation of human capital etc.) are described as malpractices on the part of wage-setting institutions on the labour supply side (unions, minimum wages regulations, dismissal protection etc.). However, unemployment through hysteresis may also be caused by efficiency wages set by employers and, in this sense, is a labour demand problem. In many industries or countries, labour markets are characterised by wage setting that results from combinations of collective bargaining and efficiency wage considerations. From an empirical point of view, a clear separation of unemployment caused by demand side factors versus supply side factors is hardly possible.

In the cases considered up to this point, involuntary unemployment and curtailment of potential output is solely caused by the process of wage setting in the labour market – as opposed to Keynesian models that explain involuntary unemployment as the result of pessimistic revenue expectations in the goods market and asset holders' liquidity preference (see section 2.4.4). Combinations of both lines

[53] See, e.g., Franz (1987) and Cross (1995). While under the keyword *hysteresis* unemployment is examined as a time sequence, the same phenomenon represents a mismatch when considered as a cross-section at a point in time: The qualifications that firms require are not matched by those offered by workers. Thus, if unemployment is explained as a phenomenon of hysteresis and mismatch, the investigation of the macroeconomic labour market is no longer confined to the dimensions of price (real wage) and quantity (employment). The quality of labour (differences in qualification and other performance criteria) is taken into account as well.

of argument are discernable in the extensive literature that explains the instability of the NAIRU in European countries since the mid 1970s by central bank rallies of disinflation following the oil price shocks OPEC I and II as well as German reunification (see, e.g., Bean, 1989; Gärtner, 1997; Ball, 1999; Spahn, 2006: ch. 4.4). In this framework, the real economic losses resulting from combating inflation by means of rising nominal interest rates are quantified as sacrifice ratios in terms of negative output gaps or cumulative changes of the unemployment rate in relation to disinflation (the decline of the inflation rate). The general explanation of the magnitudes of the sacrifice ratios invokes several transmission channels of monetary policy:

- In the labour market, the decline of inflation causes real wages to rise if nominal wages are not reduced to the same extent immediately. As individually rational contract obligations, relative wage settings and other forms of wage rigidities exist, such reductions can be expected in exceptional cases at best. Consequently, as outlined, QUERU or hysteresis unemployment may emerge.
- Unexpected or unexpectedly strong declines of inflation can cause substantial declines of aggregate demand as entrepreneurial revenue expectations are disappointed. A small open economy might be able to increase its exports due to a cost-cutting edge of disinflation; however, considering the international interest-rate nexus, generating this kind of advantage will be difficult.
- The decrease of inflation caused by the rise of nominal interest rates amounts to a substantial increase in real interest rates. This not only dampens entrepreneurial investment activity but may also bring about a devaluation of real capital by increasing real indebtedness. Thus, the decline of investment and capital devaluation diminish the capital stock and persistently reduce potential output – analogously to the losses of qualification in the labour market, which may be further aggravated by company closures and rationalisation measures due to capital shortages.
- Comparing sacrifice ratios, there is no clear evidence that central banks, which adher to clear rules and enjoy higher credibility for combating inflation have been more successful in cutting the costs of disinflation compared to central banks in "soft currency countries", which ran discretionary policies during the period in question. In some studies, the central banks of "hard currency countries" performed even worse (see, e.g., Gärtner, 1997; Spahn, 2006: 60). It is possible that the "expectation channel" of monetary policy does not quite work as suggested by models of time inconsistency in the manner of Barro and Gordon (1983) (see section 2.5.3).
- Explanations for the unexpected effects in the expectation channel range from rational price inflexibility to individually rational but macroeconomically excessive price flexibility. In the first case it is assumed that in countries with comparably low inflation rates, contract obligations featuring fixed prices are beneficial, and adaptive expectations suffice. Consequently, a comparatively moderate increase of interest rates has more substantial effects on quantities than in other countries. The second case primarily refers to the comparatively high interest elasticity of asset prices (and derivative contracts) in financial and real estate markets. It is also widely acknowledged by now that in the case of

negative supply shocks (such as OPEC I and II), restrictive demand management can cause persistent negative output gaps.

2.5.6 Interim Conclusion

Overall, the progression and present status of the Phillips curve debates can be preliminarily summed up as follows:

- By now, economists are largely in agreement that when moving upward along the Phillips curve, an *inflation-unemployment trade-off* does not exist: High employment and full utilisation of potential output cannot, in the long run, be bought with an increase in inflation.
- Also, a great majority of economists advocates rule-bound policies of inflation prevention on the part of an independent central bank.
- Primarily for reasons of research strategy, New Classical approaches still proceed on the assumption that rationally anticipated inflation (or disinflation) cannot affect potential output.
- By contrast, labour market theories and empirical studies conclude that, when moving downward along the Phillips curve, the inflation-unemployment trade-off in the process of disinflation may exist even if the central bank is credible in fighting inflation: The interplay between demand losses and various mechanisms that devaluate human and real capital on the supply side initially gives rise to a negative output gap that (in the absence of positive "counter-shocks") vanishes only because potential output correspondingly adjusts to the lower level of demand. Strictly speaking, the NAIRU, and along with it the hypothetically vertical long-term Phillips curve, is shifted within short time towards an equilibrium with higher unemployment and a diminished potential output.
- New Neoclassical Synthesis attempts to demonstrate that inefficient monetary policy may cause persistent output gaps even if the equilibrium-theoretical imperative of New Classical economics holds. Investment-theoretical extensions of the synthesis (e.g., Woodford, 2003: ch. 5) include output gaps that cause feedback effects on the progression of potential output.

2.6 Empirics and Politics

2.6.1 The Progression of National Accounting

For estimating potential output and output gaps, aggregate data on production, investments, employment and other macroeconomic variables are required. However, when gap theories had their heyday in the 1930s, no national accounting existed and labour market statistics were inconsistent and fragmentary. To wit, in response to the waves of inflation and deflation following World War I, encompassing systems of price indices had been developed, mostly at Irving Fisher's suggestion. Also, in many countries instruments for monitoring the business cycle existed, frequently designed in the style of the famous Harvard barometer, which included various indicators for the situation in the money markets, asset markets and goods markets. However, macroeconomic data giving information about potential output were scarce. In view of the reparation obligations specified in the Versailles treaty, Germany in particular, had an enormous interest in assessing productive capacities. Still, the German Statistical Office conducted only sporadic calculations but no systematic surveys.[54]

The Great Depression and especially World War II initiated extensive national and international activities aiming at a systematic collection of macroeconomic data. Aided by the Rockefeller Foundation, the League of Nations under Bertil Ohlin (1931/32), Gottfried Haberler (1934-36), and Jan Tinbergen (1936-38) commissioned comprehensive investigations of the Great Depression, the synthesis potential of business cycle theories and their empirical assessment.[55] Even so, it was not until the post-war period that a UN commission under the leadership of Richard Stone published standards for a systematic national accounting (United Nations 1947) and the large-scale, continual collection of macroeconomic data set in. In 1952, Stone's guidelines were expanded to form the first standardised *System of National Accounts* (SNA) by the United Nations and the OEEC (the predecessor organisation of the OECD), a system that was reformed in 1968 and 1993 and until today builds the international foundation of national accounting.[56]

In retrospect, the inter-war period was characterised by an interesting multitude of attempts to develop national accounting on the basis of macroeconomic theory. According to textbook folklore, chapter 6 of Keynes (1936) and its defining $Y = C + I$, $S = Y - C$, *ergo* $I = S$ is considered the decisive impetus for the progression of modern national accounting. But history is more complex and commenced prior to that. Some of the Wicksellian approaches outlined in section 2.3 as well as other initiatives played a significant part. To mention only a few examples:

- In the UK, the first estimations of national income were presented by Colin Clark in 1932, followed by Simon Kuznets (1934) in the United States. Both studies already featured the basic traits of output, income and final expenditure compilation, and especially Clark's estimations had an influence on Keynes (Patinkin, 1976).

---

[54] For example, according to Krengel (1986: 20) for the first and only time in the weekly report of the German Institute for Economic Research (DIW-Wochenbericht) No. 38/40, December 23, 1929.

[55] The best-known result of these activities is Haberler's classic on "Prosperity and Depression" (1937); see also Boianovsky and Trautwein (2006c).

[56] An extensive overview of the history of national accounting is presented by Vanoli (2005). In what follows, we merely address the evolution of national accounting. The development of labour market statistics used for estimating the NAIRU cannot be covered here.

- Since the early 1930s, Jan Tinbergen in the Netherlands and Ragnar Frisch in Norway developed econometric models of the economic cycle, which in both countries were employed as a basis for calculating national product.
- Erik Lindahl combined his cooperation in the major study on Swedish national income from 1861 to 1930 (Lindahl, Dahlgren, & Kock, 1937) with the conception of theoretical foundations for defining, in the style of Irving Fisher, national income as a flow of yields on capital, and systematically coupling stock and flow calculations (Lindahl, 1933 and 1939: Part I).
- At Harvard in 1932, Wassily Leontief developed input-output analysis based on suggestions he had gained in the course of his work at the Kiel Institute for the World Economy (1927 to 1930). By means of matrix systems that record the economy's inter-industry relations and the contributions of the individual sectors to national product, Leontief investigated the inter-industry flows necessary to achieve macroeconomic equilibrium, given the level of final demand and coefficients of technology. With this he built the foundation for structural investigations of potential output.

The emphasis put on macroeconomic aggregates in Keynes' *General Theory of Employment, Interest and Money* (1936) was doubtlessly important for the concept formation in national accounting. Keynes' definition of savings as a variable adjusting *ex post* to investment via the income mechanism (multiplier) cut the Gordian knot of prior debates about the empirical representation of the process of capital formation.

But it was not until Keynes, on account of the war, in his collection of essays [How to Pay for the War] (1940) used Clark's concepts and data to introduce the calculation of inflationary gaps that systematic efforts of establishing a system of national accounting were started. The trailblazers of this endeavour were James Meade and Richard Stone, who pointed out a theoretically consistent three-tier system for calculating national income via income, production and expenditure (Meade & Stone, 1941). This approach became decisive for the development of output, income and final expenditure compilation at the various stages of the SNA. In the beginning, however, this concept was controversial. The Meade-Stone system concentrated on national income at factor costs using simple accounting entries of monetary transaction values and entrepreneurial information on depreciation as well as nominal interest rates to capture the factor costs of real capital. By contrast, the Scandinavians around Frisch and Lundberg had developed systems that followed the principle of double-entry accounting, determined a range of national product aggregates, kept real and financial transactions apart, calculated the "real" reinvestment requirements by including repair and maintenance expenditure and tried to distinguish between market rates of interest and "real" costs of capital.[57]

---

[57] See Ohlsson (1987). The respective debates took place in the late 1940s and, thus, even before Tobin's q was developed. A concept corresponding to Tobin's q had already been developed by Myrdal (1931, 1933) according to whom real net investment rises until the present value of the net investment goods equals their reproduction costs. Tobin's q is likewise based on the relationship between the present value of an investment good and

The heydays of the Keynesian concepts of aggregate demand management were all at once the heydays of national accounting and related data systems. From the 1950s to the 1970s, survey methods and databases were forcefully expanded, mostly according to SNA standards but with numerous national peculiarities (Vanoli, 2005: Part II). The increasing impact of public sector actions on the economy's growth and stability required plentiful information that was gathered by national accounting, input-output analysis, labour market statistics and other instruments. The integration of economic theory and statistics were further advanced by the development of extensive macroeconometric models. A leading part was played by the Cowles Commission (later Cowles Foundation) in the U.S., the statistical-econometric institute INSEE in France and the Centraal Planbureau in the Netherlands. International organisations, especially the OEEC (later: OECD) and the International Monetary Fund, increasingly used national accounting for short- and medium-term forecasting. Since these institutions by their nature had (and still have) to work out international comparisons, they became driving forces in the definition of standards for macroeconomic data.

However, since the 1980s a schism has emerged in the coupling of macroeconomic empirics, theory and politics. On the one hand, the predominance of Monetarist and especially New Classical ideas in mainstream macroeconomics has substantially reduced the academic prestige of econometric and statistical research on national accounting and other macroeconomic data. Monetarist and New Classical models are by their nature kept rather "small". Their empirical versions frequently make very selective and pragmatic use of available macro data (e.g., for calibration); they are also often mixed with data and estimates from microeconometric studies. On the other hand, macroeconomic statistics have been used to an even greater extent than before in political advisory and on the basis of quite refined statistical and econometric methods (filter techniques, VAR models, cointegration and error correction models, amongst others). This expansion has been fostered by technical progress in data processing. But for the most part it is explicable by the massive need for advice in the course of macroeconomic transformations, such as the European integration and the transformation of Eastern Europe and Asian economies.

2.6.2 Potential Output in Political Advisory

Estimates of potential output, potential growth and output gaps are invoked in many realms of political advisory. They are used to determine the non-inflationary provision of liquidity by monetary policy, to ascertain structural budget positions in medium-term fiscal planning and to assess other needs for action by economic policy by distinguishing business cycle fluctuations from growth dynamics. This

its replacement costs; if $q \geq 1$, the investment pays off. Tobin's q can also be expressed as the relationship between the (expected) return on investment and the risk-equivalent market rate of interest and, thus, corresponds to Wicksell's idea of comparing the interest rate in the capital market and the money rate; see Tobin (1969).

section does not present a comparative survey of methods of estimating potential output,[58] but outlines the connections between the theories presented up to now and standard methods of estimation.

At first glance, the intersection of the multitude of standard estimation methods and the theories considered in this chapter may seem disappointingly small. A large share of the estimations are not based on economic theory, but rest solely on statistical filter methods that decompose time series of output in a trend component (potential) and a cycle component (gap). Apart from these univariate techniques, multivariate, "semi-structural" methods exist that model the relationship between output gaps and changes of the inflation rate with the aid of Phillips curve equations and Okun's law (see, e.g., Apel & Jansson, 1999; Gerlach & Smets, 1999). Most techniques based on economic theories, however, draw on macroeconomic production functions in the manner of Solow's growth theory. Predominantly, Cobb-Douglas functions (and occasionally CES functions) are utilised, and the contributions of the production factors and technological progress are mostly determined by means of growth accounting. When estimating the potential increment of labour input, capital stock and "total factor productivity" (Solow residual), often purely statistical methods are employed. Ordinarily, estimations of the labour input are based on data on labour force potential, participation rate and average working time as well as estimations of the NAIRU.

The Cobb-Douglas approach is employed since the 1960s by the Council of Economic Advisers (CEA) and the Congressional Budget Office (CBO) in the U.S., since 1973 by the German Central Bank and more recently also by the International Monetary Fund, the OECD, the EU commission (DG ECFIN) and the European Central Bank. The German Council of Economic Experts (Sachverständigenrat zur Begutachtung der gesamtwirtschaftlichen Entwicklung, SVR) does not share the common practise. Since 1968 (with the exception of 1999 to 2002 for reasons of data availability), the SVR has estimated potential output using a limitational production function that describes potential output as solely depending on the progression of estimated capital productivity. The Council explains that this approach proceeds on the assumption that cyclical fluctuations of capacity utilisation are primarily caused in the entrepreneurial domain (SVR 2003: No. 746).

The relationship between the Cobb-Douglas approach for estimating potential output and Solow's growth theory seems close and natural. Following to the common dichotomy that treats the short run and the business cycle as determined by aggregate demand and the long run and growth as solely determined by aggregate supply, estimated factor contributions are usually equated with factor supplies. Moreover, many models (e.g., those of the OECD, the IMF, and the CBO) proceed on the assumption of demand adjusting to supply and output gaps being

[58] With respect to the analysis and critique of common estimation methods, see chapter 5 in this study as well as Sachverständigenrat zur Begutachtung der gesamtwirtschaftlichen Entwicklung (2003: No. 734-64) and Cotis, Elmeskov, and Mourougane (2004). For an international survey of institutions and methods of mid-term forecasts encompassing estimates of potential output, see ZEW (2005).

closed by the end of the forecasting horizon (ZEW 2005: 28, 36, 40). But it is not imperative to interpret trends that result from purely statistical extrapolation as completely determined by supply data. Likewise, the possibility that underlying NAIRU estimates contain hysteresis components that reflect cyclical impacts of the past cannot *a priori* be excluded.

In macroeconomic studies, structural vector autoregressive (SVAR) models have become increasingly popular, and they also seem to gain influence in the business of estimating potential output (e.g., Gerlach & Smets, 1999). In vector autoregressions with no restrictions all variables are equally endogenous, i.e. determined interdependently via time lags. In SVAR models theoretical restrictions are imposed in order to permit the unambiguous identification of impulses and propagation mechanisms (according to the classification by Frisch, see section 2.4.2). These kinds of restrictions may consist in ordering variables according to degrees of exogeneity or classifying shocks according to the persistence of their effects. Conforming to the well-known classification by Blanchard and Quah (1989), shocks effective in the long run are treated as supply shocks, and transitory shocks are treated as demand shocks. However, this is merely conventional and would not have been accepted in many of the older theories outlined in this chapter since it disregards the difficulty of separating demand and supply effects of investments along the time axis.

2.6.3 Conclusion: The Evolution of Theories and Growth Regimes

In concluding this chapter, the connections between historical macroeconomic theories and the economic situation at their time of origin are examined. Since the 1920s, in both Europe and the U.S. the pendulum of macroeconomic thought has swung at least as forcefully as the rates of inflation, real interest and GDP growth.[59] This section presents an experiment that relates to those interest rate gap theories presented in this chapter that have contributed to the development of the concepts of "potential output" and "output gaps" since the 1920s. History is, after all, the biggest (and often only) laboratory available for macroeconomists.

The experiment reads:

1. Identify different growth regimes by comparing time series of real GDP growth rates and real capital market interest rates in the time period 1925-2004.
2. Examine to what extent the theories outlined in this chapter contribute to the explanation of growth regimes at their time of origin.

In this study, the experiment cannot be conducted by every trick in the book. In its simple shape it is not intended to provide "hard" empirical evidence for the conformity of theory and reality or for divergence of both. Rather it serves to give an impression of how the progression of macroeconomic theories is related to changes of variables that are closely connected with the progression of potential output in reality. In order to identify different growth regimes, a well-known tech-

[59] For three different interpretations of the evolution of macroeconomics in the 20th century, see, for example, Woodford (1999), Blanchard (2000), and Leijonhufvud (2004).

nique for empirical testing the "golden rule of capital accumulation"[60] is employed. However, it starts out from a different line of argument, which stems from the short-term to medium-term interest rate gap theories outlined in this chapter. It should be widely acceptable to macroeconomists as it is supported by a large number of theoretical approaches. It introduces the notion of growth regimes, in which a growth regime is denoted as *expansionary* if growth rates of real GDP are higher than real interest rates in the capital market. If, conversely, interest rates are higher than growth rates, a *stagnative* regime prevails. Expansionary growth regimes are associated with higher increments of potential output than stagnative regimes.

This relationship between interest rates and growth can be substantiated as follows:

- Growth rates and interest rates in the capital market are pivotal determinants of investment activity, which in turn is a strategic variable for the progression of potential output. Economic growth affects investment positively due to the accelerator effect of revenue expectations; interest rates affect investment negatively due to the cost effect.
- Real interest rates in the capital market are not "natural rates of interest" in the sense of physical yields on capital or an equilibrium interest rate that reconciles planned savings with planned investments. They are inflation-adjusted money rates of interest to be compared with expected yields from investment in real capital – in modern versions of interest rate gap theories this is commonly done in terms of Tobin's *q*. Concerning Tobin's *q,* see footnote 63.
- While observed growth rates are also a determinant for investment activity (as already described), they are first and foremost dependent on investment. As a component of aggregate demand, investment has an immediate effect on the current growth rate; as a component of aggregate supply, it influences future growth rates through its capacity effect.
- Periods of deflation and disinflation are characterised by negative or small positive rates of inflation, frequently associated with an increase in nominal interest rates. The corresponding increase of real interest rates slows down investment activity and, thus, diminishes the growth of potential output. Consequently, persistently high real interest rates are associated with real economic stagnation or a slowdown of the growth trend.
- Low real interest rates can provide for sustainable real economic expansion if they are based upon comparatively low nominal interest and inflation rates. Higher rates of inflation may temporarily be associated with low or even negative real interest rates but ordinarily cause capital supply shortages or disinflation induced by monetary policy, thus, heralding the end of an expansionary growth regime.

[60] According to the golden rule of capital accumulation deduced by Phelps (1961) from Solow's growth model, an economy reaches its maximum consumption growth path if the growth rate of real output equals the real interest rate relevant for investment.

Fig. 6. Production and Interest Rates in the U.S., 1925-1934

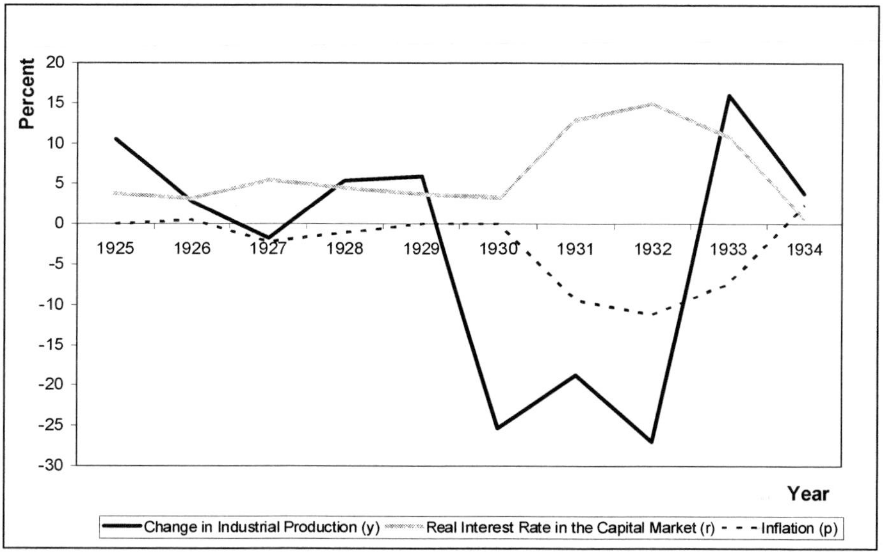

Source: NBER Macrohistory Database, FRED (St. Louis Fed)

Fig. 7. Production and Interest Rates in Germany, 1925-1934

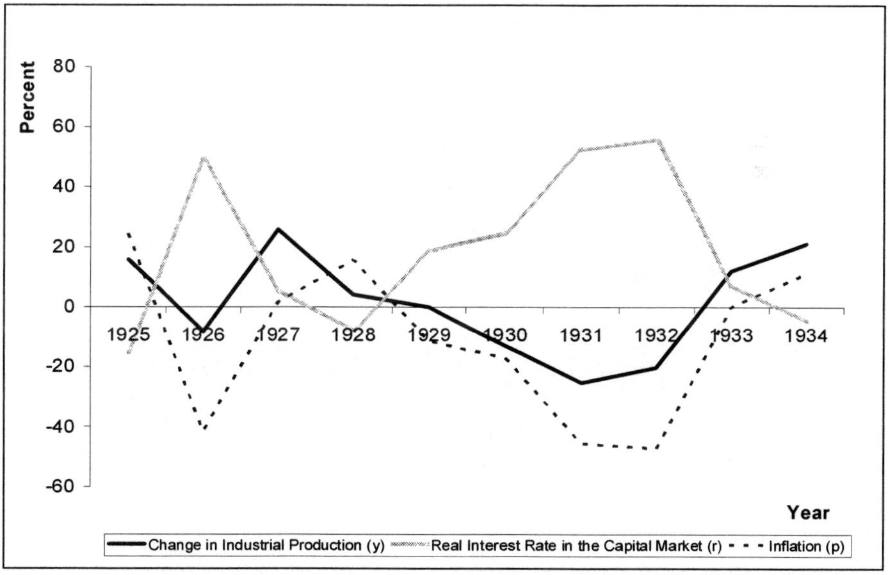

Source: NBER Macrohistory Database

Fig. 8. Growth and Interest Rates in the U.S., 1930-2004

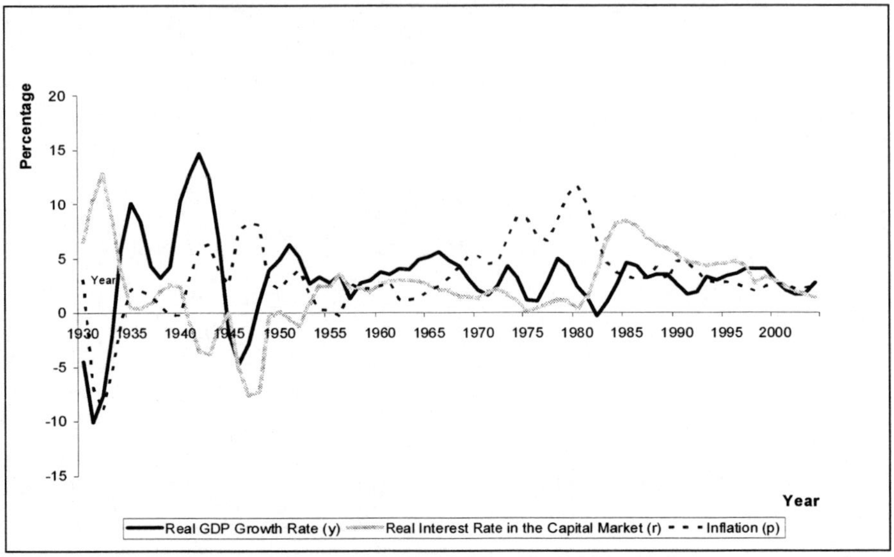

Source: OECD, NBER; FRED (St. Louis Fed)

Fig. 9. Growth and Interest Rates in the U.S., 1955-2004

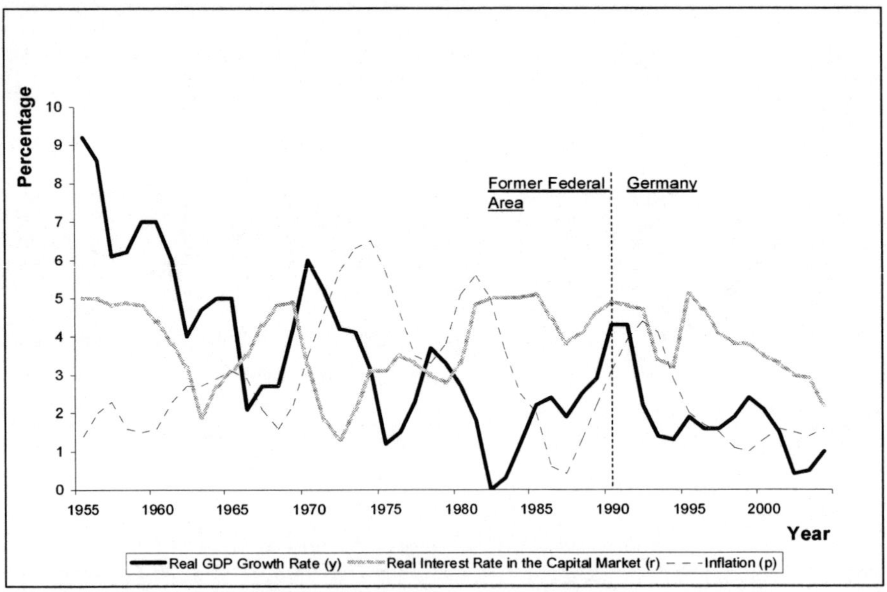

Source: German National Statistic Office, German Central Bank

This perception is supported by the data for the U.S. and Germany in the time period between 1925 and 2004 as presented in Figures 6-9. Choosing these two countries is motivated by pragmatic but also by theoretical reasons: The study commissioned is (at least implicitly) concerned with the economic progression in Germany. However, German economic history is also a particularly interesting case. Since the 1920s, it has frequently mirrored world economic progression in the extreme: In Germany, macroeconomic turbulences prior to and during the Great Depression were more pronounced than in most other countries. The ascent of the Western German economy to the most powerful economy in Europe up to 1974 is as striking as the slowdown of economic growth since then. The U.S. form a benchmark for the development in Germany in many respects. They play the leading part in the world economy since the 1920 and in economic research since the 1940s. In addition, the macroeconomic databases for these two countries are comparatively sound.

The examination starts in the mid-1920s. As there are no reliable data on GDP for the time prior to the Great Depression (see Section 2.5.1), consistent time series available for the progression of output, prices and interest rates for the period 1925-1934 were selected.[61]

The long-term time series on the progression of real GDP, inflation and real interest rates in the US capital market, 1930 to 2004 (Figure 8), bridge the pre- and post-war period and lead into the present. Due to the lack of data on comparable interest rates, for Germany (until 1990 only the old West German states) these variables are shown from 1955 onward (Figure 9).

In the following, *expansionary growth regimes* are defined as periods with GDP growth rates being positive and higher than real interest rates in the capital market $(y > r)$ over several years. *Stagnative growth regimes* are defined as converse constellations $(y < r)$. Applying this simple classification and adding some historical information yields the following rough picture.[62]

Prior to 1929	*No unambiguous assignment:* massive fluctuation of output, prices and interest rates in the aftermath of the reintroduction of the Gold Standard
1929-1933	*Stagnation:* severe recession during the Great Depression

[61] The data used here are taken from the National Bureau of Economic Research's (NBER) Macrohistory Database and the Federal Reserve Bank of St. Louis' FRED database. For the U.S., the industry production index and the consumer price index were chosen, for Germany, the production index by the Berlin Institute for Economic Research (now: DIW) was employed; inflation is represented by the "Index of Sensitive Prices" from the same source. Interest rates in the capital market for both countries are reported using inflation-adjusted current yields of long-term government bonds.

[62] It should be considered that due to the asynchrony of business cycles in the U.S., Germany and other countries, the temporal assignment is only an approximation. In addition, from Figures 8 and 9 it appears that the usage of three-year averages (for better illustration of regime changes) may cause minor deviations.

1934-1939	*Expansion: New Deal* policy in the U.S.; military build-up in Germany
1940-1949	*No unambiguous assignment:* expansion of output in the wartime economy, suppressed and open inflation, post-war recession, the early stage of the Bretton Woods system along with balance-of-payments crises and adjustments of exchange rates
1950-1970	*Expansion:* "Golden Age" of the Bretton Woods era with high GDP growth rates and comparatively minor inflation
1971-1980	*No unambiguous assignment:* collapse of the Bretton Woods system of fixed exchange rates, in the aftermath of the oil price shocks OPEC I (1973/1974) and OPEC II (1979/1980) boosts of inflation in fits and starts, massive volatility of inflation and GDP growth rates[63]
1981-1997	*Stagnation:* disinflation due to a policy of high interest rates in the aftermath of OPEC II and German reunification, period of intensive financial market globalisation, initiation of convergence processes in the run-up to the European Economic and Monetary Union
1998 to date	*No unambiguous assignment:* mild expansion with minor inflation and low real interest rates in the U.S. (accompanying both the "New Economy" and the burst of the *dot.com bubble* by means of an enormous increase of liquidity); in Germany stagnation with real interest rates higher than in the U.S. and some EU countries (after the German interest rate advantage was eliminated by the introduction of the European Monetary Union)

Examining the evolution of macroeconomic theories against this background, it turns out that it can only partly be explained as responses to real economic problems. It was to a greater extent driven by the inner logic of tackling the question how empirically observed fluctuations of real economic activity can be reconciled with a general theory of rational economic behaviour. The answer to this question had (and still has) fundamental implications for economic policy – not least for the question of how to define and utilise potential output best. The pendulum of economic doctrines has swung to and fro between the idea that deviations of current output from potential output are market failures and thus require public demand management and the idea that deviations from potential output stem from malpractices in economic policy which cause inflation and call for rigorous self-restrictions of economic policy. However, there are both older and more recent

[63] This period is frequently characterised as "stagflation", even though there were some years with high economic growth and the average growth rate in the U.S. only fell short by 0.2 percentage points compared to the following decade while in Germany it even was 1.1 percentage points higher. Thus, the choice of term has more likely resulted from retrospection to the 1950s and 1960s.

theories that combine both lines of argument and, thereby, arrive at more balanced conclusions. Moreover, from the two above-mentioned propositions, it cannot be inferred that macroeconomic mainstream theory has always taken the optimal route of scientific progress.

One by one: It is no historical coincidence that the interest rate gap theories in the tradition of Wicksell (1898), which form the basis of the concepts of potential output and output gaps, originated in the late 1920s and early 1930s (see sections 2.4.2-2.4.5). In those turbulent years, monetary policy required deep conceptional thinking, first about the reversion to the gold standard in the mid-1920s, then about (ultimately) abandoning the gold convertibility of currencies in the early 1930s. In particular, the question came up which kinds of cumulative processes of prices and output adjustments may be caused by measures of interest rate policy (or by their omission in cases of technical progress and other innovations) and to what extent the system's real equilibrium position is changed by it. In the 1920s, economic mainstream took more and more the position that, when it comes to analysing the dynamics of disequilibrium processes, the core subject of monetary and business cycle theory, Walrasian general equilibrium theory is a static and purely hypothetical reference model at best. Monetary and business cycle theory are linked by the notion that, in coordinating savings and investments, the interest rate mechanism frequently fails, thus, triggering excess demand and supply in other markets which in turn create feedbacks due to their effects on income distribution and productivity. It has been debated whether adjustment processes of wages and prices suffice to restore a general equilibrium with full utilisation of potential output and zero inflation or whether the government needs to take suitable measures of interest rate and employment policy. Both anti-cyclical fiscal policy aiming at stabilising output and rule-bound monetary policy aiming at stabilising prices had been already advocated by the early 1930s – prior to Keynes (1936) and long before Friedman (1968).[64]

Nevertheless, the common perception changed when Keynes' *General Theory of Employment, Interest and Money* (1936) was published. By that time, the mass unemployment of the Great Depression had shattered the belief that free markets always tend to produce full-employment equilibrium. Keynes attempted to demonstrate why market systems may fall into depression without being able to automatically find their way out of it. He set his principle of effective demand against Say's law and implicitly also against Walras' law: Goods and financial markets may be in market-clearing equilibrium while unemployment persists in the labour market due to rationing of labour supply. The latter cannot be equated with effective demand for consumption goods, nor do savings necessarily translate into future effective demand for consumption goods (due to asset holders' liquidity preference, among other things). Keynes argued that the interest rate mechanism does not coordinate investment and savings at all, but that income adjustments are re-

[64] Both strategies are proposed, e.g., in the translation (1939: Part II and Appendix) of Lindahl (1930) and Lindahl (1935). An international survey is given by Laidler (1999), who shows that the view that, prior to Keynes (1936) and during the Great Depression, most economists banked on the markets' self-regulating forces is largely a myth.

sponsible for reconciling savings with investment *ex post*. Rather than analysing the dynamics of cumulative price adjustments in disequilibrium, Keynes emphasised the comparative statics of underemployment equilibria (the rule) and full-employment equilibria (the ideal case exception), brought about solely through adjustments of quantities. Keynes' theory resulted in the notion that full utilisation of potential output requires continuous stabilisation of aggregate demand, largely by means of fiscal policy.

The achievements of the *New Deal* in the U.S. as well as the strong role of fiscal policy in overcoming the post-war recession seemed to confirm this belief. The lessons learnt from the planned organisation of war economies and the political competition with the Soviet Union and its sphere of influence contributed to the belief widely held after World War II that concepts of global demand management and indicative planning are the most efficient solutions for macroeconomic problems of resource allocation. Ensuring full utilisation and expansion of productive capacities by means of governmental guidelines and spending became the planning project of social engineers, who made use of recent "technical progress" in the realm of statistical data collection and econometric data processing. As recessions rarely occurred during the 1950s and 1960s and, when they occurred, were much milder than the cyclical fluctuations of the pre-war period, this was considered as a success of Keynesian stabilisation philosophy. Fostering economic growth became a major concern, and the concept of potential output began to play a key role in it.

Meanwhile, Keynes' theory was being integrated into the Neoclassical Synthesis in the form of IS/LM analysis and its AD/AS extension. In the process, the hitherto central issue of coordination failures of the interest rate mechanism causing inflationary and output gaps completely disappeared from the scene.[65] The explanation of underemployment equilibria by means of Keynes' liquidity preference theory seemed to reduce the whole story to the liquidity trap – an exceptional case, scarcely empirically observable and plausible only in the very short run if at all. Ultimately, the Neoclassical Synthesis reduced the explanation of underemployment and corresponding output gaps to the existence of wage and price rigidities. An expansionary mix of monetary and fiscal policy seemed to provide a remedy for underemployment albeit associated with inflation. That way, the Phillips curve became popular making post-war standard macroeconomic theory an easy prey for Monetarist and New Classical criticism.

Concerning Friedman's (1968) and Phelps' (1967) Phillips curve critique, it may seem as if reality for once followed theory, rather than the reverse. The rapid success of Monetarism in the 1970s was based, amongst other things, on the strong empirical confirmation that the great inflation of those years seemed to provide for Friedman's acceleration hypothesis (see section 2.5.2). It should be remembered, however, that even in the early 1930s as well as during the inflationary waves in the post-war period, attempts at fostering growth and employment by way of inflation had been widely criticised without resorting to the concept of a

[65] See Leijonhufvud (1981 and 2004). The development of Tobin's *q* and Tobin's emphasis of the importance of financing structures could be considered an exception.

"natural rate of unemployment" (sections 2.4.3 and 2.5.1). Furthermore, the oil price shocks in the 1970s can be interpreted as supply shocks (as is now customary in RBC theory) and, thus, as a shift of the long-term AS and Phillips curves to the left (Figures 3 and 4), rather than a host of short-term curves converging on a long-run vertical. Even if one follows the Monetarist and New Classical lines of argument, inflationary pushes and declines in economic growth during this period (Figures 8 and 9) can hardly be reduced to the idea that politicians have tried to displace markets from their (long-run) equilibrium position. Expansionary monetary and fiscal policy during those years was motivated by the attempt to stabilise unemployment rates considered as "natural" in the sense of an equilibrium in the labour market.

Nevertheless, in the 1970s and 1980s the pendulum of economic doctrines swung towards the notion of policy malpractices. Not only were the parallel increases of inflation and unemployment considered as signs of a complete failure of social engineering. They were considered to be the result of discretionary "stabilisation policy" that threatens to destabilise the system because it is both ineffective and inefficient: It is ineffective since the private sector anticipates the policy's time inconsistency, and it is inefficient because anticipated inflation and unexpected disinflation entails welfare losses. Monetarist theory implies the correspondence of potential output with the natural rate of unemployment. Negative output gaps emerge only in rare cases of deflation and "incredible" disinflation; more generally, positive output gaps and especially inflationary gaps tend to develop in the short run. New Classical theory even goes the extra mile and reduces short-term effects to mere surprise responses towards shocks. Thus, deviations of current output from potential output can only occur stochastically and can be reduced by self-binding monetary and fiscal policy. By then, it had become imperative to explain fluctuations in real economic activity as equilibrium phenomena rigorously deducible from microeconomic rational behaviour to the greatest possible extent.

When, during the period of stagnation in the early 1980s, the relationship between growth rates and interest rates went into reverse (Figures 8 and 9), mainstream economic theory hardly reacted at all. High real interest rates in the short run were interpreted as an indispensable investment in acquiring reputation capital that independent and rule-bound central banks have to make for the sake of their credibility. Growth rates that persistently fall short of real interest rates are harder to explain without alleging a drastic increase in consumer time preferences. The methodological imperative ultimately established with RBC theory, commanding to model any macroeconomic fluctuations in terms of continuous intertemporal equilibrium, has rendered coordination failures that result from market processes (as opposed to political malpractices) basically "unthinkable". In standard models of present macroeconomics, capital markets – in the non-trivial sense of price and other mechanisms that coordinate the supply and demand for loans – have largely vanished.[66]

---

[66] However, during the 1980s and 1990s, on the sidelines of mainstream economics attempts were made at deducing financial constraints of real economic activities by em-

Nevertheless, since the 1980s, various attempts have been made at explaining why changes of GDP growth are empirically observed to run ahead of changes of inflation (Figures 8 and 9) as well as providing micro-founded explanations for the obvious persistence of the effects of monetary policy on output and employment. Corresponding NAIRU models are supported with a substructure based on the concept of quasi-equilibrium unemployment (QUERU) (Figure 4), a hybrid between market clearing and rationing equilibrium that allows for various interpretations with respect to potential output – depending on the extent to which rationed outsiders are still considered as effective labour supply. Within the framework of the New Neoclassical Synthesis, attempts are made to substantiate the existence of persistent output gaps in intertemporal equilibrium models (section 2.3). In these models, the RBC core of intertemporal optimisation is modified by integrating nominal rigidities that emerge on the supply side of product markets in an environment of monopolistic competition. To what extent this renaissance of interest rate and output gap theories based on New Classical methods will prove tenable for a consistent definition of potential output, remains to be seen.[67]

Up to now, the dominance of New Classical methods in academic mainstream economics has carried little weight in political advisory concerning questions related to potential output.[68] In many realms of political advisory, however, using a macroeconomic production function as in Solow's growth model has become a widely accepted practice. The aggregate production function is a purely supply-theoretical concept that excludes feedback effects of temporary interest rate and output gaps on potential output from the outset. The advantages and drawbacks of this type of exclusion with respect to calculating potential output will be discussed in the following chapter.

---

ploying information asymmetries and financial accelerators. Two major advances were Stiglitz and Weiss' (1981) credit-rationing approach and the credit cost approach by Bernanke and Gertler (1989). However, both attempts employ rationing equilibria, which presently tend to be frowned upon in mainstream economics. For a survey of this *credit view* and a comparison with pre-war interest-rate gap theories, see Trautwein (2000).

67 Various problems associated with determining potentials and gaps in the New Neoclassical Synthesis are addressed in chapter 3 of this book.

68 By developing the "a-theoretical" Hodrick-Prescott filters, Edward Prescott has probably exerted a more lasting influence on methods for estimating potential output than by advancing RBC theory.

3 Historical Positions and Controversies

3.1 Introduction

Chapter 2 chronologically surveyed the development of the concepts of "potential output" and "output gaps" in macroeconomic theories. The present chapter examines key problems in four areas related to these concepts. The first area concerns the problem of aggregation. Since estimations based on economic theory mostly rest on the idea of a macroeconomic production function, we assess the explanatory power of macroeconomic aggregates within the concept of potential output (section 3.2). The second problem area pertains to the relationship between the growth trend and the business cycle. This primarily concerns the question to what extent the short run and the long run can be separated strictly according to the common dichotomy of demand and supply influences (section 3.3). The notion of non-inflationary unemployment constitutes the third problem area. Its implications for economic policy are pointed out by means of highlighting the differences between the concepts of the natural rate of unemployment, the NAIRU and the QUERU (section 3.4). The last problem area relates to the role of monetary policy. Concerning this matter, the interaction between the progression of potential output and monetary policy is discussed.

While chapter 2 presented the subject in the sense of a longitudinal section over time, chapter 3 forms an analytical cross-section: The assumptions and concepts invoked today in determining potentials and gaps are confronted with theoretical positions advocated at different points in time. Accordingly, the present chapter contains résumés concerning the above-mentioned four matters that can be drawn from the theories presented in chapter 2. Where necessary, we establish cross connections to other contributions made in the history of economic theory.[69]

3.2 Macroeconomic Aggregates

As outlined in section 2.6.2, most theory-based methods of estimating potential output rest on the notion of a macroeconomic production function grounded in

[69] By contrast, contributions made in the history of statistical and econometric theory are not included.

S. Hauptmeier et al., *Projecting Potential Output*, Zew Economic Studies,

DOI: 10.1007/978-3-7908-2177-2_3, © Physica-Verlag Berlin Heidelberg 2009

Neoclassical growth theory. The theoretical concept of a macroeconomic production function is controversial for at least two reasons: It holds problems concerning the valuation of the capital stock, and it neglects structural influences on potential variables.

With respect to the first problem, the concept of a macroeconomic production function either involves a circular argument in the valuation of the capital stock or has to resort to an independent money rate of interest. Solow's notion of an equilibrium time path of production converging to a steady state (structurally unchanging growth) is based on a strictly inverse relationship between factor prices and factor input relations, building on the concept of a natural interest rate in terms of the marginal physical productivity of capital. The capital stock increment – a pivotal factor for potential output – can, then, be described as a function of the natural rate of interest.

Wicksell (1911: III.2), Lindahl (1930: 247f.), and Myrdal (1931: 50f.) have demonstrated (section 2.4.3) that the concept of a "natural interest rate" can be rigorously and consistently deduced only for a one-good economy where output and input are homogenously identical and, therefore, measurable by the same unit or in a stationary economy with fixed prices. In a growing economy with heterogeneous capital goods and variable prices (conditions that tend to apply to estimations of potential output in the real world), the value of this aggregate can only be determined with reference to the prices of capital goods. In a monetary economy the prices of capital goods are not independent of the price of loans in terms of the money rate of interest – the more so, as in Lindahl's theory (just like in modern theories of finance) the prices of capital goods are determined by means of their present value, which in turn includes the money rate of interest as a discount factor. As the present capital stock influences the future capital stock through investment activities, it follows from Lindahl's and Myrdal's critique of the concept of a natural interest rate that the future capital stock cannot be determined independently from the present level of the money rate of interest.

With special regard to Solow's growth theory, this argument has been further developed during the "Cambridge capital controversy" between Cambridge (England) und Cambridge (Massachusetts) in the 1950s and 1960s – with similar outcomes.[70] Cambridge (England) pointed out that Neoclassical growth theory is based on Neoclassical distribution theory and, thus, given heterogeneous capital goods, includes a circular argument: The equilibrium interest rate (natural rate of interest) is regarded as the market price that reflects the marginal productivity and relative scarcity of the existing stock of aggregate capital; however, the aggregate capital stock and its marginal productivity can only be determined by means of a given interest rate. Despite several attempted rescues (invoking "jelly goods" and other metaphors), Cambridge (Massachusetts) finally admitted that the concept of a macroeconomic production function could not be considered as universally valid.

[70] The most notable protagonists of this controversy were Joan Robinson, Piero Sraffa, and Luigi Pasinetti on the British side as well as Robert Solow and Paul Samuelson on the American side. For recent surveys, see Harcourt (1999) and Cohen and Harcourt (2003).

Advanced microeconomic research in general equilibrium theory has also led to fundamental criticism of the standard practice of aggregating individual preferences to form a representative function. From the Sonnenschein-Mantel-Debreu theorem, which states that due to wealth effects a unique general equilibrium may not exist, it follows, amongst other things, that the "well-defined" macroeconomic production function of Neoclassical growth theory, which shows decreasing marginal returns, can only under extremely restrictive conditions be deduced as unambiguously resulting from the aggregation of factor supplies in individual preference functions (Kirman, 1992).

These grave analytical problems of aggregation have not stopped economists from continuing to employ the concept of the aggregate production function in the empirical realm. In principle, there is no need to object to the pragmatic use of aggregate data on gross capital assets and employment in terms of some type of production function in order to assess economic progress on an empirical basis.[71] However, one should not lend oneself to illusions of the concept of an aggregate production function being theoretically sound or even "micro-theoretically founded" – even though RBC theory and endogenous growth theory have advocated the resurrection of the macroeconomic production function by raising the latter claim for more than two decades.

The second aggregation problem consists of neglecting the effects of adjustment processes towards the presumed equilibrium state. Potential output is an unobservable quantity representing the maximum output reconcilable with minimum inflation. In the Stockholm School's parlance (see sections 2.4.3 and 2.4.7), potential output is a projection of *ex post* data, which (1) can be deduced *ex ante* from the plans of suppliers and buyers in product and factor markets and (2) is distinguished from observable *ex post data* by remaining an unobservable ideal result. Outside an environment with perfect foresight or consistent rational expectations, *ex ante* compatibility of plans cannot be safely assumed even when projecting an ideal result. Thus, in the case of incompatible plans hypotheses concerning the adjustment process need to be formed. In the simplest hypothesis there are no coordination problems, or prices are perfectly flexible. But estimations of potential output in a real economy cannot proceed from this. Rather, market structures, intersectoral dependencies and institutional framework conditions that cause quantities to adjust faster than prices (especially downward) need to be taken into account. Consequentially, the "probable potential output" might fall short of the "ideal potential output".

Theoretical foundations for incorporating adjustment processes and structural bottlenecks are provided by the contributions of Lundberg (1937), Leontief (1941), and Hansen (1951) mentioned in chapter 2 as well as the literature on QUERU. Even if it is possible to develop models of such adjustment processes that are operational in econometric investigations, some uncertainty or disagreement concerning the choice of the proper model will remain in empirical estima-

[71] There are also many problems of consistently delimitating, aggregating and consolidating the data, which are specific to the context at hand. These problems cannot be addressed here but should not be underestimated.

tions of potential output and forecasts of potential growth. A pragmatic method of dealing with this uncertainty is the technique of forecasting alternative mid- and long-term scenarios. These are based on the variation of assumptions about possible shocks (e.g., oil price or interest rate increases) as well as assumptions about the transmission channels relevant in the propagation mechanism. An early model of the scenario technique was developed by Lundberg and his colleagues at the Swedish National Institute of Economic Research, springing from the Stockholm School's method of sequence analysis (Berg, 1987; Ohlsson, 1987). In many countries and on an international level, the construction of alternative scenarios is common practice in political advisory.

3.3 Growth Trend and the Business Cycle

The progression of theories on the relationship between growth and cycle resembles a "long wave" (even longer than the Kondratieff cycle) with various states of integration and separation:[72]

1. In older theories of the business cycle – for example by Åkerman (1928; see section 2.4.2) and Schumpeter (1934) – growth of national output was included in the explanation of business cycles as a process of interference of long and short waves. There was no clear separation of trend and cycle; the trend merely indicated the direction of the progression of the cycles but had no analytical "life" of its own.
2. Various attempts at integrating business cycle theory with general equilibrium theory were made in the inter-war period (e.g., Hayek 1929, 1931; Frisch, 1933; Hicks, 1933). A controversial point was the question whether equilibrium forms a mere reference point for cyclical fluctuations in disequilibrium or a centre of gravitation, or even an observable stage of the cycle. As a rule, the underlying equilibrium was, for the sake of simplicity, treated as stationary.
3. It is only after the late 1930s that growth theory has developed into a separate branch of macroeconomics, starting out from the multiplier-accelerator analysis of disequilibria (e.g., Lundberg, 1937) and, then, focussing on the discussion of stability properties of steady-state growth equilibria (section 2.4.6).[73]
4. Due to didactical separations in economic education and other considerations, a dichotomy has become conventional since the 1950s, by which business cycle and growth theories are carefully separated in terms of the short and the long run. Gradually a consensus evolved that considers cyclical fluctuations of national product as demand-determined whereas GDP growth is believed to be purely supply-determined. This consensus shaped the Phillips curve debates

[72] Many of the beliefs outlined in these periods can be traced back even further in the history of economic thought. The issue of priority is, however, not of greater relevance in this study.

[73] "Growth theory was invented to provide a systematic way to talk about and to compare equilibrium paths for the economy" (Solow, 1988: 311).

and is best illustrated by the differences in the AS curves for the short and the long run (sections 2.5.2-2.5.3).

5. The RBC approach, which gained prominence in the 1980s and formed the basis of the New Neoclassical Synthesis, treats GDP fluctuations as optimal reactions to productivity shocks. The cycle clearly has no longer an analytical life of its own (section 2.5.4).

The standard treatment of potential output and output gaps still corresponds to the conventional dichotomy of phase 4.[74] While potential output as a trend component represents the growth aspect determined by aggregate supply, the current output gap is interpreted as a cyclical component in the sense of a varying degree of capacity utilisation that is determined by aggregate demand. At first sight the dichotomy may look plausible since many determinants of GDP and the labour supply (such as technological innovations and demographic change) are permanent in nature or irreversible in the short run while components of aggregate demand fluctuate more forcefully. In addition, the assumption in the Keynesian theory of effective demand according to which prices react more slowly than quantities is generally plausible only in the short run. In the long run, it is commonly assumed that prices are flexible and markets are cleared. This proceeds on the assumption that Say's law is valid, according to which the supply of goods results in factor incomes and, hence, automatically induces the corresponding *aggregate* demand for goods.

However, the practice of separating the supply and demand sides by means of the trend-cycle dichotomy is problematic for three interrelated reasons:

1. Business cycle fluctuations are mainly caused by "supply shocks".
2. GDP growth is not independent of the cyclical progression of aggregate demand.
3. The occurrence and intensity of cycle-generating "supply shocks" is not independent of the pace of economic growth.

Ad 1.: Many approaches to investigating the business cycle – in strands as different as those of Wicksell, Schumpeter or RBC theory – proceed on the assumption that "technological shocks" form the most important impulses that trigger fluctuations of prices and real economic activity (sections 2.4.2-2.4.3 and 2.5.4). Technological shocks are generally classified as supply shocks since productivity changes affect the costs of production. Positive technological shocks make profit expectations rise due to declines in costs (in cases of process innovations) and increasing revenues (especially in cases of product innovations). These expectations raise the demand for investment goods, inducing cumulative effects on aggregate demand and prices. The cycles (including their upper and lower turning points) can, in different manners, be represented as endogenous fluctuations, for example, as stochastically dynamic equilibria in RBC models or as multiplier-accelerator combinations or other disequilibrium models. In this kind of "gap theories", demand variables, in particular investment, are mostly treated as more responsive or more volatile than aggregate supply. The bottom line is that the demand for in-

[74] Evidence can be found in most descriptions of both concepts from Okun (1962) to the Blanchard-Quah restrictions in SVAR analysis; see sections 2.1 and 2.5.2.

vestment goods is determined by expectations on the future profit-maximizing supply of goods and, thus, by expectations on growth and future potential output. The same message is clearly contained in the connections between the "term structure of interest rates" and the business cycle, as described by Lindahl (1930) and Burns and Mitchell (1946) (see section 2.4.4).

Ad 2.: Influences of short-term changes in aggregate demand on long-term growth of aggregate supply result from the dual nature of investments, which through their income effect constitute a component of aggregate demand and through their capacity effect contribute to changes of potential output (section 2.4.6). Basically this had been pointed out by Okun (1962), when he first introduced the concept of potential output (section 2.1). The impacts of business cycles on growth are aptly described in the Nobel price lecture given by the pioneer of Neoclassical growth theory:

> "[I]f one looks at substantial more-than-quarterly departures from equilibrium growth, as suggested for instance by the history of the large European economies since 1979, it is impossible to believe that the equilibrium growth path itself is unaffected by the short- to medium-run experience. In particular the amount and directions of capital formation is bound to be affected by the business cycle, whether through gross investment in new equipment or through the accelerated scrapping of old equipment. I am also inclined to believe that the segmentation of the labor market by occupation, industry and region, with varying amounts of unemployment from one segment to another, will also react back on the equilibrium path. So a simultaneous analysis of trend and fluctuations really does involve an integration of long-run and short-run, or equilibrium and disequilibrium" (Solow, 1988: 311f.).

As section 2.6.3 shows, Germany has indeed undergone a stark deviation from the golden rule of capital accumulation since the beginning of the 1980s: For most of the time it has seen a stagnative growth regime with real interest rates higher than the real GNP growth rate (Figure 9) and a continuous increase in base unemployment (the remaining unemployment at the upper turning points of the cycles). As a possible strategy of "simultaneous analysis" taking account of such cases, Solow mentions modelling sticky prices and wages in processes of adjustment to excess supply. He concludes:

> "The economy may eventually return to an equilibrium path, perhaps because 'prices are flexible in the long run' as we keep telling ourselves. If and when it does, it will not return to the continuation of the equilibrium path it was on before it slipped off. The new equilibrium path will depend on the amount of capital accumulation that has taken place during the period of disequilibrium, and probably also on the amount of unemployment, especially long-term unemployment, that has been experienced. Even the level of technology may be different, if technological change is endogenous rather than arbitrary" (Solow, 1988: 312).

Solow's proposal of simultaneous analysis is tantamount to demanding that hysteresis (or persistence) effects of demand fluctuations on the capital stock, effective labour supply and technical progress – i.e. potential output – has to be taken into account. Within the framework of New Neoclassical Synthesis tentative attempts are made at reconciling these demands with the methodological imperatives of RBC theory (e.g., Woodford, 2003, ch. 3-5; Blanchard & Galí, 2005). The framework of endogenous growth theory has already been employed to demonstrate that business cycle fluctuations triggered by temporary demand shocks (such as increases in the quantity of money) can permanently affect technical progress (Aghion & Howitt, 1998: ch. 8).

Ad 3.: The circle is closed by considering that growth, according to Schumpeter (1934), invariably implies "creative destruction", such that innovations cause cyclical fluctuations in the growth process (see 1.). This possibility is pointed out in Schumpeterian approaches to endogenous growth theory. They allow to investigate the interaction of counteracting welfare effects as well as innovation and obsolescence effects of R&D investments within dynamic equilibrium models (Aghion & Howitt, 1998: ch. 2 and 8, 2005).

It might, thus, be speculated whether, with recent Schumpeterian approaches, the "long wave" in the relationship of business cycle and growth theories reconnects to phase 1 – of course on a higher technical level. The concept of potential output is not *per se* a supply concept but an equilibrium concept: the maximum utilisation of capacity achievable without generating inflationary pressure. Consequently, supply and demand need to coincide. The Solow quotations should not be misunderstood as arguing that every cyclical fluctuation must exert long-term effects in the sense of shifts in equilibrium positions that follow from gaps. They rather imply that clear distinctions should be made between "passive" gaps under self-regulating forces (stability) and gaps that themselves effect changes in the system (meta-stability or hysteresis). This is the methodological challenge for theories of cumulative processes in the tradition of Wicksell (1898) (see section 2.4.1).

3.4 Non-Inflationary Unemployment

The concept of an unemployment rate that is consistent with stable inflation (NAIRU) plays a major role in various techniques of estimating potential output (section 2.6.2). Still, it is by no means unambiguous with respect to its interpretation and its implications for economic policy. Again, a "long wave" of theoretical evolution encompassing different phases with respect to the voluntariness and involuntariness of unemployment can be identified:

1. According to Keynesian reading (valid since 1936), unemployment associated with a stable price level is involuntary unemployment: Given the level of prices and wages, effective demand falls short of the amount required to employ all those who are prepared to work at the prevailing market wage rate.[75] Consequently, the NAIRU can be associated with an output level lower than potential output (section 2.4.5).

[75] According to Keynes (1936: ch. 19), wage declines, if anything, are likely to aggravate the problem as they contribute to further failures of aggregate demand to match supply; see section 2.4.5.

2. According to Monetarist reading (valid since 1967), the NAIRU corresponds to the natural rate of unemployment. Since the latter represents the labour market equilibrium in the Walrasian sense, the NAIRU is basically interpreted as voluntary unemployment, determined by supply side factors. The output level associated with the NAIRU corresponds to the sustainable potential output; current output can exceed it in the short run at best (section 2.5.2).
3. According to New Classical reading (valid since 1972), the concept of involuntary unemployment is analytically useless (Lucas, 1981: 241f.). In New Classical theories, disequilibria and rationing equilibria are ruled out from the outset; all market processes are intended results of choices under rational expectations and flexible prices. As rationally anticipated inflation has no effect on employment, the NAIRU does not constitute a systematic category in New Classical theories (section 2.5.2).
4. According to New Keynesian reading (valid since the late 1980s), persistent unemployment can be explained by new theories about quasi-equilibrium in the labour market, both with and without hysteresis. As this equilibrium is associated with rationing the *outsiders* among the labour suppliers,[76] QUERU approaches include elements of involuntary unemployment (section 2.5.5).

The present mainstream view still largely corresponds to phase: In common parlance the NAIRU is equated with natural unemployment. As pointed out by Tobin (1972), there are fundamental differences between the two concepts. Firstly, the NAIRU is directly observable while the natural rate of unemployment is not. Secondly, the NAIRU is the specific unemployment rate associated with an unchanging inflation rate at the time of observation; in this sense, the inflation rate might depend on the level of unemployment – or vice versa; correlation does not *per se* indicate causality. By contrast, the natural rate of unemployment is clearly independent of inflation or compatible with any inflation rate. Thirdly, the natural rate of unemployment corresponds to a market-clearing equilibrium and is, thus, voluntary. The NAIRU, by contrast, may be a rationing equilibrium and, therefore, in part involuntary.

The discussion about voluntary and involuntary unemployment in macroeconomic equilibrium might be considered a sterile philosophical exercise. However, if the NAIRU concept is employed in estimations of potential output, the underlying theory needs to be made explicit as the different views have strongly divergent policy implications:

- If the NAIRU denotes the natural rate of unemployment in the sense of Lucas, there is no need for action whatsoever.
- If the NAIRU is taken to be the natural rate of unemployment in Friedman's sense, there might be a need for structural policy to improve the supply conditions in the labour market but no need for action on the part of stabilisation policy.

[76] "Rationing of *outsiders*" means that labour demand falls short of labour supply, thus, constituting the "short side of the market" that keeps *outsiders* out even if their wage demands undercut the equilibrium wage rate.

- If the NAIRU coincides with the QUERU, the underlying problems of imperfect information and imperfect competition need to be identified in order to employ the appropriate explanation (see the paragraph below).
- If the NAIRU implies Keynesian unemployment, there is a need for action on the part of stabilisation policy in order to stimulate effective demand.

With respect to the QUERU, it should be noted that approaches exist that attribute persistent unemployment exclusively to dysfunctional structures in the labour market, such as organised market power of *insiders*, mismatches due to unemployability or false incentives in terms of excessive reservation wages. In these cases, the QUERU diagnosis leads to recommendation of microeconomic policies to make changes in labour market structures, qualifications and social security. Other approaches explain persistent unemployment with failures of monetary and fiscal policy that affect the labour market. Accordingly, even given an efficient structure, the labour market is not in a position to process interest rate shocks, substantial declines of public spending or other demand shocks without resulting in extensive downgrading of workers and other long-term effects on effective labour supply. In this case, the QUERU diagnosis gives rise to recommendations in favour of macroeconomic stabilisation policy in order to minimise employment losses (section 2.5.5).

In NAIRU explanations that include hysteresis effects of disinflation, the current rate of unemployment is co-determined by past inflation and interest rate responses of monetary policy.[77] This leads to a problem that resembles the difficulty of valuing the aggregate capital stock as discussed in section 3.1: The NAIRU as an (implicit) benchmark for present monetary policy is not independent of past monetary policy. If one follows the current mainstream and makes the assumption of rational expectations, the difficulty arises that present monetary policy depends on earlier, self-fulfilling expectations about present monetary policy.

3.5 The Role of Monetary Policy

The discussions in the previous sections have introduced several controversies about the non-neutrality of monetary policy in the short and the long run. As already argued in sections 2.3, 2.4.3 and 2.6.3 in particular, two strongly differing views prevail with respect to the role of monetary policy and, hence, also to the significance of estimations of potential output:

- Current mainstream macroeconomics describes the main task of monetary policy as preventing itself from becoming a disruptive factor.[78] For market forces to be able to work in such a way that potential growth can actually be achieved, central banks need to ensure an immediate adjustment of money rates of inter-

[77] This type of approaches can be found as early as in the 1950s, for example, in writings of Lindahl (Boianovsky & Trautwein, 2006b); for a general survey, see Bean (1989).

[78] Within this framework fiscal policy needs to be "budget compatible" with monetary policy.

est to the uniquely determined "natural" rates of interest, growth and unemployment.

- According to the Wicksellian theories of the early 1930s, the task of monetary policy is to coordinate the activities of market agents. For potential growth to be achieved, the central bank ought to set interest rates in such a fashion that the agents' plans are compatible. In this way it generates rational expectations (instead of following *ad hoc* assumed rational expectations) – and it needs to do so since a "natural" rate of interest rate does not exist independently of its interest rate setting behaviour.

Advanced extensions of the New Neoclassical Synthesis deal, nevertheless, with interactions of central banking and potential growth that may cause long-term non-neutrality of monetary policy – even within the framework of intertemporal equilibrium models. Following the Taylor rule, monetary policy oriented at potential output can in turn influence the capital stock and, thereby, potential output (Woodford, 2003: ch. 5). Models of this type are still the exception rather than the rule. But if long-term non-neutrality can be deduced even under the restrictive conditions of intertemporal equilibrium models, it is to be expected that the incorporation of other frictions (other than sluggish price adjustments) will lead to even more powerful interactions of potential output and monetary policy.

In this process, however, modern modelling strategies are confronted with problems of consistently defining the equilibrium interest rate (and implicitly the "normal" capital stock and corresponding potential output) similar to those recognised by Lindahl and Myrdal in the early 1930s (section 2.4.3). To serve as a benchmark for assessing the effectiveness and efficiency of monetary policy, the equilibrium rate needs to be independent of policy influences even though it is co-determined by monetary policy. This problem can only be solved if the equilibrium interest rate is defined as a path-dependent variable: Impacts of past monetary policy enter the determination of the current equilibrium interest rate, and impacts of present monetary policy enter the determination of the future equilibrium interest rate. The standard assumption of (Muth-)rational expectations may lead to another circular argument or it brings back the traditional Swedish criticism of the concept of a "natural rate of interest". The equilibrium interest rate would, then, be simply determined by the given money rate of interest and the deduced expectations of the private sector with respect to real economic growth. That hypothesis can in fact be tested by way of assessing the forecasting power of the term structure of interest rates with respect to economic growth. Accordingly, this approach is evaluated in chapter 7 of the present study.

4 Epistemological Subsumption

4.1 Introduction

This part of the study discusses the implicit epistemological assumptions of the concept of potential output with respect to the key characteristics of the economic system as well as the resulting prospects and limitations for forecasting potential output. As a theoretical framework for this discussion we employ the conception of general systems theory, which is designed for the investigation of the properties and dynamic behaviour of various types of systems.

The first section introduces the notion of a "system" as well as some basic concepts of general systems theory according to von Bertalanffy (1949) and briefly outlines their influence on economic and social science theory (section 4.2). Subsequently, we sketch the natural science paradigm that forms the basis for the idea of closed systems along with their properties and systems behaviour (section 4.3). We then discuss the influence of the paradigm and presumptions relevant for closed systems on economic modelling as well as the implications resulting with respect to systems behaviour and, in particular, the possibilities for forecasting (section 4.4). After that, the underlying paradigm and the properties and systems behaviour of open systems are discussed (section 4.5). Finally, we examine the options for modelling the economic system as an open, dynamic system and discuss the consequences for systems behaviour and forecasting potentials (section 4.6).

4.2 System-Theoretical Concepts and Paradigmatic Considerations

The term "general systems theory" traces back to biologist von Bertalanffy (1949), who also introduced the essential concepts of systems theory relevant for the topic at hand.[79] In the sense of methodological holism, von Bertalanffy's general systems theory is an attempt at detecting and formalising regularities and principles

[79] Other important fields of systems theory have their origins in cybernetics (Wiener 1948) and information theory (Shannon & Weaver, 1949). However, in the context of the topic at hand they are of minor importance.

S. Hauptmeier et al., *Projecting Potential Output*, Zew Economic Studies,

DOI: 10.1007/978-3-7908-2177-2_4,

that are valid for all systems exhibiting certain characteristics – irrespective of whether they are physical, biological, economic or social systems.

Von Bertalanffy was motivated by his critical attitude towards the classical scientific approach that is based on deductive methodology and the corresponding isolated treatment of components, which he countered with the suggestion to consider systems instead. A system in the sense of systems theory is an entity that consists of several components that are interconnected. Examples for systems in the sense of systems theory are physical, chemical and biological systems but also social and economic systems, like a competitive market economy. The realm outside the system is the system's environment, into which the system is embedded. The frontier that delimitates the system and its environment with respect to space and time is called the system's boundary. Of course, when applying systems theory the exact specification of these system's boundaries often proves to be anything but trivial.

A system in the sense of general systems theory possesses an internal structure, which is determined by the properties of the system components and their interactions and which is significant for the system's functionality and performance. Systems theory is aimed at investigating the interrelations and interactions of and within systems in order to be able to explain the performance and progression of a system.

In general systems theory, the following basic types of systems are distinguished:

- A system is called *isolated* if it has neither inputs nor outputs. This means that the system exchanges neither matter nor energy or information with its environment.
- A system is called *closed* if it exchanges energy but not matter with its environment. Consequently, closed systems can have any number of inputs and outputs but at least one of either.
- A system is called *open* if it exchanges both energy and matter with its environment.

Perfectly isolated systems are a theoretical ideal case that does not exist in reality. Likewise, closed systems that show no exchange of matter with their environment whatsoever do not exist outside laboratory conditions. Accordingly, all biological, economic and social systems are open systems. Therefore, common parlance does not distinguish between isolated and closed systems, but subsumes isolated and closed systems under the notion of a closed system and narrows the distinction down to closed versus open systems.

The properties of the system components and their interactions define the system's state at a given point in time. The essential variables characterising the system's state are called state variables while the essential factors characterising the system's environment are called parameters. Changes in the system's state can either be caused by external impacts or by processes within the system itself. The resultant system's performance is determined by the properties of the system's components, their interrelations and the system's type. Depending on whether the system under investigation is an open or a closed system and on the nature of the interrelations between the system's components, different characteristics and manners of dynamic performance are to be expected (see sections 4.3 and 4.5).

If changes in the state variables have an effect on these state variables themselves, meaning that the state variables are a function of their own lagged values, this is called a feedback loop. In the presence of feedback loops, the system may develop an autonomous manner of performance that is independent of environmental influences and cannot be related to external impacts. In principle, positive and negative feedback loops need to be distinguished. While the former induce self-reinforcing systems reactions, the latter have an extenuating effect. For the system to exhibit complex behaviour, at least one interrelation between the systems component needs to be non-linear, and at least one feedback loop needs to exist. In systems of such a kind, an incidence cannot be traced back to a single cause or even a sequence of causes. The system's progression is not so much generated by external impacts but by the system's internal dynamics.

The passage toward a system-theoretical perspective initiated by von Bertalanffy out of a critique of the classical deductive approach can be considered as part of a paradigm shift (in the sense of Kuhn, 1962). Von Bertalanffy explicitly designed his system-theoretical approach as a counter-draft to the modelling procedure in classical physics, in particular classical mechanics, as he was critical with respect to its deductive and reductionist strategy. He reasoned that the individual entities investigated in reality never exist as isolated phenomena and, therefore, need to be examined using a model of "organised complexity" that takes account of their interconnectedness. According to von Bertalanffy, the deductive scientific methodology transferred from classical mechanics is capable of successfully explaining "unorganised complexity", but when it comes to the investigation of "organised complexity" it reaches its limits. At this, "unorganised complexity" means entities that are connected by linear relationships while with "organised complexity" entities are linked by non-linear relationships and interconnections.

With respect to the phenomenon of scientific paradigms not only Kuhn but also von Bertalanffy himself as well as economic authors have pointed out that the analytical instruments of contemporary science are significantly influenced by prevailing perceptions concerning regularities that are considered as universally valid for all processes in nature and society. Physics, in particular, shapes the common worldview and, in doing so, also influences theory construction in other branches of science.[80] As mentioned, von Bertalanffy himself explicitly emphasised the influence of classical physics, in particular mechanics, on the approaches in other disciplines. In transferring these analytical instruments, the presumptions about significantly adopted system-theoretical characteristics shape the perception concerning the properties, behaviour and options for progression of the system investigated.

[80] See Biervert and Held (1994), Hsieh and Ye (1991); for a discussion of the influences of the prevailing worldview on the perception of nature in economics, see also Priddat (1993) and Skourtos (1994).

4.3 Characteristics and Systems Performance in Closed Systems

From the viewpoint of systems theory, the model formation in the manner of classical mechanics criticised by von Bertalanffy represents the prototype of a closed system. The epistemological and analytical foundation of classical mechanics originating in the 17th century is considered to be Cartesian rationalism, which treats nature as a perfect machine that operates according to exact and universally valid laws. By means of analytical geometry, as introduced by Descartes, as well as reductionist methodology stating that all properties of a total system can be deduced from the properties of the system components, these natural laws can be mathematically specified (Hsieh & Ye, 1991).

This paradigm was elaborated by Isaac Newton to form an encompassing physical system of explanations. In Newton's classical mechanics, systems are treated as an assemblage of indistinguishable and in nature unalterable particles of matter. They maintain no material exchanges with their environment and follow the linear Newtonian laws of motion and the universal law of gravitation.[81] These properties correspond to the system-theoretical criteria of closed systems whereby each systems component is ascribed a proper motion constant with respect to direction and speed. Changes of this proper motion can only be caused by external force impacts and consequently occur with the least possible effort, according to the so-called „Principle of Least Action". The path and the result of this alteration can be mathematically calculated by means of constrained optimisation. The basic equations are linear and the equilibrium states achieved are invariably unique and stable. Linearity of relationships between the systems components is accountable for the behaviour of the total system being deducible from the behaviour of the system components and, thus, for the applicability of classical deductive and reductionist methodology.

Thus, for closed mechanistic systems the options for progression can be characterised by the following two statements:

- closed, mechanistic systems are characterised by *continuous changes* and *unique equilibrium states;*
- closed, mechanistic systems exhibit simple equilibrium states unalterable in nature, space and time.

From these two items, the following consequences concerning the determinacy and predictability of closed, mechanistic systems can be derived. The implications of continuous change and uniqueness of equilibrium states give rise to a strictly deterministic worldview:[82] As the properties of the total system can be deduced

[81] See Hsieh and Ye (1991). Gravitation was explained as an invisible "distant effect" determining all motions while the coordination process itself remained unexplained. In the Cartesian worldview distant effects of that kind were unknown.

[82] That linearity of interconnection is a necessary prerequisite for reductionist methodology, since it implies that all changes of magnitude occur proportionally and, thus, guar-

from those of the system components and as all particles are subject to Newton's laws of motion, all incidents are completely predetermined and predictable (Hsieh & Ye, 1991). The determinism of classical mechanics articulately appears in the image of Pierre-Simon Laplace's demon, who, provided with exact knowledge of all initial conditions, is in a position to completely and perfectly forecast the future of the universe. Furthermore, Newton's system excludes the possibility of irreversible qualitative change: As all systems components are unalterable in nature, any change in Newton's system is caused by relocations of systems components and proceeds continuously. By contrast, qualitative changes of systems components are impossible. But as distinguished to qualitative change, changes in location are inherently reversible. Accordingly, all of Newton's laws can be calculated in the reverse direction, rendering an exact restoration of the initial state theoretically possible. Moreover, since the equilibrium states are both simple and unalterable with respect to nature, space and time, the equilibrium state is determined by the same state variable values at any point in time.

4.4 Modelling the Economy as a Closed System: Systems Behaviour and Forecasting

Due to the enormous success of classical mechanics in physics, the impact the worldview implicit in this discipline had on the perspective and modelling approaches in other contemporary branches of science can hardly be overestimated.[83] Newton's system seemed to comprise the laws governing the course of the world and it made scientific research conducted at the desk an actual option.[84] In the following time period, for a multitude of phenomena that seemed to relate to regularities, equilibria or a natural order, analyses employing Newtonian instruments were presented.

This impact of classical mechanics on modelling strategies is also noticeable in economic theory, with respect to both the presumptions of continuous changes and unique equilibrium states and the properties of equilibrium states as being simple and unalterable in nature, space and time. Classical political economy already proceeded on the notion that interactions of systems components follow mathematical regularities and lead to a unique and stable equilibrium state, characterised by so-called "natural" figures. In early Neoclassical economics the analytical instruments of classical mechanics were formally adopted. Edgeworth, Jevons, and Walras, in particular, explicitly refer to classical mechanics as a standard for their

anties that the properties of the system as a whole can be inferred from the sum of the properties of the systems components. See Hsieh and Ye (1991).

[83] For an impressive narrative see Prigogine and Stengers (1984: ch. I).

[84] The most famous example is the discovery of the planet Neptune solely by means of theoretical calculations, which was confirmed later on by empirical observations. See Sebba (1953) and Georgescu-Roegen (1979).

economic theory.[85] Corresponding to the basic principles of classical mechanics, this generation of models treats the economy as a closed system that leaves its equilibrium position only as a reaction to external interference factors and invariably converges towards a new, stable final position. This final state can be calculated according to universal laws, ordinarily presuming linear functions. With the assumptions of profit and utility maximisation, classical mechanic's "Principle of Least Action", which amounts to the technique of constraint optimisation of an objective function, was also transferred into the formal instruments of economic theory – the variables and parameters were merely ascribed a different interpretation.[86]

Contemporary Neoclassical models also explicitly or implicitly include the suppositions of classical mechanics (Hsieh & Ye, 1991). For instance, models of perfect, atomistic competition assume identical and unchangeable economic agents, whose interrelationships are described by log-linear functions. Examples are the usage of linear-homogenous production functions or the supposition of linear-homogenous fields of indifference curves. Linearity assumptions of such a kind are essential for the possibility of deriving aggregate demand and supply functions for goods and production factors as the sum of the supply and demand functions of the individual agents. Thus, they are accountable for reductionist methodology, i.e. explaining the behaviour of the total system by summing up the behaviour of the system components. Furthermore, the presumptions that economic agents are indistinguishable and that their interrelationships are linear ensure that the system does not exhibit complex internal structures – thus, endogenous influences on its progression cannot emerge. As a result, equilibrium states are determined by exogenous parameters and are both unique and stable at all times (see also section 3.2).

The assumptions of classical mechanics are also found in Neoclassical growth theory, which in turn is based on Neoclassical models of perfect competition including the implications mentioned. The prototype of the Neoclassical growth model according to Solow (1956) and Swan (1956) is based on a linear-homogenous production function that determines the growth path of national income and capital accumulation (see also section 2.4.6). In this model, the system converges to a unique long-term equilibrium growth path, the characteristics of which are determined by exogenous parameters. The Neoclassical model of opti-

---

[85] See, e.g., Thoben (1982), Georgescu-Roegen (1979). While Jevons considered the economy as "the mechanics of utility and self interest" (Jevons 1970), Walras referred to it as "... a physico-mathematical science like *mechanics* or *hydrodynamics*" and stated: "... economists should not be afraid to use the method and language of mathematics" (Walras, 1909). An impressive narrative of the influence of classical mechanics and energetics on modern Neoclassical theory is provided by Mirowski (1984a and 1989); concerning the influence of energetics on modern Neoclassical theory, see also Mirowski (1984b).

[86] A detailed comparison of modelling structures is presented by Khalil (1994). Neoclassical growth theory, in using the Hamilton function, also employs the same instruments as classical mechanics. See Hsieh and Ye (1991).

mal growth also implies deterministic predictability. The model includes the choice of optimal time paths of some strategic variables, the solution being calculated by means of constrained dynamic optimisation. Pivotal is the optimisation of the Hamilton function, the dynamic equivalent of the Lagrange method of optimisation: Again, log-linear relationships are presumed, and the mechanistic "Principle of Least Action" comes into use. As a result of the explicit and implicit mechanistic model suppositions, Neoclassical growth theory exhibits the same deterministic worldview as Newtonian mechanics – a consequence that is explicitly highlighted in the introductory paragraph of *[Mathematical Theories of Economic Growth]* (1970) by Burmeister and Dobells:

> "The mathematician Laplace is reputed to have said, „Give me only the equations of motion, and I will show you the future of the Universe." Likewise, economists studying the evolution of a large general equilibrium system ask only for the equations of motion in order to bring their work to completion."

Concerning growth theory, the perception of the economy as a mechanistic, closed system is particularly important with respect to the predictability of actual and potential growth. Most theory-based estimation approaches rest on Cobb-Douglas or CES production functions in the style of the Solow-Swan growth model (see section 2.6.2). As mentioned, models of this type include suppositions that imply predictability of the system's progression and exclude multiple equilibria as well as effects of hysteresis and path dependency. As such, the modelling procedure itself, due to its implicit assumptions, presupposes the existence of a unique path of potential growth that is log-linear in course. Consequently, most basic approaches proceed on the assumption that the progression of potential growth is basically unambiguously predictable, log-linear and cannot be affected by measures of economic policy. As outlined in the following sections, there is the possibility that economic policy's presumed incapacity to act may well become a self-fulfilling prophecy, in case the economy, contrary to these assumptions, is not structured as a closed, mechanistic but as an open system.

4.5 Characteristics and Systems Behaviour in Open Systems

The system-theoretical assumptions inherent in classical mechanics and the inevitably resulting perceptions concerning the operating mode of a system were recognised early. This prompted especially biological and social scientists to warn against an unreflecting transfer of mechanistic modelling into other branches of science – especially in cases for which the modelling assumptions referring to closed, mechanistic systems are obviously unrealistic. At an early stage, the search for analytical instruments alternative to those of classical mechanics brought thermodynamics into focus since this discipline explicitly sets out to investigate the total system (as distinguished from its components). More recently, due to new developments in modern disequilibrium thermodynamics, interest has grown enormously since this discipline explicitly focuses on the investigation of properties, performance and progression of open, complex systems.

Classical thermodynamics, originating around the middle of the 19th century, in physics marked a leadoff departure from the worldview of classical mechanics in many ways.[87] As distinguished from classical mechanics, which focuses on the analysis of systems components, thermodynamics examines the properties of the total system and, thus, proceeds on a macroscopic perspective. Concerning the analysis of open, complex systems, the explanatory model of disequilibrium thermodynamics developed by Ilya Prigogine[88] and his co-workers is particularly important since it investigates the performance of open systems far from thermodynamic equilibrium. This discipline is also known as non-linear thermodynamics since the relationships between the systems components are non-linear and systems behaviour may be determined by positive and negative feedback loops (Prigogine & Stengers, 1984). Due to the presence of positive feedback effects, the stability of the system's performance can no longer be taken as guaranteed. Rather there is the possibility that stochastic fluctuations of systems components or external random influences are reinforced by feedback effects and cause the system to deviate from its original state and to approach a new regime that may exhibit completely different qualities compared to the old equilibrium state. After the distance from equilibrium has reached a certain threshold, the system can begin to exhibit structured and organised behaviour in the form of a dynamic equilibrium state. These kinds of equilibrium states, enforcing a distinctive behaviour once the system enters their sphere of influence, are called *attractors*. In the simplest case, they are so-called fix point attractors that draw the system's development to a single state of equilibrium invariable in nature, space and time. This corresponds to the equilibrium state of a closed, mechanistic system as discussed in the previous section. The equilibrium state of closed mechanistic systems, thus, represents a special case within a wider range of possibilities. In cases of open systems, however, attractors can take on far more complex shapes, forcing the system to exhibit a cyclical or spiral-shaped behaviour in equilibrium. At this, there is the possibility that various attractors coexist allowing for the possibility that even under otherwise identical conditions the system may follow different paths of progression, depending on the impact of random fluctuations.

The performance of an open system can be illustrated with the aid of so-called bifurcation diagrams that represent the system's progression as depending on the distance to equilibrium, measured by means of a control parameter λ.

---

87 See Prigogine and Stengers (1984). Concerning the philosophical implications of thermodynamics, see also Hsieh and Ye (1991), Georgescu-Roegen (1971).

88 The interdisciplinary research group around Prigogine stationed in Brussels investigates, amongst other things, the implications of the results achieved in disequilibrium thermodynamics for scientific branches outside thermodynamics (see Prigogine and Stengers, 1984). In 1977, Prigogine was awarded the Nobel price for chemistry for his work on dissipative structures.

Fig. 10. Bifurcation Diagram

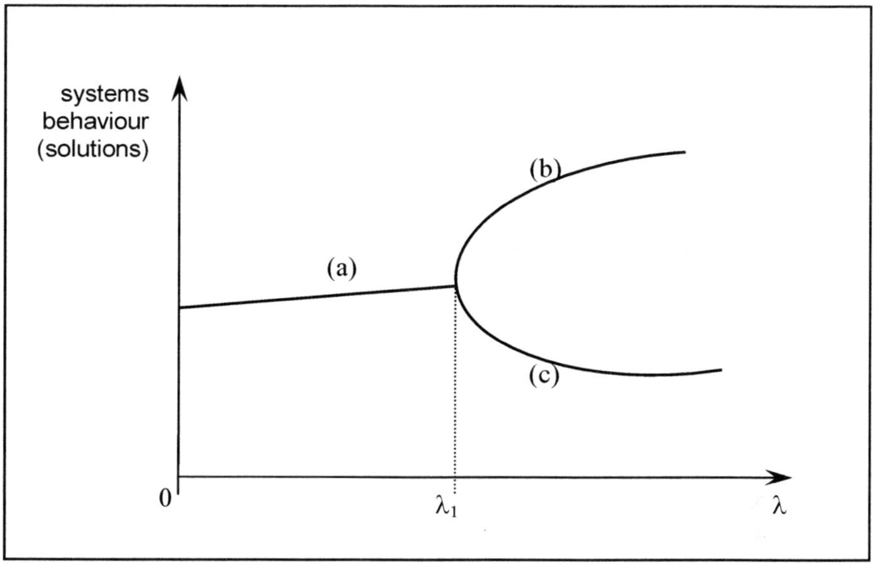

Source: Drawing on Prigogine and Stengers (1984: 161).

In Figure 10 the values 0 to λ_1 represent the realm of linear systems progression. In this realm, a unique and stable path of the system's development, denoted by (a), exists. If starting from the initial value 0, the distance to equilibrium is increased, the system approaches the point λ_1, which is known as the "bifurcation point". At this point, path (a) becomes unstable, and the system's further progression can follow either of the paths (b) and (c). Which path the system eventually follows is determined by random fluctuations.

After the first bifurcation point has been passed, the system may assume a spatially or temporally structured behaviour, which is called "self-organisation".[89] The observable pattern is stable in the sense of repeating itself without deviations, but it does not possess any optimality properties in the sense of common methods of optimisation. The system's choice between different paths at bifurcation points can be understood as a decision between the sphere of influence of different attractors, which do not necessarily need to be fix point attractors but can exhibit complex spatial or temporal patterns of organisation.

[89] See Prigogine and Stengers (1984). Within this general concept of self-organisation, the economic idea of a market equilibrium emerging as a result of individuals' interactions (Smith, Hayek) is a special case, which is characterised by a fix-point attractor. The general case, however, allows for the existence of more complex attractors.

Fig. 11. Bifurcation Diagram

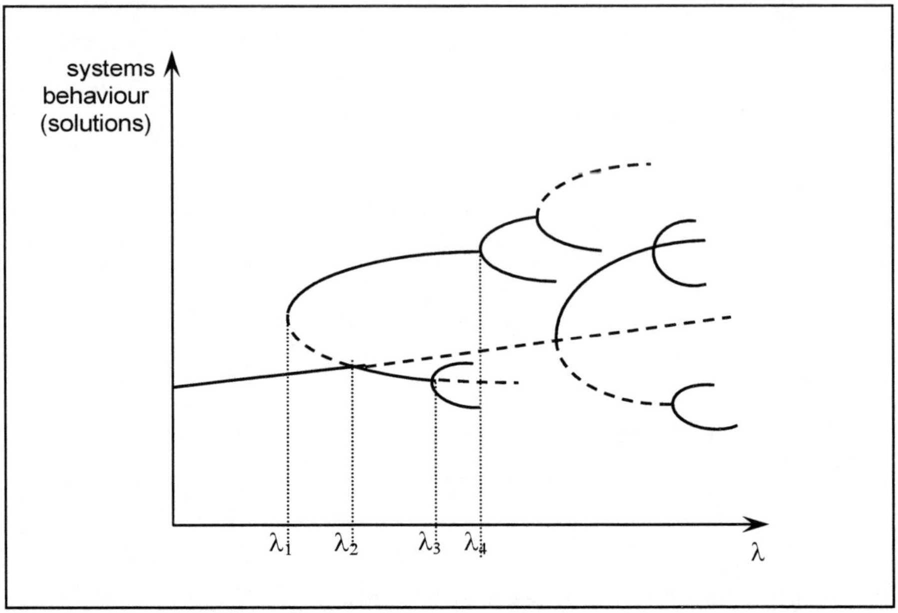

Source: Drawing on Prigogine and Stengers (1984: 170).

The system can now assume a multitude of possible evolutionary paths whereat stable as well as unstable paths (dotted lines) may exist (Figure 11). The historical path of the system's actual progression consists of a sequence governed by deterministic regularities and unstable regions close to the bifurcation points. If the distance to thermodynamic equilibrium is increased, new bifurcation points appear that cause the paths to further split up and allow for a multitude of attractor shapes. Eventually, the succession of critical points becomes so tight that the branches intersect and the possibilities for the system's further evolution become infinite. This is the realm of so-called *deterministic chaos,* where highly complex, so-called "strange" or "chaotic" attractors govern the system's progression. In the sphere of influence of a chaotic attractor, systems behaviour is still governed by deterministic laws, but even marginal differences in the initial situations can give rise to completely differing evolutions.

With respect to their properties and progression, open systems, thus, show fundamental differences compared to closed, mechanistic systems. For one thing, in open systems the presumption of linear relationships between the systems components, which is vital for deductive and reductionist methodology, and according to which the behaviour of the total system can be understood by studying the systems components, is no longer applicable. Since open systems are characterised by nonlinear interactions between systems components, they can exhibit complex behavioural patterns. At this, in systems with more than one state variable any separation of the variables' influences becomes unfeasible. Thus, as distinguished from closed, mechanistic systems with linear relationships between systems components, in open systems the behaviour of the total system cannot be deduced as the sum of the behaviour of its systems components. Furthermore, crucial propositions by chaos theory with respect of the behaviour of dynamic systems directly contradict those of Laplacian determinism, according to which systems progression is perfectly predictable, provided the initial conditions are known. Poincaré, one of the pioneers of chaos theory, had already pointed out that in systems in which minor alterations are amplified by cumulative effects, unpredictable self-reinforcing phenomena might occur:

> "[e]ven if it were the case that the natural laws had no longer any secret for us, we could still only know the initial situation approximately. If that enabled us to predict the succeeding situation with the same approximation, that is all we require, and we should say that the phenomenon had been predicted, that it is governed by laws. But it is not always so: it may happen that small differences in the initial conditions produce very great ones in the final phenomenon. A small error in the former will produce an enormous error in the latter. Prediction becomes impossible, and we have the fortuitous phenomenon" (Poincaré, 1903).

Thus, according to chaos theory, empirically observable irregular time series need not necessarily be purely random in nature but can be governed by deterministic, albeit non-linear regularities that generate complex chaotic behaviour. Consequently, as opposed to the Laplacian proposition, despite being governed by deterministic laws, chaotic systems are in principle unpredictable since even the smallest deviations from the observed initial value may be amplified to the extent of rendering long-term forecasting unfeasible. The first concrete example of a chaotic system was discovered in 1963 by Lorenz within the realm of meteorology; in the 1970s and 1980s similar chaotic pattern were detected in other realm of science, for instance, in ecological and social systems.

As distinguished from closed, mechanistic systems (see section 4.3), with open systems the possibilities for evolution can be characterised by the following two statements:

- In open systems, there is the possibility of *cumulative* processes and *multiple equilibria:* Due to the existence of non-linear interactions of systems components, self-reinforcing instabilities can occur and the system's state may change by leaps and bounds. Contrary to closed, mechanistic systems, the progression of open systems can follow not one but several different paths, the change towards a new equilibrium state being discontinuous. At such points of bifurcation, the choice of paths may be affected by both changes of external parameters and internal fluctuations.
- In open systems, there is the possibility that complex equilibrium states may emerge, the shape of which differs from the classical fix point attractor. At this, both spatially and temporally structured systems behaviour may occur as well as seemingly irregular progressions that are, nevertheless, deterministic since they are governed by chaotic attractors.

From these two items, the following consequences concerning the determinacy and predictability of open systems can be derived. As illustrated by the bifurcation diagrams in Figures 10 and 11, the progression of open systems is governed by deterministic rules as well as random influences: On the branches of the bifurcation tree, the system is in the area of influence of whatever kind of attractor which dominates the influence of random factors. The system's behaviour in this realm is, therefore, essentially governed by deterministic regulations. At the points of bifurcation, however, these paths become unstable: Positive feedback effects cause cumulative processes that reinforce the system's internal fluctuations and, as a consequence, the attractor's influence can be overcome. The following systems progression depends on random factors, where both minor changes of external parameters and the behaviour of individual systems components become pivotal for the evolution of the total system. At this, drastic changes in systems behaviour can occur since the transition to another path implies entering the area of influence of a different attractor. The existence of several stable paths to be chosen from is at the basis of the hysteresis phenomenon, which is observable not only in physical and chemical but also in economic systems (see also section 2.5.5).

As a result of the interaction of random influences and deterministic rules, in open systems irreversibility attains pivotal significance. Since the random influences that are decisive at the points of bifurcation cannot be reproduced at will, a path, once chosen, cannot be simply reverted. The choice of paths itself, in turn, is crucial for the system's further possibilities of development as different options present themselves, depending on the path entered. This property is known as *path dependency of development*: A system's future evolutionary options are determined by the choices of paths in the past. Beyond the possibility of saltatory and irreversible developments, forecasting the progression of open systems is rendered completely impossible if the system at hand is a chaotic system since in this case predictability is ruled out in principle.

4.6 Modelling the Economy as an Open System: Limits to Forecasting

As all economic systems are connected with their environment by exchange relationships, they are open systems in the sense of general systems theory. It is, therefore, not surprising that attempts have been recently made at linking the theory of open systems with the progression of economic systems. With respect to the options of progression for open systems as discussed at the end of the previous section, the influence of the theory of open systems as well as similarities in model formation are recognisable in several of the economic approaches discussed in chapters 2 and 3.

Concerning the possibility of *cumulative effects* and *multiple equilibria,* the alterability of "natural" figures due to parameter changes, as discussed by Wicksell, Lindahl and Myrdal, resembles ideas of multiple equilibria in the theory of open systems. As outlined in sections 2.3, 2.4.1, 2.4.2 and 2.4.4, these approaches consider the possibility that, due to feedback loops and cumulative effects, equilibrium states of natural figures may arise that are completely different from the original regime. This property reflects the well-known imagery of the bifurcation diagram, where changes in control variables, such as parameters of technical progress or monetary policy, may induce a change of the future system's state (here: investment and growth) – a possibility that is negated in strictly Classical or Neoclassical models characterised by unique and unalterable equilibrium states. Similar properties are to be found in Keynes' (1936) theory. In this case, the focus lies on the significance of entrepreneurial expectations for investment demand: Again, due to cumulative processes there is the possibility of different equilibrium constellations characterised by full- and underutilisation, which may differ from the initial state (see section 2.4.5). Here, even more than in theories by Wicksell, Lindahl and Myrdal, the possibility of endogenous systems progression as well as the options of stabilisation policy for bringing the system onto another path are addressed. In the framework of the QUERU and hysteresis approaches developed later and outlined in section 2.5.5, which also allow for the possibility of cumulative processes and multiple equilibria, the properties of the systems components and their interactions responsible for these phenomena were also discussed. As distinguished from Classical and Neoclassical models with perfect competition and identical agents, these kinds of models presume monopolistic competition and, thus, include the idea that agents are distinguishable and supply and demand curves may be non-linear. Consequently, the corresponding systems exhibit a complex internal structure, which renders the linear relationships prevailing in closed, mechanistic systems untenable - same as the reductionist conclusion that the behaviour of the total system can be deduced from the sum of the reactions of the systems components.

The approaches discussed so far still focus on deviations from potential output rather than potential output and its progression itself. The transition from national income to potential output and potential growth is accomplished by models including an investment multiplier, for instance, by Lundberg (1937), Harrod (1939), and Domar (1946), which, by discussing cumulative processes and the possibility of unstable growth equilibria also show similarities to the theory of open systems (see also section 2.4.6). New growth theory, by modelling increasing returns to scale, network externalities and product innovations, has also extensively addressed possible impacts of positive feedback effects on the growth path even if these approaches continue to focus on the determination of equilibrium growth paths in a Neoclassical sense.

An explicit transfer of the basic principles of the theory of open systems was undertaken by W.B. Arthur, who investigated the significance of historical events and path dependencies for the technological progression of an economy (Arthur, 1988, 1990; Arthur, Ermoliev & Kaniovski, 1987). In Arthur's models, path dependency is caused by non-linearities in the form of increasing returns to scale, which can arise as a result of learning effects, fix cost degression and network externalities, and imply non-linearities in the progression of revenues. In the presence of increasing returns to scale, random historical events, such as personal preferences of decision makers, the influence of lobby groups and contract partners or political factors play an important part for the progression of the market shares of competing technologies: Once one particular technology due to a historical accident has acquired a competitive edge, learning effects, scale effects and network externalities lead to further competitive advantages. As a typical example, the almost exclusive usage of the QWERTY keyboard for typewriters is mentioned, which was developed in the 19th century and since then, despite several ergonomic inefficiencies, has prevailed over all new developments. The imperfections of the QWERTY keyboard were not considered as a disadvantage in the beginning as the contemporary mechanical typewriters were prone to jammed type bars, therefore, typing too fast was not desirable anyway. When, as a result of improved typewriter technology, this problem became obsolete, the QWERTY keyboard was already established to the extent that all attempts at replacing it by ergonomically superior models were doomed to failure (cf. David, 1985). Further examples are the developments in the markets for personal computer operating systems and VCR systems. The impact of increasing returns to scale amounts to a positive feedback loop and eventually leads to a market-dominating position of this technology whereas the competing alternatives are driven out of the market (so-called *lock out effect*).

Likewise, concerning the possibility of *complex equilibrium states,* among the economic approaches presented in chapters 2 and 3, there are many examples that show similarities to the propositions of the theory of open systems. Questions of dynamic macroeconomic developments were investigated in gap theories by Lindahl, Myrdal, Åkerman, and Frisch as outlined in section 2.4.6. Åkerman's spectral-analytical model, in particular, is governed by deterministic non-linearities that lead the system to a complex equilibrium in the shape of cyclical behaviour, which is characteristic for a system in the catchment area of a complex attractor (see section 2.4.6). The multiplier-accelerator models dating from the 1930s (see Frisch, 1933; Lundberg, 1937; Samuelson, 1939) as well as non-linear multiplier-accelerator models developed later by Hicks and Goodwin also show properties akin to systems under the influence of complex attractors. But none of these models incorporate the degree of non-linearity that would suffice to cause chaotic behaviour. Only Grandmont (1985) applied chaos theory to economic systems in a seminal paper in order to explain persistent endogenous and deterministic business cycles. However, attempts at empirically substantiating deterministic chaos in the progression of GDP empirically have so far remained unsuccessful (Hsieh & Ye, 1991).

Currently no formalised models derived from the theory of open systems for the purpose of analysing and forecasting actual and potential economic growth exist. However, the treatment of the economy as an open, dynamic system with non-linear relationships between systems components points to the possibility of employing the self organisation paradigma in macroeconomics in a heuristic manner, at least, in order to arrive at important statements concerning the forecasting of potential growth. Firstly, the theory of open systems suggests that when forecasting potential growth the possibility of several alternative and not necessarily linear growth paths exists. At this, over- and underutilisation of potential output in one period may affect the path of potential output in future periods via cumulative effects. Furthermore, the significance of parameter changes at bifurcation points, as illustrated in bifurcation diagrams, suggests that for the choice of the path the system ultimately follows parameter decisions in economic policy may be of vital importance. A commendable practical solution is the employment of scenario techniques, investigating potential growth under different presumptions with respect to political strategies.

METHODOLOGICAL-EMPIRICAL PART

5 Analysis and Criticism of Conventional Methods of Estimation

5.1 Introduction

The history of the idea of potential output (chapters 2 and 3) shows how difficult it is to pin down this concept even from a purely theoretical perspective. How much more difficult must it, therefore, be to come up with an empirical definition of potential growth? A series of standard procedures for determining potential output have, nonetheless, been established in recent decades and are considered in the following. While theoretical criticism of these concepts and doubts about a strict dichotomy between growth and the business cycle have been discussed in detail in chapter 2, this chapter spotlights the empirical features and data requirements of these methods.

Section 5.2 begins by reviewing the literature and the findings of a project performed by the ZEW in 2005 on behalf of the German Federal Ministry of Economics and Technology and briefly sketches the most important procedures for estimating potential output and potential growth. The ZEW project dating from 2005 examined medium-term macroeconomic projection methods used by government agencies in major industrialised countries and international institutions. As shown by both a questionnaire survey conducted by the ZEW and an appraisal of the relevant literature, official institutions use a vast array of different methods and models for the purpose of constructing medium-term projections. In each case, however, key importance is attached to the concept and empirical implementation of potential output.

This is not the place to present all these models and methods. The following discussion will, therefore, be limited to typical representatives of particular categories which are used especially frequently to estimate potential output and – drawing on such estimates – to make medium-term projections with a time horizon of 3 to 5 years. The following digression also takes a critical look at the empirical implementation of the NAIRU concept. Since there is such a close correspondence between the NAIRU concept and potential output and potential growth, the NAIRU plays a central role in both the production function method and sys-

S. Hauptmeier et al., *Projecting Potential Output*, Zew Economic Studies,
DOI: 10.1007/978-3-7908-2177-2_5, © Physica-Verlag Berlin Heidelberg 2009

tem-based methods of evaluating potential output.[90] This digression will focus, in particular, on presenting different empirical methods and estimates of the non-accelerating inflation rate of unemployment ("NAIRU").

Section 5.3 follows with a comparative appraisal of the results of different procedures for estimating potential growth for the total economy by using the entire observation period from 1970 to 2004 for the estimate. The object of interest is whether the different methods produce fundamentally similar assessments of fluctuations in real changes in GDP from the estimated long-term growth trend or whether the different methods imply extremely different ideas about the development of potential growth and the business cycle over time.

Methods of estimating potential output are usually not only used to trace overall economic developments in the past and present but to draw up medium- to long-term projections. One key element of the study will, therefore, be section 5.4 which will examine whether the forecasts of overall economic developments generated using these methods meet minimum quality standards over a medium-term period in terms of bias and variance in forecast errors. These analyses are based on recursive "out-of-sample" forecasts, which are contrasted with actual outcomes in each case in order to formally examine the resulting forecast errors. As all the procedures examined here are retrospective in nature (the presumed interactions and estimated parameters are only derived from historical economic time series), the present study is restricted to the systematic errors in medium-term projections that this focus on the past may possibly induce. In practical terms the statistical and structural procedures for forecasting medium-term growth are not usually used in a purely mechanistic manner but are complemented with qualitative estimates and expert opinions ("add-factors") in the hope that this will take the sting out of the tail of the design-induced defects in the formal methods. A comparison of purely statistical economic, recursive forecasts with actual five-year projections of medium-term changes in German GDP drawn up by the German government and the International Monetary Fund will then demonstrate in what direction official projections are influenced if such qualitative assumptions are set.

The discussion of specific methods and their practical implementation in the next section illustrates which official statistical data is usually used to estimate potential output and which methods are used to deal with possible structural breaks in the data. Cotis et al. (2004) have formulated some fundamental requirements which need to be met by procedures for estimating potential output to enable these to be used as aids for economic policy decisions at all: theoretical consistency, transparency, consistency and precision of estimates. These fundamental criteria are used to determine the usefulness of the reviewed methods in the following sections.

---

[90] Theoretical aspects of the NAIRU and similar concepts are discussed in detail in section 2.5.

5.2 Methods of Estimating Potential Output and Potential Growth

There are a number of empirical methods for estimating potential output or trend components of overall production in the economy. The following sections describe and examine the most commonly used representatives of particular categories. Given the content focus of the project, a particular slant is taken on the various variants of production function methods. As far as the significance of the following procedures in the work of government agencies and international organisations is concerned, reference is made to the findings of the ZEW project "Methods of Medium-Term Economic Projections" completed last year. This project report does not take any account of the significance of macroeconometric structural models, which are used as standard in policy consulting and projection contexts alongside the methods presented here. We have not included very much in the way of detailed formal descriptions of any of the methods in the following and the reader is referred to the relevant literature or technical appendix. Detailed overviews of various methods of estimating potential growth can be found, for example, in Bjørnland, Brubakk, and Jore (2005), Carnot, Koen, and Tissot (2005), Njuguna, Karingi, and Kimenyi. (2005), Sachverständigenrat zur Begutachtung der gesamtwirtschaftlichen Entwicklung (2003), Cotis et al. (2004), Weyerstraß (2001), Chagny and Döpke (2001), Cerra and Saxena (2000), or Dupasquier, Guay, and St-Amant (1997).

5.2.1 Univariate Methods of Estimating Potential Output and Potential Growth

Univariate methods of estimating potential output and potential growth are based on time series procedures which only take account of the historical values of target variables with the aim of fitting trend lines to observed time series. Typically trend lines are equated with a potential variable or a long-term development while the difference between actual observations and trend paths are defined as gaps, which can be interpreted as excess demand or weakness in demand. Proponents of the New Neoclassical Synthesis and more recent macroeconomic theories take a critical stance towards these methods, however, as they produce results that agree only coincidentally, if at all, with analytically determined potential values. Trend-related procedures of this type project past values into the future without taking the fact into account that potential output is also determined by future expectations (cf. section 2.3).

Potential estimates carried out using univariate or most multivariate methods should be regarded as proxies of normal capacity utilisation given that the observed values can run above or below the estimated trend capacity utilisation. Full use of potential in the sense of full capacity utilisation is usually not computed as this would only allow negative gaps. One of the few exceptions in this context is the capital stock method used by the German Council of Economic Experts

(*Sachverständigenrat zur Begutachtung der gesamtwirtschaftlichen Entwicklung*) which results in technically driven potential output which is at all times greater or equal to actual production (cf. section 2.6.2). The term *potential* is used in the same way as *trend components*, which reflect normal or full capacity utilisation in the following. The concept to which these procedures refer is apparent from the context in each case.

Table 1 in section 5.3 provides an overview of the univariate methods covered by the study. The following explanations are limited to brief and intuitive descriptions of each method. This report does not provide a technical description of univariate methods, and the reader is referred to the original papers or the literature referred to above.

The *symmetrical moving average* uses the arithmetic mean of present, past and future values to compute the long-term components. *Spline regression* adapts linear slopes to the rate of change in GDP for various past cycles.[91]

Both the *Baxter-King filter* and the *Christiano-Fitzgerald filter* are "band-pass filters" which eliminate the trend and irregular components of a time series while preserving business cycle components. Both procedures are based on the modification of two-sided moving averages to the time series and only differ in terms of the estimation of the weights; both filter variants require the specification of a typical cycle length.

The *Hodrick-Prescott filter* obtains the trend components of a time series after selecting the degree for smoothness of trend components or adjusting of the trend to the actual series. The central variable used in this method is the smoothing parameter λ which is used to input indirect assumptions about the typical duration of reference cycle in the computing procedure. If λ is close to zero, the smoothed components are equal to the original time series. This corresponds to the assumption of the standard real business cycle theory (e.g., Kydland & Prescott, 1982) according to which all output movements are equal to fluctuations in the potential value. In contrast, very large values of λ produce a series of smoothed components that correspond to a linear time trend, and all actual output developments around this time trend are assigned to the cyclical components. In practice λ values of 1,600 for quarterly data and 100 for end-of-year data have become established.[92] In line with the recommendations of Ravn and Uhlig (2002), the rate of change in German GDP is also filtered using a smoothing parameter of 6.25.

In the *univariate model of unobserved components*, observed aggregate production is composed of an unobserved trend and unobserved cycle components. The long-term trend is usually assumed to follow a random walk while the cyclical components can be described by a stationary autoregressive process. The model is

---

[91] The different business cycles are differentiated according to Sachverständigenrat zur Begutachtung der gesamtwirtschaftlichen Entwicklung (SVR, 2003). Cf. Figure 33 in Appendix AI.2.

[92] Refer to Chagny and Döpke (2001) for a discussion of the pros and cons of the Hodrick-Prescott filter.

recursively estimated after transformation into a state space formulation with the help of the *Kalman filter*.[93]

The evaluation of the state space model using the Kalman filter leaves a degree of arbitrary scope for the input of initial values and restrictions relating to the variance of cycle and trend components, which has a substantial impact on the results. The advantage of the filter is that, in addition to smoothed estimated values for the individual components, additional confidence areas are given which enable the uncertainties in the estimated components to be captured. This is a decisive feature of the model of unobserved components given that the remaining univariate methods do not usually allow the statistical lack of accuracy of the estimated components to be quantified.

A problem often discussed in relation to statistical filter methods is the so-called *end-point problem*. One dimension of this problem concerns the proneness of these methods to deliver up-to-date and reliable estimators of potential output and the resulting capacity utilisation - publications of current economic statistics are usually preliminary in nature and are often modified as times goes by. This can result in incorrect estimates of aggregate capacity utilisation and potentially to inappropriate implications for possible economic policy decisions. All the methods are beset by this problem to some extent - in fact this problem is inherent in the recording and processing of official statistics. It is for this reason that leading indicators of economic trends are usually used in practice to close any information gaps.

The second dimension of the end-point problem concerns the filter methods that are based on the use of symmetric moving averages in such a way as the Hodrick-Prescott filter or the Baxter-King and Christiano-Fitzgerald filters. It is not possible to use symmetric averages on the end of the observation period owing to a lack of data so that use is made of asymmetric moving averages such that recent developments in the time series have a major impact on the estimation of trends at the current data points. In practice this end-point problem is usually dealt with by extending the reference series by the forecast values for immediate future periods.

Although purely statistical methods are sufficient without the need to formulate the economic framework and, thus, offer considerable advantages over structural methods (about which more below), they also draw on ideas about the type and duration of business cycles (as in the case, for example, of the filters of Baxter & King, 1999 or Christiano & Fitzgerald, 2003). The clear advantage of univariate methods is that they require only minimal assumptions to be made and do not require any additional time series other than the target variables. What is more, it is also possible to break down the components for all the relevant economic time series and not just for central variables such as GDP or the NAIRU.

The univariate methods are not suitable for applications in which identifying the influencing factors of the trend or cycle components is of key importance. The

---

93 Cf. Cerra and Saxena (2000) for a formal presentation of the model touched on here. Hamilton (1994: 372f.) describes the technical implementation of the Kalman filter method in great detail. Refer to the digression in section 5.2.2.1.

purely mechanistic separation of components is merely undertaken from the information in the time series itself, and interactions with other important variables are neglected. Another critical characteristic of univariate methods is that a permanent output gap per assumption is usually excluded by construction and is not based on empirical results. When applied to GDP, this inevitably shows a flattening out of trend components if the period of full capacity utilisation is longer than the presumed cycle duration. Univariate methods have not per se been developed for forecasting purposes but are, nonetheless, often used as tools to smooth series in interaction with economic structural procedures for estimating and projecting potential output.[94]

5.2.2 Multivariate Methods of Estimating Potential Output and Potential Growth

This section takes a critical and analytical look at conventional multivariate procedures for estimating potential growth making explicit reference to economic interrelationships. This presentation primarily focuses on the production function method and the numerous variants used, for example, by the German Council of Economic Experts, the German Bundesbank, the OECD and the European Commission. Although the analysis in this section is based on our own calculations, account is also taken of the results of a ZEW study from 2005 undertaken for the German Federal Ministry of Economics and Technology, which addressed similar issues.

Furthermore, this section analyses the structural vector autoregressive (SVAR) model developed by Blanchard and Quah (1989). These methods are extremely influential in the real business of estimating potential output and are consequently examined as alternatives to the production function approach.[95] A brief review is made of the system approaches adopted by Apel and Jansson (1999) and other procedures originating in empirical growth economics based on analyses of country cross-sections.

5.2.2.1 Production Function Methods

The concept of potential output suggests that a macroeconomic production function exists which combines various input factors at any current level of available technology and that potential output may be conceived of as the output of an economy subject to a given quantity of non-variable input factors and sustainable

[94] As a rule the Hodrick-Prescott filter is used in this context. Refer also to section 5.4 for the use of this filter when producing projections based on the production function method.

[95] For applications of the SVAR models, refer to Scacciavillani and Swagel (2002), Gottschalk and van Zandweghe (2001), Dupasquier et al. (1997). System estimators are used, for example, by Ögünc and Ece (2004), Benes and N'Diaye (2004).

quantities of variable input factors. This is the conceptual underpinning of the methods described in the following.

Parametric Production Function Method

These methods typically take a Cobb-Douglas or CES-type production function for the private sector (gross value added excluding the public sector) with the production factors labour and capital.[96] The method uses the Cobb-Douglas function and requires knowledge of the following variables and parameters which are estimated or taken either directly (e.g., employment) or indirectly (e.g., capital stock) from the national accounts of the relevant OECD countries:[97]

- total gross value added for the private and public sector (Y_t, Y_t^p, Y_t^g);
- potential labour input in the private and public sector (L_t^{*p}, L_t^{*g});
- potential capital input in the private sector (K_t^*);
- development of total factor productivity (u_t^*);
- partial factor elasticities (α, $1\text{-}\alpha$).

Potential production in the private sector is determined by the functional form of the production function combined with the values of the potential input factors. The usual procedure for obtaining the potential production of the total economy is to add actual gross value added in the public sector to potential production in the private sector. This is based on the assumption that gross value added in the public sector corresponds to its potential value at all times. As gross value added in the private sector is by far the largest element of total gross value added, this assumption does not have a major influence on the calculation of aggregate potential outputs and its development.

The production function method is not only subject to the theoretical criticism already outlined in sections 2 and 3, it also suffers from a number of empirical shortcomings which are usually regarded very pragmatically by institutions using the method. The problems relate to the unobservability of the potential input factors, which can only be resolved by adopting additional assumptions and tools, such as statistical smoothing methods.

---

[96] Cf., e.g., Carnot et al. (2005), McMorrow and Roeger (2001), Giorno, Richardson, Roseveare, and van den Noo (1995), or Torres and Martin (1990). The presentation of the parametric production function methods in this section is largely based on Carnot et al. (2005) and Giorno et al. (1995). Refer to Appendix AI.4 for the concrete implementation of these methods. The OECD recently revised its methods and now directly calculates potential output for the total economy. What is more, new estimates of capital input are used which take better account of the relative marginal productivity of various capital goods in particular. This mainly affects the use of information and communications technology inputs. Refer to Beffy, Ollivaud, Richardson, and Sédillot (2006) for a description of the revised method.

[97] In order to be able to use the empirical wage ratio to determine the partial factor elasticities of the Cobb-Douglas production function, it is also necessary to assume constant returns to scale, i.e. the partial factor elasticities must add up to 1 (this corresponds to first degree homogeneity of production functions).

The potential capital input is usually approximated by drawing on actual capital stock. However, as the capital stock cannot be directly observed either, this is usually calculated from past investment flows and appropriate assumptions about capital depreciation.[98] The total factor productivity is usually obtained as the Solow residual of the production function and smoothed-using statistical filters (in most cases the Hodrick-Prescott filter) to calculate a trend value.[99]

It is much more difficult, in contrast, to derive potential labour input. The starting point is the relationship between demographic and institutional labour market factors which can be summarised as follows:

$$L_t^{*p} = P_t^w \times PR_t^* \times (1 - U_t^*) - L_t^{*g}, \tag{5.1}$$

where P_t^w represents the working age population, PR_t^* the trend labour force participation rate and U_t^* the (time-variable) NAIRU.

Potential labour input in the public sector is usually approximated via the actual value. The trend labour force participation rate is typically determined using a filter for the observable labour force participation rate. Estimating the NAIRU can be a treacherous business and is ultimately dependent on the choice of concept used to measure unemployment. Empirical concepts and typical data problems relating to the measurement of NAIRU are addressed in the digression in section 5.2.2.1. A theoretical critique of the concept of non-accelerating inflation rate of unemployment (NAIRU) as well as a critical approach to its interpretation and implications for economic policy can be found in section 3.4.

The procedure outlined here clearly shows what a priori information is required and what assumptions need to be made about the macroeconomic production process in order to be able to estimate potential output and make projections based on the production function procedure. For the purpose of projections it is basically necessary to specify development paths to potential labour input, to capital investments and to productivity or to extrapolate the current development of these factors over the projection horizon on the basis of appropriate trend values. It is standard practice to feed qualitative assumptions about the anticipated development of total factor productivity, for example, into the projection process in addition to technical forecasts of input factors.[100] Provided that the assumptions and specified development paths of the influencing factors have been adequately derived and substantiated, this can also be seen as an advantage of the method in terms of the transparency and communication of the projections. What is more, alternative assumptions (e.g., regarding labour market developments) can also be used to describe different scenarios that reflect the uncertainty of the projection

[98] Cf. OECD (2001) for the OECD method of measuring total capital stock and input. These calculations in this study are based on these figures.

[99] Carnot et al. (2005) describe an alternative method in which a simple trend line is modified to the Solow residual. Breaks can also be modelled in the trend if required.

[100] Cf. the results of the ZEW project "Methods of Medium-Term Economic Projections" dating from 2005 which describes in detail the performance of medium-term projections by government bodies in selected industrial countries and of international organisations such as the OECD and IMF.

and also underline the fact that the projections are based on specific conditions and assumptions.

If it is not possible to identify restrictions for capital formation – such as low return on investment –, the medium- to long-term potential output of given labour productivity in this model approach is limited only by labour supply (Chagny & Döpke, 2001). The key factor in the production function method is, therefore, the potential labour input, which the NAIRU concept aims to capture. However, this also shifts uncertainty about the most relevant potential components of GDP and attributes to the uncertainty inherent in the empirical implementation of the NAIRU concept. Theoretical problems also arise if the potential output is identified on the basis of the NAIRU (cf. section 2.3): On the one hand the logic of the New Keynesian Phillips curve suggests that, as a result of output reactions at nominal rigidities, a low rate of inflation may be linked with inefficiently high rates of unemployment. On the other hand, no account is taken of the fact that full inflation stability only occurs as a response to monetary policy, which itself requires an independent determinant of potential output.

Digression: Empirical Concepts Relating to the Estimation of the NAIRU

The NAIRU (Non-Accelerating Inflation Rate of Unemployment) is – like potential output – unobservable, which means that there are several (in principle solvable) problems attendant in its empirical calculation.

As the NAIRU is derived from the Phillips curve concept, its equation is also the starting point for the calculation.[101] The following baseline model is also referred to as a "triangle model" since, as well as containing price rigidities, it reflects influences from both the supply and demand sides:[102]

$$p_t = a(L)\, p_{t-1} - b(L)\, (U_t - U^*) + c(L)\, z_t + \varepsilon_t, \tag{5.2}$$

where upper-case letters stand for levels and lower-case letters for the initial differences in logarithmic variables; L stands for the lag operator and ε_t for an error term with $\varepsilon_t \sim N(0, \sigma_t^2)$. p_t and p_{t-1} stand for current and delayed rates of inflation, U_t and U^* for the current and constant natural rate of unemployment; vector z_t contains possible shock variables such as raw material prices, currency fluctuations or administrative price determinants (such as tax wedge or value-added tax).

U^* forms part of the constant d for the following estimation equation:

$$p_t = d + a(L)\, p_{t-1} - b(L)\, U_t + c(L)\, z_t + \varepsilon_t. \tag{5.3}$$

As the NAIRU is defined in terms of stable inflation $p_t = p_{t-1}$, typically the sum of the polynomials in the lag operator of the rate of inflation is restricted to 1: $a(1) = 1$. Assuming that on average z_t is not the source of supply shocks (thus $z_t = 0$), the "no shock-NAIRU" is identical with U^* and can, thus, be determined from the constant d as $d \equiv b(1)\, U^*$.

[101] Alternatives include univariate methods (e.g., using the Hodrick-Prescott filter) or structural approaches which estimate the determinants of a price and wage equation. Beissinger (2004) provides a good overview of various models.

[102] The term "triangle model" originated with Gordon (1997). Refer to Franz (2005: 132) and Staiger, Stock, and Watson (1997) for the following model.

The NAIRU is not necessarily constant, however, but may vary over time as a result, for example, of shocks or hysteresis effects. The time-varying NAIRU is usually modelled as *random walk with zero drift* as follows (e.g., Franz, 2005, Gordon, 1997 and Beissinger, 2004).[103]

$$U_t^* = U_{t-1}^* + \eta_t \text{ with } E(\eta_t) = 0 \text{ and } var(\eta_t) = \sigma^2. \quad (5.4)$$

The selection of data for estimating the NAIRU is an additional challenge. The next paragraph sketches out three basic considerations regarding the selection of data for the empirical implementation of the NAIRU concept.

Data Problems

The unemployment rate – the central variable to go into the calculation – varies depending on how it is defined. Rates of unemployment determined and published by the Federal Statistical Office are based on the general census concept and differ from values obtained using the definitions proposed by the International Labour Organization (ILO). The interpretation of estimated non-accelerating rates of employment is, of course, linked to the underlying concept used.

Consumer price indices and GDP deflators are suitable variables for measuring inflation rates. The first of these better reflects the price developments, which are relevant to workers engaged in negotiating their consumer wages. The GDP deflator, on the other hand, better reflects the production prices, which are decisive from the point of view of the employer. Both price indices are, however, inflation indicators. The selection of the price measure used is decisive for the estimated outcome.

Finally, it is important not to forget that the relationship between the rates of inflation and unemployment is influenced by inflation expectations (Friedman, 1968; Ball & Mankiw, 2002; Beissinger, 2004). Assuming adaptive inflation expectations, this is reflected in this model by delayed rates of inflation. These expectations may be better approximated by direct measures, such as those found in surveys undertaken by the European Commission. There is usually only a limited amount of relevant data available, however, so that an adaptive expectation formation process is usually assumed.

Time Constant NAIRU: OLS

If the NAIRU is assumed to be constant over time, its value may be determined by means of estimating eq. (5.3) with the help of the ordinary least square (OLS) method. As described above, the "no-shock NAIRU" U^* results from the estimated constant term d of the relationship (5.3).

However, as the underlying assumption that $p_t = p_{t-1}$ (zero inflation) does not reflect the real situation in Germany, a rate of inflation regarded as tolerable must also be defined (e.g., the ECB inflation target of 2% p.a., see Franz, 2001).

Integration and Cointegration

Unit root tests of the German unemployment and inflation rates diagnose these time series typically the property of non-stationarity so that cointegration tests are necessary for econometric estimates to test whether a long-term connection can be described by an equation such as (5.3) and the concept of a long-term Phillips curve is empirically confirmed at all. If this is the case, the concept of long-run neutrality between inflation and the unem-

[103] Laubach (2001) compares specifications of the NAIRU as random walk with and without drift.

ployment rate may be seriously questioned, thereby, weakening the evidence for an empirical NAIRU.

Time Variable NAIRU: Kalman Filter

For the most part, current research is for the most part based on a time-variable NAIRU. The rationale for the empirical modelling of a time-variable NAIRU is the hysteresis effect: Erosion of qualifications, stigmatisation and the discouragement experienced by the long-term employed – as well as the institutional regulation of the labour market which reduces incentives to look for work – can result in rising non-accelerating unemployment rates over time. The time variable NAIRU is usually estimated with the Kalman filter method (e.g., Greenslade, Pierse, & Saleheen, 2003; Richardson et al., 2000; Fabiani & Mestre, 2004). This method is based on the state space model and has the advantage that it enables a time variable NAIRU to be simultaneously estimated with a Phillips curve.

$$p_t = a(L)\,p_{t-1} - b(L)\,(U_t - U_t^*) + c(L)\,z_t + \varepsilon_t \qquad (5.5)$$

with $E(\varepsilon_t) = 0$ and $var(\varepsilon_t) = \sigma_\varepsilon^2$ and

$$U_t^* = U_{t-1}^* + \eta_t \qquad (5.6)$$

with $E(\eta_t) = 0$, $var(\eta_t) = \sigma_\eta^2$ and $cov(\varepsilon_t, \eta_t) = 0$.

If $\sigma_\eta^2 = 0$, this again produces the model of a constant NAIRU.

In the Kalman filter the frequent repetition of information forecasting and correction over the entire period is optimally used. The Kalman smoothing recursion is used for the recursive calculation of the NAIRU. The parameters of the Phillips curve are usually estimated with the help of the maximum likelihood method. Confidence intervals for recording estimate uncertainties relating to time variable NAIRU can be determined with "bootstrap" methods.

Non-Parametric Production Function Method

In contrast to the parametric production function method, this procedure formulates a more general form of the aggregate production function: $Y_t = F(L_t, K_t)\,A_t$. The practical implementation of this method runs analogously to the parametric variants (see also Annex AI.4). Growth rates of macroeconomic production are determined as the weighted rates of change in the input factors labour and capital arising from production elasticities and the total factor productivity. Assuming constant returns to scale (sum of elasticities of production = 1) and that wages equal their marginal productivity, the production elasticities can be determined on the basis of the wage share, which is directly taken from the National Accounts as the ratio of income in the total economy and the compensation paid to employees. If a constant wage share is assumed over time, the non-parametric method corresponds to the parametric production function method based on a Cobb-Douglas production function. For a detailed explanation of the method, refer to Sachverständigenrat zur Begutachtung der gesamtwirtschaftlichen Entwicklung (2003).

Capital Stock Method Used by the German Council of Economic Experts

The capital stock method that was mainly used in the early studies issued by the German Council of Economic Experts also falls within the category of production function methods. The method differs from the statistical filter methods and other production function methods by calculating a potential that, by construction, is always greater or equal to actual production. Probably the biggest disadvantage of the capital stock method, however, is that potential output is only derived from the potential capital productivity of the private sector. This approach has recently been dropped by the German Council of Economic Experts and is not examined in any further detail here either.

5.2.2.2 Structural Vector Autoregressive (SVAR) Models

SVAR methods draw their theoretical motivation from the neoclassical synthesis in which the long-term production capabilities are determined by the overall supply capacity in the economy, and business cycle movements are based on the aggregated dynamics of demand. This approach consequently focuses primarily on the identification of supply and demand innovations. Potential output is, then, regarded as the sum of all supply innovations while the aggregated demand elements reflect the output gap. The SVAR method is based on a vector autoregressive (VAR) model, the original variant of which consists – according to Blanchard and Quah (1989) – of changes in GDP and trend-adjusted rates of unemployment. In order to be able to identify supply and demand innovations at all the assumption is made that only supply innovations have a long-term influence on the GDP level while demand elements only have a temporary effect on GDP.[104]

Numerous modifications and additions to the standard approach by Blanchard and Quah (1989) can be found in the empirical literature and in practical use. Bayoumi and Eichengreen (1993), for example, show that the use of price variables instead of the trend-adjusted rate of unemployment or other measures for supply-side capacity utilisation delivers the same identification restrictions as the original model. Fritsche and Logeay (2002) estimate a trivariate SVAR model for Germany that – in addition to the rate of unemployment and real GDP – also takes account of real wage developments. The estimates drawn up by DeSerres, Guay, and St-Amant (1995) estimating the potential output of the Mexican economy are also based on a trivariate SVAR system. This system consists of time series for industrial production, oil price and the money supply. Claus (2003) uses an SVAR model to estimate the potential output for New Zealand based on time series of real GDP, number of employees in full time work, survey data on capital utilisation and the oil price. Many more applications of this method could be cited. The sole purpose of this brief survey of the literature is to clarify which strategies for

[104] A good introduction to the SVAR method can be found in Gottschalk (2001). Various bivariate SVAR models for Germany are examined in Gottschalk and van Zandweghe (2001). Refer to Appendix AI.3 for an estimation of a SVAR model.

identifying supply-side and demand-side shocks have been pursued and which empirical options are made possible by this procedure.

The addition of higher dimensional systems to the standard approach is primarily a response to the criticism that concentration on just two shocks is too restrictive, particularly in the context of complex macroeconomic models. A further fundamental criticism of the Blanchard-Quah methodology is that it assumes that all shocks are strictly assigned to either supply or demand factors and that it leaves no room at all for a mixture of the two. The problem inherent in such a strict separation of supply and demand shocks along the time axis in SVAR context has already been plausibly described in section 2.6.2. The fact that it is not always possible to assign shocks so simply is immediately apparent in the example of the shock on the nominal exchange rate that is influenced by factors on both the supply and demand sides.

The results of an SVAR estimate also raise the question as to whether shocks are correctly identified. This is an important issue for the application of this method for the purpose of calculating long-term output components and the cycle components since those are calculated as the sum of the identified shocks. Faust and Leeper (1997) therefore propose checking the correlations between supply and demand shocks in different models. If minor correlations are measured, doubts may be legitimately raised about the reliability of the shock identification and the various models may mix both types of shock. In their analysis of different bivariate SVARs for Germany, it is clear that both types of shock exist, but that different models also identify more or less similar supply shocks while there are greater discrepancies as far as demand shocks are concerned. If the shocks are plausibly identified, the SVAR method offers the advantage – particularly with respect to the univariate methods – of omitting the automatic assignment of persistent demand shocks on long-term output components.

Although a decomposition of the components of total production in the economy on the basis of an SVAR model is somewhat more "economic" than in pure time series models, the idea that potential output development and cyclical fluctuations are exogenous is also dominant here given that the really interesting components merely result from the sum of two types of shock ("shock-accounting"). The central variables for boosting potential output cannot be identified in this context nor is it possible to perform transparent scenario analyses.

5.2.2.3 State Space Models and Panel Data Models

State Space Models

The typical system approach based on Apel and Jansson (1999) simultaneously estimates potential output and the NAIRU as unobservable components with the help of the Kalman filter. These components are explicitly identified on the basis of the formal relationship between the NAIRU and inflation (Phillips curve) and Okun's law of the rate of unemployment and GDP growth. The explicit formulation of fundamental relationships ground in economic theory as well as a consistent identification of the potential components both underlining the attractiveness of this approach in the context of economic policy analysis.

The attractive theoretical features of the system approach contrast with the empirical implementation, which encompasses all the difficulties connected with the Kalman filter. The Kalman filter provides a well-founded, versatile and flexible instrument for calculating forecasts and unobserved state variables such as potential output or the NAIRU. In most cases, however, the calculations are sensitive to variances and covariances in the state and observation equation and in the selected start values for unknown parameters to initialise the filter.

Panel Data Models

These methods basically extend the production function method by taking account of much more extensive information about the development of overall economic productivity and technology than does the standard model. The theoretical concept is derived from neoclassical growth theory, on the one hand, which regards technological progress as the only enduringly effective engine for growth and, on the other hand, insights provided by new growth theory which identify a number of other factors influencing potential growth. The stock of human capital and its production, endogenous technological development and institutional quality and efficiency are just a few examples of the potential influencing factors discussed in the context of new growth theory.[105]

This method no longer empirically identifies factors that may influence potential output and potential growth on the basis of single country analyses. Larger cross-country panels, which combine cross-sectional and time series data, are used in this context to facilitate the identification and quantification of the factors which do not vary over time but over the cross-section.[106]

The econometric method is defined by Pesaran, Shin, and Smith (1999) and in subsequent literature issued by these researchers. Pesaran et al. (1999) have developed a method of simultaneously estimating long-run relationships and short-term adjustment processes drawing on panel data. It is assumed that the long-run relationships, which can also be interpreted as equilibrium relationships, are homogeneous while short-term deviations or adjustments to this equilibrium are heterogeneous. When applied to the case of overall production in the economy and its determining factors, this means that business cycle movements are modelled on a specific country basis while the long-term interactions between production and explanatory factors are identical for all countries. Even if these methods basically allow for heterogeneous modelling of short-run and long-run relationships on the basis of single country observations, the real strength of this method is the account taken of cross-country variations in data for identifying and quantifying produc-

[105] Temple (1999) provides an overview of new insights into the theory and empirical study of growth.

[106] Macroeconomic indicators of the stock of human capital in an economy – such as the average number of years of schooling of the working age population – are a typical example. These time series vary little over time but substantially from one country to the next.

tion growth factors. These methods can consequently be used to estimate how specific institutional reforms can alter the potential of a country.

The Deutsche Bank, for example, has recently begun using panel data methods to forecast long-run growth in particular countries. These models are also used in the projections produced by the International Monetary Fund (cf. Batista & Zaldu-endo, 2004); the ZEW also draws on these methods in its evaluations of the determining factors of potential growth in OECD countries. Kappler (2004) outlines the basic procedure and demonstrates its practical application for 12 OECD countries. Panel data methods start off with the factors which potentially influence long-term GDP and GDP growth in the areas of human capital, real capital, fiscal policy, monetary policy, research and development, international trade, financial market developments, labour markets and demography. Long-run relationships are identified with the help of panel cointegration tests and error correction models based on Pesaran et al. (1999) and are used to measure production trends or potential in a particular country.

Panel methods require high levels of data input and – despite the econometric benefits they offer in the field of panel data analysis – are still problematic in a number of ways. The extent to which estimated factors must be homogeneous and to which country-specific characteristics can be taken into account are largely determined by the econometric method. Econometric estimating methods usually also assume that countries are independent of each other or, at the most, only allow for very rudimentary modelling of patterns of dependency. Many of these and other issues relating to the technical implementation of these methods are currently the subject of ongoing research.

5.3 "In-Sample"Analysis

The evaluations in Tables 1 to 3 are based on an ex post calculation of the potential growth components and the corresponding GDP cycle components for each univariate and multivariate method. The entire observation period from 1970 to 2004 is used. Up to the year 1991, the rates of change in GDP relate to the territory of former West Germany and subsequently Germany as a whole.[107] As the entries in the second column of Table 1 show, the average rate of change in estimated potential growth corresponds to the actual rate of change, more or less regardless of the method used. However, it would be unrealistic to expect any other outcome using this method given that the results are based on the standard utilisation (normal activity) concept; estimated potential growth is bound by definition, therefore, to correspond on average with actual growth.

Consideration is also given to whether the method produces an output gap which is non-stationary and would not, therefore, automatically lead to the closing of this gap (see the last column of Table 1). This cannot be diagnosed for any of

[107] Refer to Appendix AI.1 for a detailed description of data and data sources.

the methods. Most of the methods considered here close this gap anyway simply by construction.

The standard deviation of potential growth is a measure of the smoothness of these components: High volatility suggests erratic potential growth paths and vice versa. There are no significant differences between each of the methods as far as this measure is concerned. They all generate a potential component that, as one would expect, is smoother than the original series of GDP changes. The lowest standard deviation is produced by the model of unobserved components, and the greatest level of volatility is measured for the structural VAR. With the exception of the Hodrick-Prescott Filter with the standard value parameter $\lambda = 100$, the purely statistical filters basically agree, in the first and second order moments, with the rate of change in the trend components. The results for the two versions of the Hodrick-Prescott Filter do, however, show that in this case the choice of smoothing parameter only impacts the volatility and not the average trend growth.

The average rate of change in the cyclical components is almost zero for all methods, and the standard deviation is larger in all of them than for the trend components. This corresponds to the assumptions made in the component models of classical business cycle theory, which postulate a non-permanent output gap that symmetrically fluctuates about the potential output. As most methods are based on this component model anyway, the results of the "in-sample" analysis are not surprising. Figures 12 and 13 show the results of long-run and cyclical components of the rate of change in real GDP in Germany.

The high correlation coefficients between the various estimates of trend growth and cyclical changes (refer to Tables 2 and 3) confirm the visual impression conveyed by the graph of a relatively high level of homogeneity over time of the results produced by these methods. The correlation coefficients in Table 2 assume values between 0.43 and 0.99. The lowest overall correlation coefficients are produced for the structural VAR model followed by the estimated trend components of the non-parametric production function method. The statistical filters and parametric production function method both show a high degree of agreement. This agreement corresponds to expectations in the case of the statistical filters given that they are based on very similar methodological approaches. The high correlation of the production function method with the statistical filters is most probably due to the use of the Hodrick-Prescott Filter to smooth the underlying input factors.

All in all one can say that retrospectively the various methods of distinguishing long-term and cyclical components in the rate of change of German GDP largely coincide over time. The correlation coefficients suggest that the estimated results are even more accurate for the cyclical components than for the trend components. The correlation coefficients for the former are between 0.59 and 0.99. This correlation calculation does not, however, alter the fact that the concrete numerical values for the various methods at specific points of time produced very different levels of trend growth. The range of the estimated trend components for the year 2004 extends from 0.39% to 2.16%, for example. This degree of uncertainty with regard to trend growth is unlikely to be insignificant for many economic decisions.

Table 1. Descriptive Statistics and Characteristics of Methods of Estimating Potential Growth in Germany

	Rate of change in trend components (in %)		Rate of change in cyclical components (output gaps)		Non-stationary output gaps?
	Arithmetic mean	Standard deviation	Arithmetic mean	Standard deviation	
Actual rate of change in GDP (Δy)	2.1	1.8			
Univariate methods					
Symmetric moving average over five years (MA)	2.3	1.1	0.0	1.5	No
Spline regression (SP)	2.2	1.1	-0.1	1.5	No
Baxter-King Filter (BK)	2.3	1.1	0.0	1.4	No
Christiano-Fitzgerald Filter (CF)	2.3	1.1	-0.1	1.4	No
Hodrick-Prescott Filter $\lambda = 100$ (HP100)	2.2	0.8	0.0	1.6	No
Hodrick-Prescott Filter $\lambda = 6.25$ (HP6.25)	2.2	1.0	0.0	1.4	No
Model of unobserved components (SSP)	2.2	0.7	-0.1	1.6	No
Multivariate methods					
Structural VAR (SVAR)	2.1	1.2	0.0	1.4	No
Production function method (parametric, PFAa)	2.3	0.9	-0.1	1.5	No
Production function method (non-parametric, PFAb)	2.2	0.8	-0.1	1.7	No

Note: Evaluation for the period 1970-2004. The entries in column 3 are based on the results of an ADF test for the resulting cyclical level components (output gaps) for each filter method; refer to text for further comments.

Fig. 12. Trend Components of Methods of Estimating Potential Growth

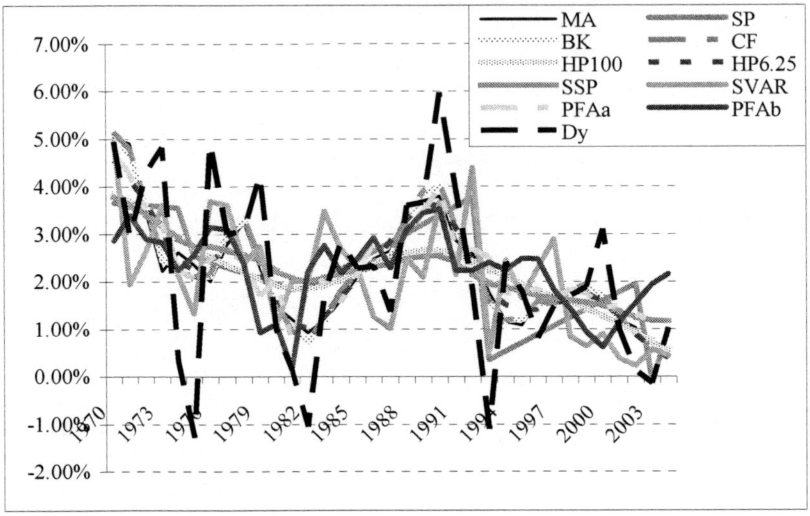

Note: Refer to Table 1 for designation of variables.

Fig. 13. Cyclical Components of Methods of Estimating Potential Growth

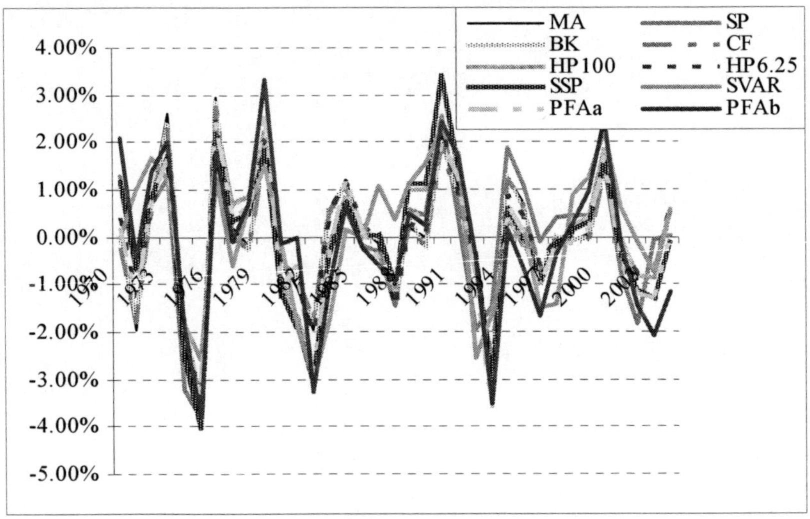

Note: Refer to Table 1 for the designation of the variables.

Table 2. Correlation Matrix for Trend Components of Methods of Estimating Potential Growth

	Δy	MA	SP	BK	CF	HP 100	HP 6.25	SSP	SVAR	PFA a	PFA b
Δy	1.00										
MA	0.81	1.00									
SP	0.84	0.88	1.00								
BK	0.81	1.00	0.87	1.00							
CF	0.80	1.00	0.87	0.99	1.00						
HP100	0.93	0.92	0.91	0.91	0.91	1.00					
HP6.25	0.86	0.98	0.92	0.98	0.98	0.96	1.00				
SSP	0.94	0.91	0.91	0.90	0.90	0.99	0.95	1.00			
SVAR	0.81	0.61	0.74	0.59	0.59	0.80	0.67	0.80	1.00		
PFAa	0.88	0.95	0.88	0.95	0.95	0.96	0.97	0.94	0.71	1.00	
PFAb	0.85	0.83	0.85	0.84	0.93	0.89	0.91	0.78	0.94	0.85	1.00

Table 3. Correlation Matrix for the Cyclical Components of Methods of Estimating Potential Growth

	Δy	MA	SP	BK	CF	HP 100	HP 6.25	SSP	SVAR	PFA a	PFA b
Δy	1.00										
MA	0.81	1.00									
SP	0.84	0.88	1.00								
BK	0.81	1.00	0.87	1.00							
CF	0.80	1.00	0.87	0.99	1.00						
HP100	0.93	0.92	0.91	0.91	0.91	1.00					
HP6.25	0.86	0.98	0.92	0.98	0.98	0.96	1.00				
SSP	0.94	0.91	0.91	0.90	0.90	0.99	0.95	1.00			
SVAR	0.81	0.61	0.74	0.59	0.59	0.80	0.67	0.80	1.00		
PFAa	0.88	0.95	0.88	0.95	0.95	0.96	0.97	0.94	0.71	1.00	
PFAb	0.85	0.83	0.85	0.84	0.93	0.89	0.91	0.78	0.94	0.85	1.00

5.4 "Out-of-Sample" Forecasts

The accuracy issue cannot be adequately resolved using "in-sample" analyses given that no observations of the actual development of potential growth that could be used for comparative purposes are available. The different methods substantially differ in many cases also in terms of the assumptions made and envisaged analysis purposes – in most cases it is not entirely clear which specific comparative measures should be drawn on in particular instances. However, if the methods are assessed in terms of their suitability for forecasting actual medium-term growth, accuracy analyses can offer an appropriate instrument of analysis.

The following "out-of-sample" analysis produces GDP forecasts using the various potential methods for points in time in the past based on information which was actually available at the relevant point in time and compares these with actual GDP figures. Recursive forecasts of this nature are produced for time periods of 3, 4 and 5 years to enable the forecasted potential rates of growth in GDP to be compared with the actual rate of GDP growth. The differences between forecasts and actual developments (forecast errors) provide the starting point for a formal investigation of the forecast precision of each method.

The following projection analysis focuses on the production function method, which is particularly frequently used for projections over medium-term periods. The structural VAR model is also regarded as a further benchmark forecast of methods in the category of multivariate procedures. The time series filters are not designed for forecasting purposes and cannot be directly used in the projection analysis. Medium-term forecasts based on an ARIMA model which are smoothed to extract the trend components with the Hodrick-Prescott Filter are examined in the following, however. It is also usual practice when comparing forecasts to use a naive forecast which only contains information about the forecast time series as a comparative benchmark. A useful approach for medium-term GDP forecasts is using a random walk with drift in which forecasts are only created using the historic mean value known at the time the forecast is made. A detailed description of the forecast design for the structural VAR model and for the production function method can be found in Appendices AI.3 and AI.4.[108]

As a rule, recursive forecasts are performed on the basis of quarterly data. Data for West Germany was linked with data for Germany as of the first quarter of 1991. The resulting break in the data was remedied using an impulse dummy regression to ensure that the test statistics on forecast precision are not distorted by these data inconsistencies.

The first forecast was drawn up on the basis of all the observations for the relevant time series up to the fourth quarter of 1979, and, beginning in the first quarter of 1980, forecasts were produced over 12, 16 and 20 horizons. The next step was to extend the relevant period by one quarter and to use this new information to produce new forecasts over 12, 16 and 20 horizons. The last forecasts are calculated with information up to the fourth quarter of 2000. In total 92 three-year forecasts, 88 four-year forecasts and 84 five-year forecasts were used to evaluate forecast accuracy. The forecasted development of real GDP – measured in terms of the cumulative quarterly rates of change over the forecast horizon – is, then, compared with the actual development over the corresponding period.

---

[108] The analysis of the predictive quality of the yield curve in chapter 7 is performed in a similar way.

5.5 Formal Assessment of Forecast Precision and Accuracy

This section assesses the predictive quality and accuracy of forecasts produced using the production function method, the structural VARs, the ARIMA model and the random walk model drawing on the usual statistics for analysing the quality and accuracy of forecasts. The problem arising in this context is the unobservable nature of potential growth. For this reason the average development of real GDP is used as a reference value over a period of 3, 4 and 5 years.

Quality criteria are the mean forecast error (ME), the mean absolute forecast error (MAE), the root mean squared error (RMSE) and Theil's inequality coefficient. The RMSE is defined as follows:

$$RMSE = \sqrt{\frac{1}{T}\sum_{t=1}^{T}(R_t - F_t)^2},$$

where T stands for the number of observations and R_t (F_t) for the realisation (forecast). Theil's coefficient U also provides a suitable measure of forecast precision: In this context the RMSE of the model under examination is placed in relation to the RMSE of a benchmark model:

$$Theil's\,U = \frac{RMSE(Model)}{RMSE(Benchmark)}.$$

The forecast accuracy of models is identitical if Theil's U equals 1. If the coefficient is smaller than 1, the model under examination is preferable to the alternative model. The opposite is the case if Theil's U is bigger than 1.

As Theil's U is merely descriptive in nature and does not allow for any statements of significance regarding the differences in the dispersion of two contrasting forecast models, the Diebold and Mariano (1995) test is performed. In the version examined here this test verifies whether the difference in the squared forecast error of the reference model and the naive model significantly deviates from zero. If this is the case, one of the models – in the best possible case, the reference model under assessment – shows less dispersion than the other and would be the preferred model for producing forecasts in practice.

These indicators of forecast precision have become established as the standard for the purpose of evaluating projection procedures designed to produce point forecasts with as little forecast error variance as possible. This need not necessarily be the main concern of the relevant potential growth method. More to the point, a method may come out rather badly from this comparison and still be perfectly suitable for the purpose of calculating an economically substantiated potential measurement whilst being less suitable for the practical purpose of estimating medium-term GDP growth.

The insights these measurement figures can deliver on the projection characteristics of different methods in this context are illuminated by the interpretation of the mean forecast error ME that is normally used to test the systematic bias of a forecast. This measurement figure can provide information about deductions relating to the forecast development of economic activity – which one would have obtained in retrospect using projections produced by various methods – as follows:

- *ME is significantly positive*: The method forecasts average potential which is systematically lower than the actual medium-term rate of GDP development. In the past the method has very frequently predicted capacity underutilisation or a weakness of aggregate demand.
- *ME is significantly negative:* The forecasted potential tended to be higher than actual potential. The method primarily forecasts phases of the business cycle in which utilisation outstrips capacities or in which there is excess supply.
- *ME is insignificant:* The forecasted output gaps cancel each other out over the long term, and the method is suitable for an unbiased forecast of medium-run normal capacity utilisation.

Figure 14 shows the five-year forecasts produced using each method together with the actual development of GDP over the relevant period. All five-year forecasts are consistently smoother than actual mean GDP growth. This is the inevitable outcome of the design in the case of the random walk given that only the average past rates of growth are extrapolated into the future in this case. The forecasts produced by the SVAR model and the ARIMA model are based on a similar design: In the case of the SVAR forecasts, the influence of the mean past rates of change in total supply-side shocks dominates as soon as the forecast horizon is increasing. The forecasts produced by the parametric production function methods are similar in process to those of the SVAR and random walk forecasts albeit at a lower level and closer to actual GDP development. On the whole the ARIMA forecasts supply the most optimistic five-year forecasts over the period observed. Table 4 summarises the results of the accuracy tests.

The average forecast error for the production function method does not significantly differ from zero across all three forecast horizons while the SVAR model, the random walk model and the ARIMA model produce forecast errors which are significant around the 5% level. A classic interpretation of this test would be that the forecasts produced by the SVAR, random walk and ARIMA models are biased. This formally confirms what is plainly apparent in Figure 12: The production function method generates forecasts which – on average – correspond to the actual development of GDP and consequently – again on average – have successfully delivered a forecast of overall normal capacity utilisation in the economy over the period observed which has been consistent with actual developments.

Fig. 14. Mean Five-year Forecasts of GDP Development and Realisation (Years Refer to the Final Year of the Projection Period)

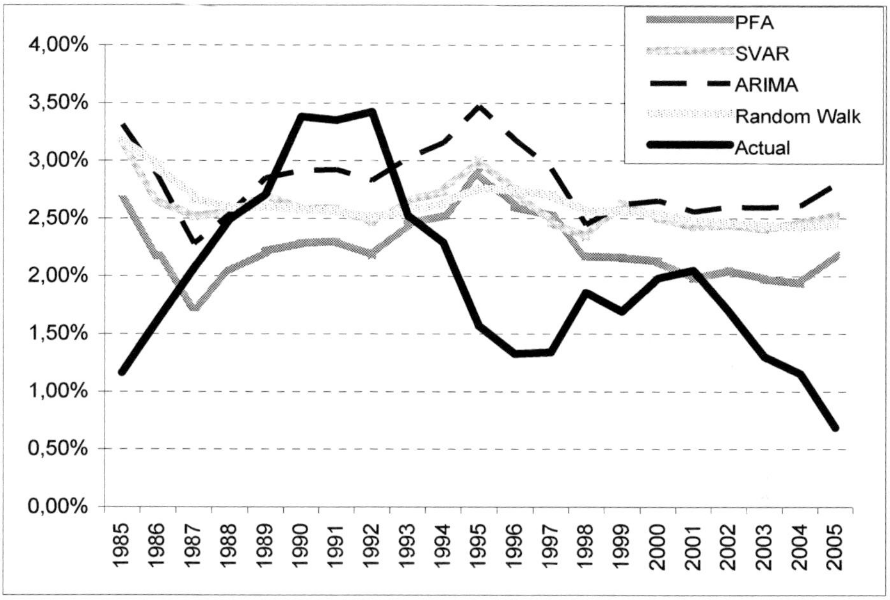

Table 4. Indicators of Forecast Precision of Methods of Producing Medium-term Forecasts of Trend Growth

	Production function	**Structural VAR**	**Random walk**	**ARIMA**
Horizon = 3 years				
Number of cumulative forecasts	92	92	92	92
Mean forecast	2.12	2.50	2.60	2.57
Mean realisation	1.87	1.87	1.87	1.87
Mean forecast error (ME)[a]	-0.25	-0.63**	-0.73**	0.70**
Mean absolute forecast error (MAE)	0.96	1.06	1.10	1.09
Root mean squared error (RMSE)	1.23	1.33	1.35	1.43
Theil's U^b	0.91	0.98	-	1.06
Diebold Mariano test[a,c]	-0.33	-0.06	-	0.21

	Production function	Structural VAR	Random walk	ARIMA
Horizon = 4 years				
Number of cumulative forecasts	88	88	88	88
Mean forecast	2.20	2.56	2.61	2.50
Mean realisation	1.93	1.93	1.93	2.72
Mean forecast error (ME)[a]	-0.26	-0.63**	-0.68**	-0.79***
Mean absolute forecast error (MAE)	0.84	0.98	0.99	1.06
Root mean squared error (RMSE)	1.05	1.17	1.18	1.30
Theil's U^b	0.89	1.00	-	1.10
Diebold Mariano test[a,c]	-0.28	-0.01	-	0.31
Horizon = 5 years				
Number of cumulative forecasts	84	84	84	84
Mean forecast	2.25	2.60	2.62	2.82
Mean realisation	1.99	1.99	1.99	1.99
Mean forecast error (ME)[a]	-0.26	-0.61**	-0.63**	-0.83***
Mean absolute forecast error (MAE)	0.74	0.89	0.89	1.01
Root mean squared error (RMSE)	0.93	1.06	1.06	1.22
Theil's U^b	0.88	1.00	-	1.14
Diebold Mariano test[a,c]	-0.25	0.01	-	0.36

[a] ***/**/* Significance at 1%, 5%, 10% level based on t-distributed Newey West standard errors. All the entries in the table are based on cumulative forecasts of quarterly rates of change in German gross domestic product. All figures are for mean rates of annual growth. The entry "mean realisation", for example, reflects the annual mean actual percentage change in GDP across the relevant horizon.
[b] RMSE of the reference model in relation to the RMSE of the random walk model.
[c] Difference of the mean squared forecast error between the reference and the random walk model.

The fact, however, that the ME is capable of providing only limited information about the quality of the forecast is clearly demonstrated by Table 4. Although forecasts using the production function method are not biased, they only provide a relatively inaccurate picture of average five-year forecasts over the course of each single year. The differences between the forecasts and actual developments are relatively strongly dispersed. The root mean squared error (RMSE) is a measure to capture this dispersion and – in addition to the mean forecast error – an additional important measure of accuracy.

Fig. 15. Histograms of Forecast Errors of Five-year Forecasts

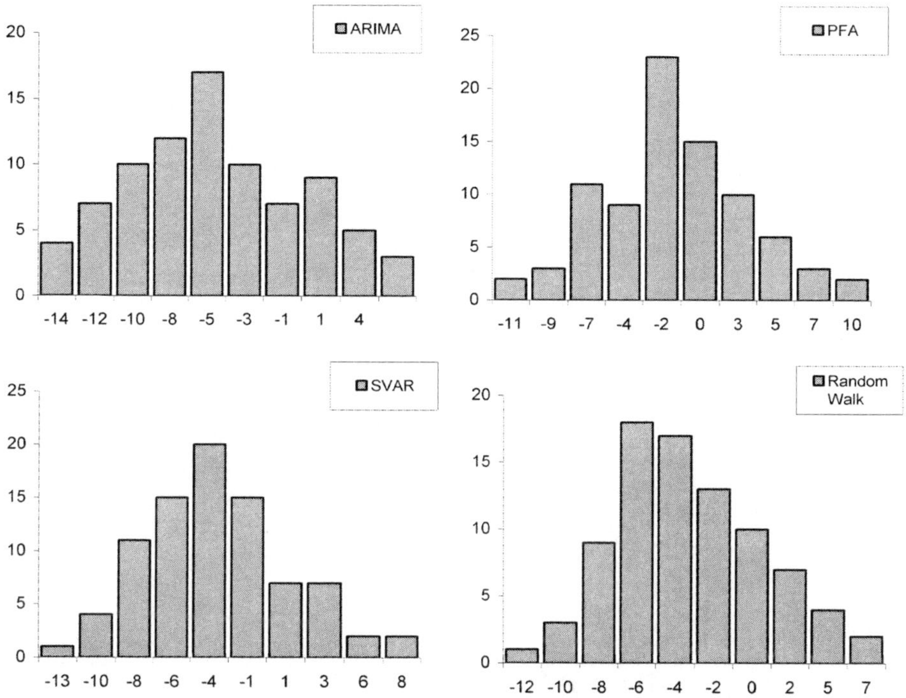

The largest RMSE and, thus, the biggest forecast error variance is measured for the ARIMA forecasts. The smallest RMSE value is generated by forecasts based on the production function. Correspondingly, the most favourable Theil's *U* values are also produced for these forecasts. This applies to all three forecast horizons. The Diebold-Mariano Test does not, however, refute the null hypothesis of equality between the squared forecast error of the model under assessment and the squared forecast error of the random walk model for any forecast model. In other words, on the basis of this test alone it is not possible to provide a statistically substantiated judgement regarding the selection of forecast model, which is statistically superior to the naive model. The value of the Diebold-Mariano test statistics is negative for the forecasts produced by production function method across all horizons, however, and suggests the dominance of this procedure as regards error dispersion compared with the naive model. Figure 15 shows the histograms of the forecast errors of the models. It is useful to recognise that the variance in forecast errors does not revolve around zero and that the errors for all models are dispersed across a very wide interval. An evaluation of all the indicators in Table 4 shows that the forecast precision of the production function method of producing medium-term forecasts is superior.

The recursive five-year forecasts produced using the production function method are, then, compared with German government projections and those of the International Monetary Fund. Owing to the lack of availability of earlier IMF projections this comparison is based on the period 1994 to 2004. The German government's and IMF projections are usually not purely mechanistic but take account of qualitative assumptions and expert assessments. The recursive forecasts are, however, based on statistical and econometric methods and are consequently by their very nature highly retrospective. The purpose of this comparison is to check whether integrating the future-oriented assumptions of these institutions in the years 1994 to 2004 offers any advantages over purely technical procedures. The relatively low number of empirical observations restricts this comparison, and the results must, therefore, be interpreted with caution.

Fig. 16. Five-year Forecasts Based on the Production Function Method Compared With the Corresponding Projections Produced by the German Government and the IMF

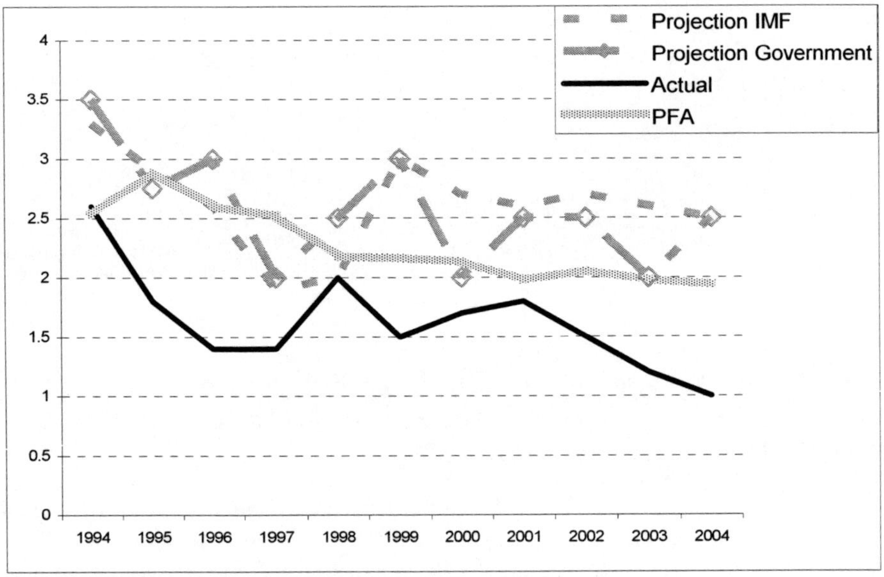

The overall economic predictions produced by the German government for the end-years 1995, 2000 and 2003 are identical in almost every point with the synthetic forecasts produced using the production function method; the projections made by the institutions for the remaining end-years – except for 1997 – are higher (refer to Figure 16). All in all, the projections produced by the institutions deviate more strongly from the realisations than the synthetic forecasts. The trend of forecasts based on the production function method is also more consistent than the trend shown by projections made by the IMF, the German government and the actual development of GDP.

It is, of course, very difficult to reach any general conclusions on the basis of this comparison. The institutional projections for the periods considered here cannot, however, be said to be more accurate than purely mechanistic forecasts. The IMF projections were, in fact, all less accurate than the technical forecasts produced using the production function method.

5.6 Conclusions

An economy's potential output and potential growth are unobserved and must, therefore, be estimated on the basis of generally available data. As there is little agreement on the concrete specification of these variables, there are many methods of estimating these indicators – indicators, which play a key role in economic analysis. This project section has discussed several important examples of such methods and analysed the corresponding empirical results for the estimation of potential growth in Germany. The design of most of the methods does not allow potential growth to be estimated in the sense of potential maximum production under conditions of full capacity utilisation but – instead – tends to measure normal capacity utilisation of total output in an economy.

Economic analyses very often make use of univariate methods, which are based on few theoretical considerations or none at all. As a result these methods are less demanding and require less previous knowledge of users. This can be advantageous, for example, if the potential components are not the actual focus of the analysis. These concepts undoubtedly fail to meet the requirements for an investigation of potential output, its evolution, its determinants and resulting economic policy recommendations.

Multivariate methods, which are based more on economic relationships and interactions between central aggregate economic figures, require many additional assumptions – such as statistical filters – before they can be used in practice. This is also why objective measurements of actual potential output cannot be made using these methods. It is, however, easier to run through scenarios based on a baseline scenario using these methods. Multivariate methods also facilitate identification of primarily supply-side or demand-side determined aggregate capacity utilisation. This is especially useful for arriving at economic policy conclusions. The example of the SVAR models clearly shows, however, that identifying these elements creates considerable scope for this model type at least.

Even in cases where the results of the in-sample analysis in this project section show a relatively high correspondence of the different methods in assessing the evolution of business cycle and trend components, considerable differences in judging the macroeconomic situation appear at single points in time. The theoretical and empirical results do not provide any grounds either for recommending one particular method or type of model. It would not, therefore, be appropriate in practice to draw on the results produced by one particular method alone to evaluate the cyclical and trend components of GDP and growth.

An analogous recommendation arises from the results of the "out-of-sample" analysis. This analysis also suggests the use of several projection procedures to check for the robustness of the overall outcomes. According to the formal analysis of forecast precision, the production function approach showed sound practical results at least for the time periods considered in the present study for German medium-term GDP growth.

6 Analysis of the Declining Trend in Germany's Potential Growth Performance

6.1 Introduction

Germany's relatively weak growth performance since the mid-1990s in comparison with other countries has given rise to policy and academic debate in recent years focusing on the possible reasons for this decline in economic dynamism. Figure 17 outlines the decline in real economic growth in Germany since the mid-1980s. A substantial growth gap has also opened up with respect to the euro area and OECD countries since the middle of the 1990s.

Fig. 17. Real Growth Rates

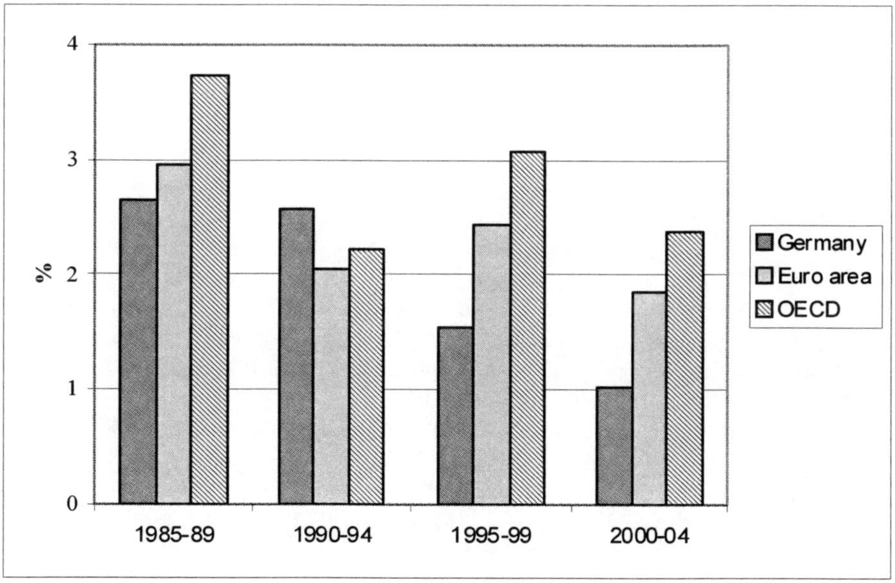

Source: OECD database, Destatis, and ZEW calculations.

S. Hauptmeier et al., *Projecting Potential Output*, Zew Economic Studies,
DOI: 10.1007/978-3-7908-2177-2_6, © Physica-Verlag Berlin Heidelberg 2009

This ongoing decline in real economic growth in Germany cannot be explained by a cyclically determined under-utilisation of production capacities alone. On the contrary, adjusting the underlying growth data for business cycle effects reveals a declining trend in potential growth for the German economy in recent decades. This development is illustrated in Figure 18.[109]

Fig. 18. Development of Trend Growth in Germany

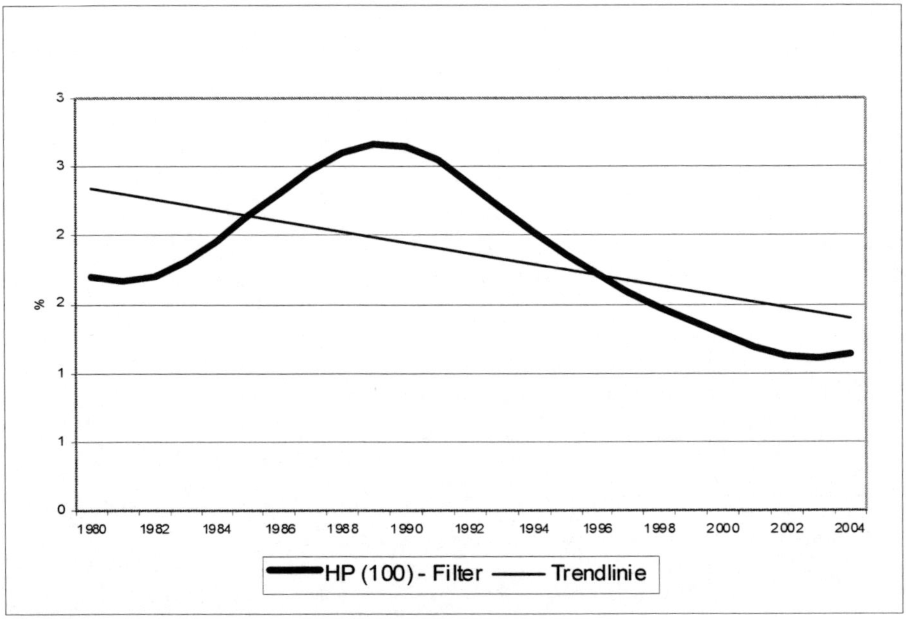

Source: OECD database, Destatis, and ZEW calculations

The trend line shows the sustained decline in long-term trend growth resulting from a systematically weak growth performance of the German economy. Bearing the fundamental theoretical, epistemological and empirical problems regarding the calculation of potential output addressed in chapters 2 to 5, this slowing down in trend growth cannot be simply equated with a slowing down in potential growth. Nonetheless, the analysis in this chapter does clearly show that a whole series of factors suggest that Germany has fallen behind in terms of potential growth and that this downwards trend at least partially corresponds to a decline in potential growth.

What is not clear is which factors have influenced the slowing down in German trend growth – particularly during the 1990s. Various factors frequently cited in the literature to explain weak growth in Germany are discussed in the following. These include direct growth factors, such as the development of the volume of labour, the formation of human capital, the accumulation of real capital and techno-

109 The potential growth rate has been calculated using the Hodrick-Prescott filter.

logical progress. Indirect influencing factors include regulations on goods and labour markets as well as fiscal policy. Factors that may be specific to Germany include the impact of EMU on real interest rates in Germany and the German reunification.

6.2 Direct Factors Contributing to Growth

A typical starting point for analysing growth developments is an examination of the relative contributions made to growth as a result of boosts to input and efficiency (Temple, 1999). Growth in potential output is broken down using a Solow growth decomposition equation for the contributions made by individual factors of production. This empirical approach, referred to as "growth accounting", is used to determine what proportion of volume changes in the available factors – in other words, development of labour potential, accumulation of real capital or the formation of human capital – or quality improvements in existing factors have contributed to potential growth and how increases in efficiency resulting from technological progress have impacted the development of potential output. As technological knowledge is not a quantifiable measure, the rate of growth of total factor productivity can only be roughly determined as a residual referred to as the Solow residual (cf. the history of this idea, its classification and criticism in sections 2.4.6 and 2.6.2).[110]

Table 5 shows a Solow growth decomposition of real gross domestic product for Germany, the U.S. and the OECD area. In addition to the relatively low rates of growth and the consistent decline in growth since the beginning of the 1990s, what really stands out from a comparison with the economies of the U.S. and OECD is the negative contribution made by the factor labour at the outset and end of the period of observation. This may provide an initial clue for an explanation of the relatively weak growth performance of the German economy. Another striking factor is the continuous drop in the contribution made by capital. Compared with the U.S., total factor productivity has also unfavourably developed since the mid-1990s.

[110] Assuming factor remuneration corresponding to marginal productivity, the production elasticity of a particular factor may be approximately determined by the share that the applicable factor income contributes to GDP. The production elasticities estimated in this way and the measured rates of growth in GDP, capital and labour input enable the rate of growth of technical knowledge to be calculated as a non-explained residual of these factors (Solow residual).

Table 5. Solow Growth Decomposition

	Capital	Labour	TFP	GDP
Germany				
1992 - 1995	0,89	-0,47	1,69	2,11
1996 - 2000	0,50	0,57	0,42	1,48
2001 - 2004	0,38	-0,12	0,89	1,14
USA				
1992 - 1995	0,65	1,05	1,43	3,13
1996 - 2000	1,13	1,30	1,67	4,10
2001 - 2004	0,57	0,30	1,44	2,31
OECD				
1992 - 1995	0,86	0,55	1,04	2,44
1996 - 2000	0,92	0,56	1,17	2,66
2001 - 2004	0,84	0,54	0,98	2,36

Rounding differences; $\alpha = 0{,}3$ (cf. SVR, 2002).
Source: OECD Economic Outlook No. 77, own calculations.

6.2.1 Labour Volume Trends

The previous growth decomposition shows that comparably weak economic trend growth in Germany in recent years is in particular determined by the factor labour. This is also clearly demonstrated by Figure 19, which outlines the development – in an international comparative context – of annual labour input in the period between 1990 and 2005. While it proved possible in the reference economic areas to increase annual hours worked since 1990 from between 8.7% (EU15 excluding Germany) and 17.5% (USA), the volume of labour input in Germany fell during the same period by an average of 0.67% per year.

The reasons for this development become apparent when the volume of labour is broken down into its constituent components. Table 6 shows the development of the working age population and annual time worked for Germany – separately for the territories of former West and East Germany. While the decline in annual working time in West Germany of 117 hours or approximately 7.5% was partly compensated by an increase in the working age population of 5%; developments in East Germany went in the opposite direction: While annual working time declined by just about 3% – less than half the rate in West Germany – the East German states lost around 1.27 million inhabitants – 15% of the working age population – which meant that in total the volume of labour fell in East Germany by around 17.5% compared with 1991.

Altogether there was a slight increase in the size of the employed labour force in Germany between 1991 and 2004 that was achieved in the West German states by an increase in part-time employment and a larger number of self-employed people in particular. At the same time annual working time substantially dropped so that the actual volume of labour input in the German economy has fallen by around 6% since the beginning of the 1990s.

Fig. 19. Labour Volume Trends in International Context

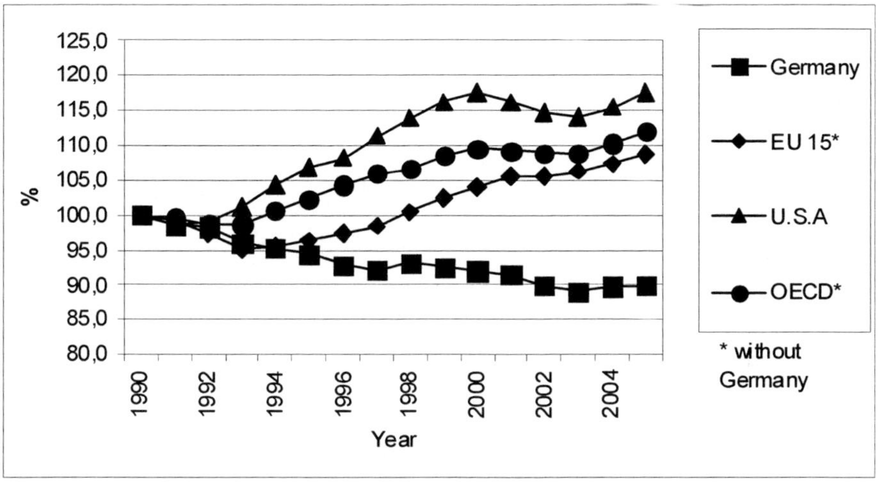

Source: The Conference Board and Groningen Growth and Development Centre.

While actual labour volume is determined by factors such as labour force participation, unemployment, number of working days and weekly working time, the labour force potential reflects the maximum possible labour input – in other words, the working age population as a whole. Labour force potential is, thus, fundamentally determined by the demographic forces: population growth and ageing as well as the immigration/emigration balance. These factors are consequently extremely important in terms of analysing trend growth. Table 7 provides an overview of the most important demographic trends since the beginning of the 1990s. Compared with other reference economies – the U.S. and OECD in particular – Germany has clearly developed unfavourably both in terms of population figures and labour force participation. Germany's total population has only grown by around 3% since 1991 while the U.S. and OECD states reported double-digit growth in the same period. Labour force participation even declined in Germany in the period under consideration. The relative size of the working age population (15–64-years) compared with the population as a whole (the "old-age dependency ratio") has fallen in Germany over the last 15 years. The same ratio has increased in the U.S. and OECD over the same period. While the old-age dependency ratio fell within the EU15, it did so by only a relatively modest margin.

Table 6. Labour Volume Trends

	1991	1994	1997	2000	2004	1991-2004 Change
Germany						
Working age population (in 1000)	38,621	37,516	37,463	39,144	38,853	+232
Change in %		-2.86	-0.14	4.49	-0.74	+0.60
Annual working time (in hours)	1,545	1,543	1,504	1,468	1,440	-105
Change in %		-0.13	-2.53	-2.39	-1.91	-6.80
Labour volume (in millions of hours)	59,669	57,898	56,326	57,456	55,964	-3,705
Change in %		-2.97	-2.72	2.01	-2.60	-6.21
West Germany						
Employed labour force (in 1000)	30,153	29,953	29,967	31,662	31,658	+1,505
Change in %		-0.66	0.05	5.66	-0.01	+4.99
Annual working time (in hours)	1,542	1,511	1,476	1,445	1,425	-117
Change in %		-2.01	-2.32	-2.10	-1.38	-7.59
Labour volume (in millions of hours)	46,506	45,244	44,237	45,760	45,107	-1,399
Change in %		-2.71	-2.23	3.44	-1.43	-3.01
East Germany						
Employed labour force (in 1000)	8,468	7,563	7,496	7,482	7,195	-1,273
Change in %		-10.69	-0.89	-0.19	-3.84	-15.03
Annual working time (in hours)	1,555	1,673	1,612	1,563	1,509	-46
Change in %		7.59	-3.65	-3.04	-3.45	-2.96
Labour volume (in millions of hours)	13,164	12,653	12,087	11,694	10,856	-2,308
Change in %		-3.88	-4.47	-3.25	-7.17	-17.53

Source: Wanger (2006), own calculations.

The figures shown in Tables 6 and 7 suggest that not only actual labour input has declined since the beginning of the 1990s, but that the potential labour force has also decreased. International comparisons also underline the fact that one of the important reasons for this development is the relatively weak growth of the German economy.

Table 7. Demographic Trends

	1991	1995	2000	2004	1991-2004 Change
Germany					
Population (in 1000)	79,984	81,661	82,160	82,491	3.1
Labour force participation (in % of pop.)	49.5	48.2	48.1	48.5	-1.0
Old age ratio (in % of pop.)	69.2	67.9	67.5	66.4	-2.8
USA					
Population (in 1000)	252,981	266,278	282,192	293,655	16.1
Labour force participation (in % of pop.)	50.1	50.2	50.9	50.6	0.5
Old age ratio (in % of pop.)	65.6	65.4	66.2	66.9	1.3
EU15					
Population (in 1000)	365,811	370,969	376,517	383,251	4.8
Labour force participation (in % of pop.)	46.2	45.3	46.4	47.2	1.0
Old age ratio (in % of pop.)	67.2	66.9	66.8	66.5	-0.7
OECD					
Population (in 1000)	1,050,916	1,088,207	1,128,516	1,160,738	10.5
Labour force participation (in % of pop.)	-	46.7	47.4	47.6	0.9
Old age ratio (in % of pop.)	66.1	66.2	66.5	66.7	0.6

Source: OECD database.

6.2.2 Human Capital Formation

Of course, the quality of labour input in the production process – as well as its pure volume – is also of decisive importance. The creation of human capital – in other words, of labour force skills and know-how – boosts labour productivity and innovative power. The creation of human capital is also closely linked to technological progress and is consequently of key interest in endogenous growth theory.

Bearing in mind the lack of direct yardsticks, empirical studies on the role of human capital formation in the growth process must fall back on indicator variables. The literature often resorts to proxies for levels of educational attainment, such as the percentage of the population achieving a specified level of education or the average education and training time per member of the working age population, which are, then, used as indicators of the stock of human capital (refer to OECD, 2003a). Table 8 outlines the development of per capita education and training time in Germany compared with other countries.

Table 8. Average Education and Training Times in the Working Age Population

	1980	1985	1990	1995	1998	1980-1998
Germany	11.4	12.1	12.9	13.4	13.5	+ 2.1
USA	12.2	12.5	12.6	12.6	12.7	+ 0.5
Japan	10.2	10.5	10.9	11.3	11.5	+ 1.3
France	9.5	9.8	10.0	10.5	10.6	+ 1.1
Italy	7.3	7.8	8.4	9.2	9.8	+ 2.5
United Kingdom	10.1	10.5	10.9	11.6	11.9	+ 1.8
Finland	9.6	10.0	10.4	10.9	11.2	+ 1.6
Sweden	10.1	10.6	11.1	11.5	11.6	+ 1.5
Switzerland	11.5	12.1	12.6	12.9	12.9	+ 1.4

Source: OECD (2003b).

Germany is a frontrunner both in terms of changes between 1980 and 1998 and in terms of absolute levels. Numerous empirical studies have demonstrated positive interactions between the level of investment in education, human capital and rates of growth. The analysis performed by Bassanini, Scarpetta, and Hemmings (2001) for a sample of 21 OECD states finds that average per capita education and training times exert a significant impact on long-term growth of per capita production. The fact that average education and training periods are an indicator for the quality of human capital and that Germany holds a leading position in this regard ought to suggest a positive contribution to Germany's economic growth. At the same time, however, international comparative studies of school performance – such as the TIMSS study undertaken by IEA or the OECD's PISA study – indicate qualitative deficiencies in the German educational system. The OECD (2004a) also urges Germany to reform its system of higher education: Germany may have relatively high per capita spending on education, but it also has a much higher student dropout rate of around 30% and its students only finally complete their studies at a relatively late age.

One interesting aspect in this context is an indicator of human capital accumulation proposed by the OECD (see OECD, 2005a), which reveals the share of GDP invested in knowledge. Spending on research and development, software and investments in higher education are regarded as knowledge investments as they are essential for the creation and diffusion of knowledge and, thus, for economic growth. Figure 20 clearly demonstrates that with knowledge investments of around 4% of GDP in 2002, Germany occupied a middle position in comparison with other European countries whilst being well below the value for OECD states of over 5%. What is more, investments have only increased in Germany by 0.5 percentage points since 1994 – not even half as great as the figure for the leading country group (Sweden, Finland, Japan, and USA).

Fig. 20. Investments in Knowledge in 2002

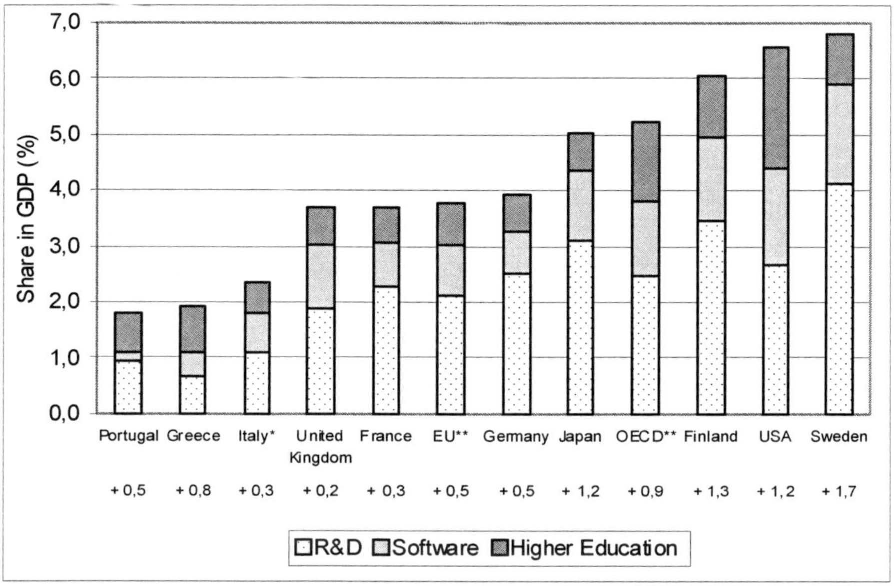

Changes compared to 1994 in percentage points. *Data for 2001; ** without Greece and Italy.
Source: OECD (2005).

6.2.3 Accumulation of Real Capital

According to the neoclassical growth model, real capital investments only influence the overall level of production in the economy but not the rate of growth as the marginal returns on capital fall while the stock of capital increases. While investments in real capital raise production levels accordingly, they only kick off a temporary growth effect that – owing to lengthy adjustment processes – can continue over a long period of time. Endogenous growth models, on the other hand, allow for constant marginal returns on real capital if such capital produces positive external effects as a result, for example, of learning effects or capital-related innovations promoting the adaptation of new technologies and productivity. Even if the significance of real capital in growth theory is contingent on context, the accumulation of capital, nonetheless, plays a key role in studies of the accumulation of capital.

Figure 21 shows the development of gross and net investment ratios in the German economy (public and private sector) since 1991 in an international context. It is immediately apparent that German gross investments – which, in terms of GDP, are traditionally significantly higher than in other industrialised countries – have been falling quite dramatically since 2001. In relation to productive investments, Kuhnert (2005) has even ascertained a marked downward trend over the last 30 years, which has only accelerated since the collapse in capital formation in mid-2001. This has meant that the gross investment ratio in Germany in 2005 was lower than that in the U.S. and the EU15.

This is another reason for the relatively weak growth performance in Germany given that falling volumes of investment and the tailing off of capacity effects of investments since 2000 have resulted in a real net investment ratio in 2004 of around 65 billion euros – a little over 40% of the value for the year 1991. At real annual GDP growth of around 1.4%, the net investment ratio of 8.9% in 1991 was cut to a third, or 3.0%, in 2004. In contrast, the reference economic areas of the EU15 and the U.S. showed constant or increasing gross and net investment ratio trends.

Fig. 21. Investment Ratio Trends

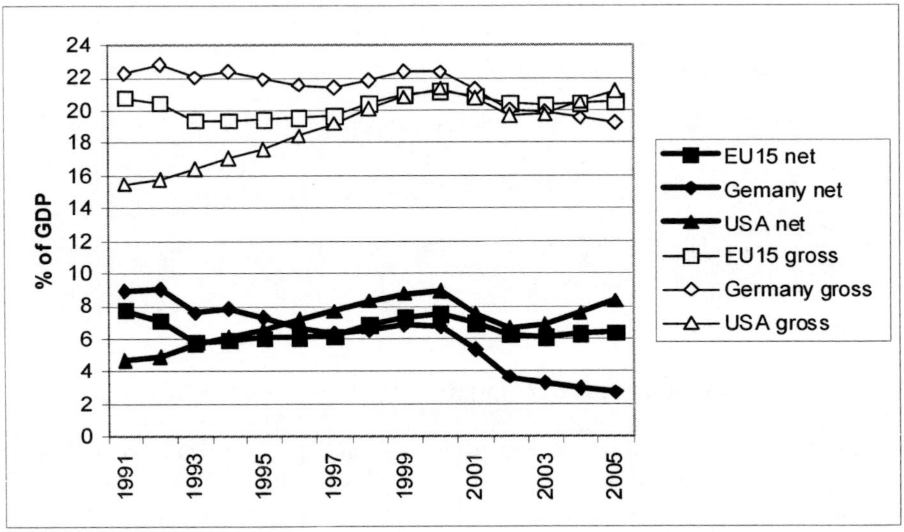

Source: AMECO.

This persistent reluctance to engage in investment activity has resulted in a noticeable slowdown in the growth of the German capital stock as shown in Table 9. It should be stressed that, while the capital stock shrank in Germany, growth in capital stock during the period of observation in the EU15 remained stable and even accelerated in the United States. While a study undertaken by Bassanetti, Döpke, Torrini, and Zizza (2006) also shows how capital accumulation has slowed in a similar way in France and Italy, it also underlines a German peculiarity: Linked with less favourable labour cost developments, the capital intensity of production has increased faster than in other comparable economies (refer to Table 9). This means that pure factor substitution cannot be the cause of the slowing down in capital accumulation. Bassanetti et al. (2006) assume that the decreasing contribution to production potential made by capital combined with lethargic labour market trends reflects difficulties in making profitable use of the factors of production.

Table 9. Capital Stock, Capital Intensity, and Capital Productivity

Period	1991-1996	1996-2001	2001-2005	1991-2005
Annual growth rate of real net capital stock				
Germany	2.34	1.91	0.92	1.78
EU15	2.04	2.31	1.96	2.11
USA	2.46	3.47	3.02	2.98
Annual growth rate in capital intensity				
Germany	3.78	1.91	1.82	2.55
EU15	2.62	0.91	1.51	1.69
USA	0.74	1.65	2.65	1.61
Annual rate of change in capital productivity				
Germany	-0.92	0.15	-0.37	-0.38
EU15	-0.44	0.54	-0.47	-0.10
USA	0.80	0.07	-0.01	0.31

Source: AMECO.

The major improvement, in comparative terms, in capital endowment in Germany is more the outcome of a loss of employment than an acceleration of investment activities. Kamps, Meier, and Oskamp (2004) also claim that consistently higher rates of capital intensification in continental European countries such as Germany, France or Italy compared with those in the Anglo-Saxon countries are the result of significantly lower employment dynamics in those countries. Permanent and disproportionate increases in labour costs have induced companies to replace labour with capital, to transfer lower productivity jobs abroad or cut them altogether (Deutsche Bundesbank, 2002). This has resulted in ongoing capital intensification of domestic production. As a result of sinking marginal returns, this is also associated with a fall in average capital productivity. This is balanced out, however, by a recent trend towards an increase in working times without extra payment, which is having a corresponding impact on labour costs (Deutsche Bank Research, 2005).

6.2.4 Technological Progress

Technological progress boosts the productivity of all the factors of production and is, consequently, extraordinarily important for the long-term economic development. Total factor productivity (TFP) can be increased by introducing state-of-the-art technologies and related forms of organisation in the production process.

Measurement problems lead to the fact that empirical analyses which look at the influence of technological progress on economic development often draw on proxy variables, such as the level of R&D spending and number of new patents registered (cf. OECD, 2004a). Table 10 highlights international developments in research and development spending and new patent registrations.

Similar to the reference economic areas, there has been very little dynamism in the research and development field in Germany since 1991. The level of R&D spending and its relative spread between the public and private sector does not markedly vary from one country to the next. Around two thirds of R&D spending is undertaken by the corporate sector. The level of R&D spending in Germany during the period reviewed is somewhat lower than in the U.S. but higher than the EU15 or OECD ratios. In other words, the German economy has a fairly strong competitive position internationally with regard to research and development spending. Another frequently used indicator of the innovation capacity of an economy – the number of triadic patent families – firmly places Germany at the top of the international league. Germany is way ahead of the reference economic regions both in terms of growth and absolute numbers. A large number of these patent registrations are for "medium high-tech industries" such as mechanical engineering, automotives or the chemical industry, however, and only a relatively small (in international terms) number are for high-tech industries such as information and communication technology or in the biotechnology sector (see Table 10). This is noted critically in the latest "OECD Science, Technology and Industry Scoreboard 2005". The relatively low level of investments in I&C technology in Germany, in particular, is regarded as a potential cause of weak growth in the second half of the 1990s. I&C technology is referred to in several studies as a key technology in terms of accelerating growth of total factor productivity. As it is not only in the production process for the I&C goods themselves in which substantial productivity gains are made owing to their cross-sectional character, positive network externalities are also created in every area of the economy and the world of work. An empirical analysis undertaken by Timmer, Ypma, and van Ark (2003), for example, deploys a growth accounting approach to examine the contribution made to growth by investments in I&C capital. Given that the share of I&C investment in German GDP has hovered around the EU level since the 1980s and is consequently around 1.0, i.e. 1.5 percentage points lower than in the U.S., this is regarded as one of the reasons for the relatively low contribution to growth made by I&C capital of around 0.3 percentage points. A recent study by van Ark and Inklaar (2005) also suggests that the gap between American and European productivity growth has widened since the year 2000 owing to a significant acceleration in US American TFP growth.

Table 10. R&D Spending and Patents

	1991	1995	2000	2002	1991-2002 Change
Germany					
R&D spending (total, as % of GDP)	2.47	2.19	2.45	2.49	0.02
R&D spending (public, as % of GDP)	0.36	0.34	0.33	0.34	-0.02
R&D spending (corporate, as % of GDP)	1.71	1.45	1.73	1.72	0.01
Number of triadic patent families* (per million inhabitants)	46	59	87	88	91.6
Number of patent registrations in the ICT and biotechnology fields (EPO)**	19.1	21.0	29.3	28.7	50.4
USA					
R&D spending (total, as % of GDP)	2.71	2.51	2.74	2.65	-0.06
R&D spending (public, as % of GDP)	0.40	0.35	0.28	0.32	-0.08
R&D spending (corporate, as % of GDP)	1.93	1.77	2.05	1.86	-0.07
Number of triadic patent families	40	45	62	64	57.3
Number of patent registrations in the ICT and biotechnology fields (EPO)	37.9	41.8	48.6	44.5	17.4
EU15					
R&D spending (total, as % of GDP)	2.20	2.08	2.23	2.24	0.04
R&D spending (public, as % of GDP)	0.32	0.30	0.26	0.28	-0.04
R&D spending (corporate, as % of GDP)	1.50	1.39	1.55	1.52	0.02
Number of triadic patent families	28	32	43	-	53.1
Number of patent registrations in the ICT and biotechnology fields (EPO)	32.4	34.2	40.8	39.8	22.9
OECD					
R&D spending (total, as % of GDP)	1.87	1.78	1.87	1.91	0.04
R&D spending (public, as % of GDP)	0.32	0.29	0.25	0.24	-0.08
R&D spending (corporate, as % of GDP)	1.19	1.10	1.20	1.23	0.04
Number of triadic patent families	25	31	43	42	69.6
Number of patent registrations in the ICT and biotechnology fields (EPO)	22.7	25.4	33.7	33.0	45.1

*"Triadic" patent families include patents registered with the European Patent Office (EPO) and the Japanese Patent Office (JPO) as well as those issued by the US Patent and Trademark Office (USPTO).

** These are registrations with the European Patent Office.

Source: OECD database.

6.3 Indirect Influencing Factors

Having analysed direct contributions to growth in section 6.2, this section looks at indirect factors influencing the general decline in growth in Germany. The institutional framework, such as the extent to which goods and factor markets are regulated, is analysed in terms of its impact on growth. The influence of fiscal policies on the long-term economic development is then addressed. Finally, two special factors – the German reunification and the European Monetary Union – are discussed in section 6.4.

6.3.1 The Institutional Framework

The institutional framework influences the incentives affecting economic subjects in a number of different ways. Political and institutional factors can both exercise an influence on the overall economic activity and, consequently, on the long-term growth trends affecting an economy (OECD, 2003b). Theoretically the market mechanism ensures that resources are allocated as efficiently as possible. Allocation arguments for state intervention do, however, arise where market failure occurs for a number of reasons, the regulation of monopoly markets being one good reason. As soon as the state intervenes in the market mechanism for reasons other than pure allocation motives, however, the danger of over-regulation and potential negative impacts on resource allocation and production efficiency arises (cf. Nicoletti, Scarpetta, and Boylaud, 2000). In this context the next section examines whether the level of regulation to which German goods and factor markets are subject could be a possible reason for the relative weak growth of the German economy.

Regulation of Goods Markets

The regulation of goods markets has both an impact on the foreign trade relationships of a national economy and on the development of domestic markets. Excessive regulation of goods markets will impair both economic growth by restricting free global trade and, consequently, putting a brake on improved efficiency and will lead to disproportionate bureaucracy and state control which has a negative impact, in turn, on corporate productivity. High levels of regulation also make it more difficult to adjust to changing structural constraints (cf. Kamps et al., 2004). In this respect, deregulation can contribute to higher production and employment. Recent studies for OECD countries show a significant positive effect of deregulation and privatisation on the formation of real capital. The liberalisation of entry into potential competitive markets, in particular, also appears to have a strong impact on private investment activities (cf. OECD, 2004c). In order to determine the strength of the impact of regulation on the competition intensity on goods markets, Nicoletti et al. (2000) have developed indicators for OECD countries that encompass regulations on goods markets as well as economic and administrative regulations.

Fig. 22. Regulation of the Product Market in 2003

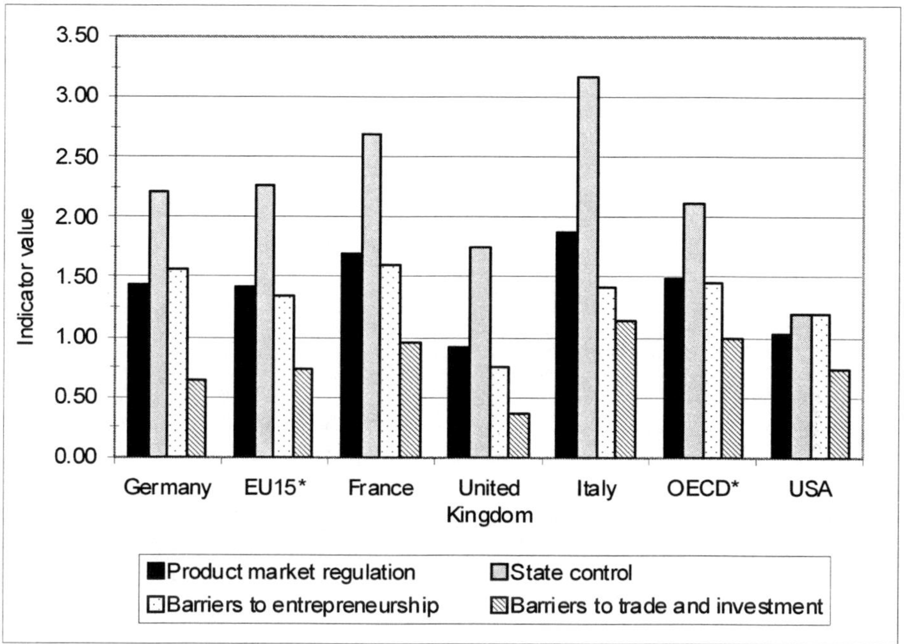

*) member state average exclusive Germany.
Source: Conway, Janod, and Nicoletti (2005).

Figure 22 provides an international comparison of selected indicators of product market regulation in which the first indicator, "product market regulation", represents an aggregation of the remaining indicators.[111] The international comparison of indicators shows that the Anglo-Saxon countries (USA and United Kingdom) are characterised by liberal domestic market regulations and foreign

---

[111] The indicator "state control" takes account of the overall size of the public sector, its weight in the relevant market, state controlling and special rights over companies, the existence of price controls and the use of mandatory regulations. The second indicator, "barriers to entrepreneurship", encompasses features of the licensing and approval system, the communication and simplification of rules and processes, the tangle of administrative red tape affecting the formation of new companies, the sheer breadth of statutory entry barriers and antitrust-exceptional regulations for public corporations or for government mandated action. Finally, the third indicator, "barriers to international trade and investment", includes restrictions on shareholdings for non-residents, discriminating procedures relating to international trade or competition policy, trade restrictions and average customs rates.

trade policies. The continental European countries (Germany, France, and Italy), in contrast, pursue liberal foreign trade policies but have relatively strongly regulated domestic markets. As far as the German economy is concerned, barriers to entrepreneurship as a result of administrative regulations are very high in comparison with other countries.

Schiantarelli (2005) has reviewed the empirical literature on the macroeconomic effects of regulation of the goods market. One finding that is supported by the overwhelming majority of studies undertaken in this field is the negative impact of regulations of product markets on corporate productivity. In particular sectors, at least, evidence is also found for the positive investment and employment effects of deregulation. There are many indications, therefore, a fairly dense pattern of regulations – at least in international terms – on German product markets does seem to be one of the reasons for the relative weak growth of the German economy.

Labour Market Regulations and Wages Policy

The persistently high levels of unemployment in Germany are regarded as one of the main causes of the country's unfavourable economic development in recent years. In this context the Sachverständigenrat zur Begutachtung der gesamtwirtschaftlichen Entwicklung (2005) has referred in this context to a "hysteresis phenomenon" which describes an ever-growing number of hard-to-place unemployed after each business cycle. There has also been an increasing divergence in the qualification-specific unemployment figures since the onset of the 1980s, which is largely due to the substantial increase in rates of unemployment among the low and unskilled. Apart from the inherent transfer payments it generates, the social costs of unemployment also arise from the lost economic input of unemployed people.

Table 11. Unemployment rates (in %)

	1991	1995	2000	2005	1991-2005 Change
Germany	4.2	8.0	7.2	9.5	5.3
United Kingdom	8.6	8.5	5.4	4.7	-3.8
USA	6.8	5.6	4.0	5.1	-1.7
Euro area	7.9	10.5	8.2	8.6	0.6
OECD	6.8	7.3	6.2	6.6	-0.2

Source: OECD database.

Table 11 spotlights the development of unemployment figures in an international comparative context. Germany tops the table with an unemployment rate of 9.5% – one percentage point above the average for the euro area. The difference between the German figures and the OECD average is almost 3 percentage points. In the U.S. and United Kingdom, unemployment is around 5% of the working age population and, consequently, significantly lower than the continental European level. The substantial dynamism of the figures since German reunification is also striking. The unemployment rate in Germany has increased by 5.3 percentage points since 1991 compared to 0.6 percentage points in the euro area. The usual reference economic areas in many cases report substantial reductions over the same period.

The reasons for the relatively high rates of unemployment in Germany and other continental European countries have been the subject of numerous empirical studies. Institutional framework conditions on labour markets, in particular, have often been cited as the cause for the strong increase in unemployment (cf. Nickell, Nunziata, and Ochel, 2005).

Fig. 23. Employee Protection Legislation in 2003

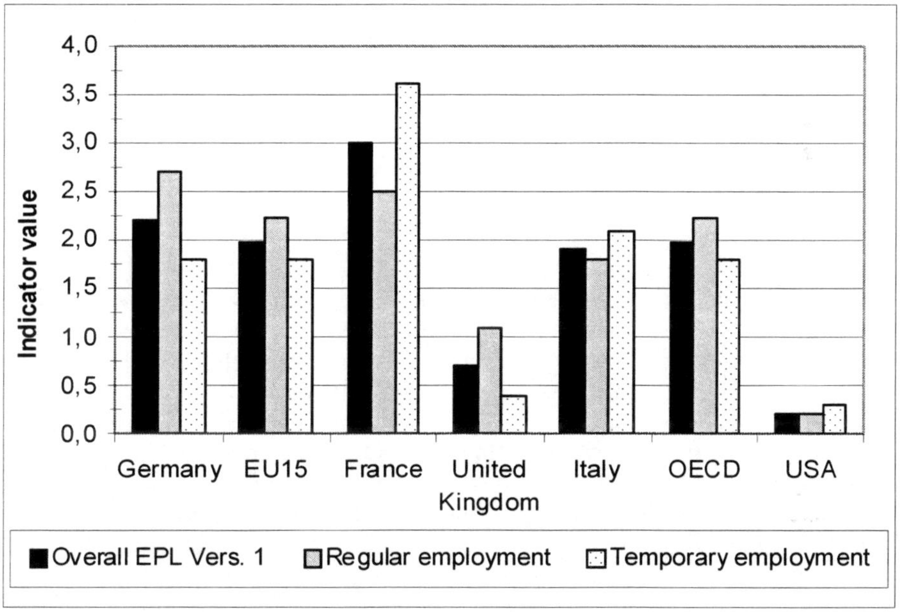

Source: OECD (2004b).

Employment protection legislation reduces flexibility on the labour market and consequently reinforces persistent unemployment. Figure 23 shows indicators developed by Nicoletti et al. (2000) on the stringency of employee protection legislation in different countries and economic areas. A distinction is made in this context between permanent employment contracts on the one hand and temporary jobs on the other hand. The "Overall EPL Vers. 1" indicator (overall employment protection legislation) constitutes the arithmetical mean of both sub indicators. The table shows that Germany has the most highly regulated permanent employment relationships while regulation of temporary employment – a field that has dramatically expanded throughout the 1990s – roughly corresponds to the EU15 levels. A comparison of the indicator values for the U.S. in particular, but also for the United Kingdom, clearly shows how highly regulated the German and other European labour markets are.

Another reason for persistently high levels of unemployment is often thought to be the negotiating strength of trade unions. The so-called "insider-outsider theory", for example, assumes that company "turnover costs" give employees or their trade union representatives (insiders) negotiating power in the wage negotiation process. "Turnover costs" are the sum of the cost of dismissing an insider and taking on and inducting a newly recruited employee. The negotiating power in the hands of employees ultimately results in a wage level which constitutes a barrier to additional employment. The fact that Germany has higher levels of employee protection than other countries (cf. Figure 23) is also likely to play a role in this context given that highly developed employee protection increases a company's "turnover costs" and, thus, the ability of employees to extract rents in the wage setting process. This may be a reason for chronic unemployment in Germany (cf. also Sachverständigenrat zur Begutachtung der gesamtwirtschaftlichen Entwicklung, 2005). Empirical evidence for the "insider-outsider hypothesis" can also be found in a recent study undertaken by the Institute of Labour Market and Work Research (Möller, 2005).

6.3.2 Fiscal Policy

Fiscal policy can have a long-term impact on the growth of a national economy in many different ways. Public investments in infrastructure or in education and research can elicit positive growth effects if they produce spillovers and positively influence technological progress. On the other hand, an excessive increase in pure consumption spending tends to impede growth, particularly if such spending is financed by a distorting system of taxes and fiscal charges. The quality of public finance is also significant with regard to economic growth. Empirical studies also suggest a relationship between government debt and long-term growth trends. The various channels via which fiscal policy influences economic growth are discussed in the following.

Taxes and Fiscal Charges

Owing to its distorting impact the system of taxes and fiscal charges exercises a significant influence on the long-term growth of an economy given that taxes and fiscal charges distort the prices of goods and factors of production leading, in turn, to inefficient allocations or an inefficient use of resources. In the case of Germany two problem areas need to be stressed in this context: the very high burdens placed on employees and employers by income tax and non-wage labour costs and the high – in international terms – taxes paid by companies.

Fig. 24. Effective Average Rate of Corporate Taxation Across Europe

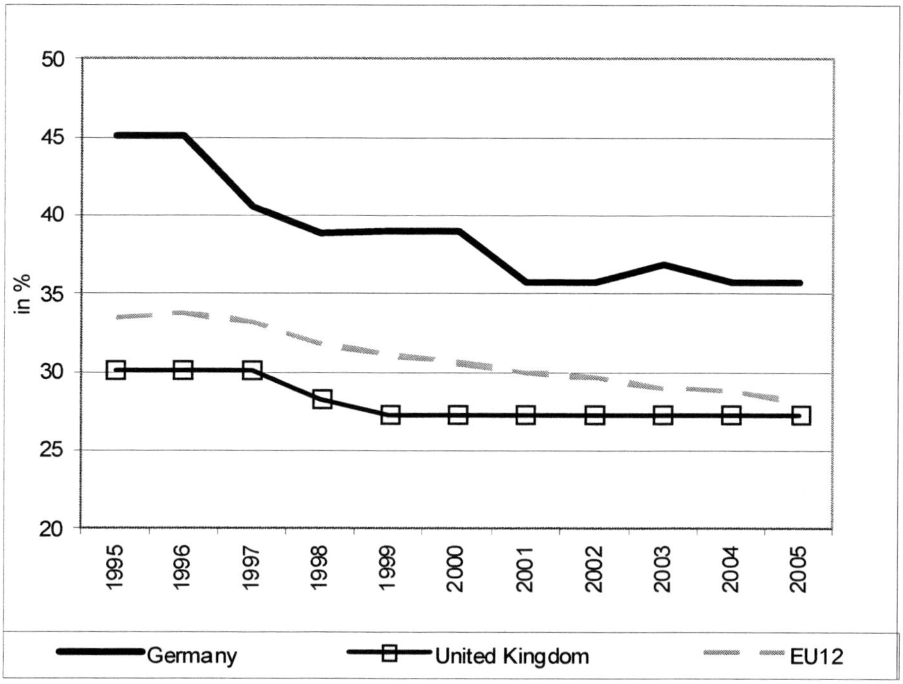

Source: Overesch (2005).

Figure 24 shows the effective average tax rates for companies in Germany, the United Kingdom and the corresponding EU12 average. The rates of tax have been calculated on the basis of the approach used by Devereux and Griffith (1999) and reflect the tax incidence on a hypothetical investment project.[112] The figures clearly show that the effective average rate of tax in the United Kingdom at the outset of the 1990s was significantly lower than the EU12 level, but that the tax rates have converged more recently. The effective average tax rate for Germany, on the other hand, is substantially higher than that in the EU12. Although tax rates were reduced between 1991 and 2004 by around 10 percentage points, they nevertheless remained around 7.7 percentage points above the EU12 average. As the level of effective average tax rates has a major impact on company's choice of international location, the comparatively higher tax burden in Germany is likely to lead to negative growth effects arising from a lack of investments or from the relocation of production to more tax friendly environments. This is suggested by the development of German rates of net investment (cf. Figure 21).

The burdens borne by the factor labour show a similar picture. Figure 25 shows the average level of income tax – plus non-wage labour costs and transfer pay-

[112] See Overesch (2005) for a more detailed description of the approach.

ments – for the U.S., Germany, and EU12. These income taxes refer to an average family with two children and one parent employed.

Fig. 25. Income Taxes Plus Non-wage Labour Costs and Transfer Payments

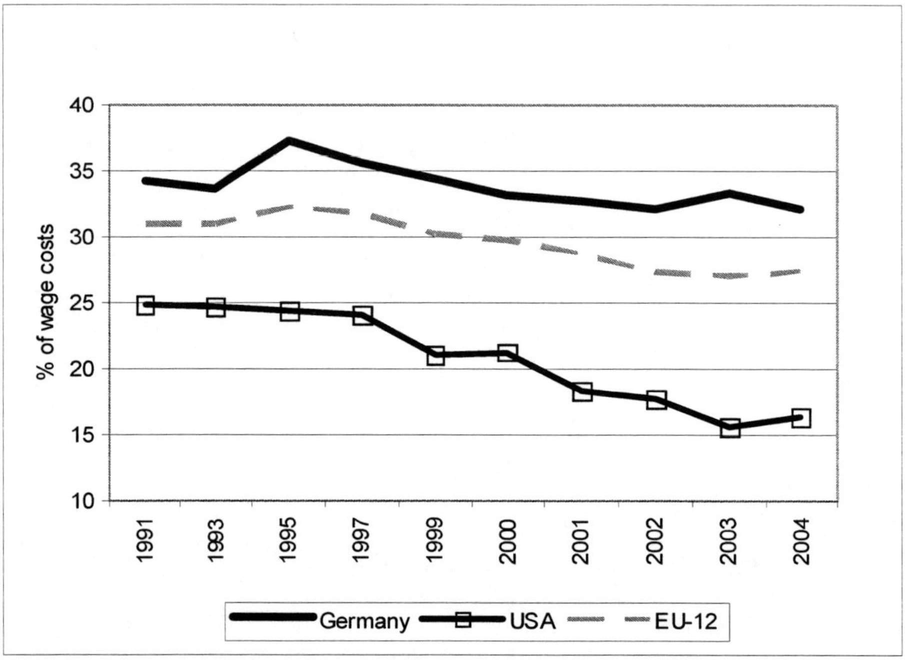

Source: OECD database.

As shown in the graph, income taxes and non-wage labour costs are lowest in the United States. In fact they fell by almost 10% in the period 1991 to 2004. In Germany, in contrast, the burden on the factor labour is substantially higher than in the reference economic areas and has only slightly decreased over the relevant period. The very high – in comparative international terms – levels of income tax and non-wage labour costs in Germany work as a brake on the sustained generation of employment in Germany. The high levels of tax and social security levies paid by companies are likely to lead to a shifting of labour-intensive production stages to more cost-effective production locations abroad. This thesis is supported by a current empirical study by Becker and Jaeckle (2005), which draws on a comprehensive data record of German direct investments in Eastern Europe.

All in all one can, therefore, assume that, in combination with the high effective tax rate on corporations, the comparatively high levels of taxes and non-wage labour costs bearing down on the factor labour will have substantially negative location effects for Germany. The German Council of Economic Experts also stresses the need for an international competitive tax system and warns in its current annual report (Sachverständigenrat zur Begutachtung der gesamtwirtschaftlichen

Entwicklung, 2005) of the need for reform – particularly in the realm of corporate taxation.

Total Government Outlays as Percentage of GDP and Spending Structure

The literature also discusses the impact of fiscal policy on growth in the context of the scope and structure of state activities. Unproductive state spending which is financed by a distorting system of tax and fiscal charges, in particular, will have negative effects on long-term economic growth.

Numerous empirical studies suggest that state activities have a negative impact. A regression analysis undertaken by Fölster and Henrekson (2001) based on an extensive panel of OECD states shows that an increase in public spending of 10 percentage points (as a ratio of GDP) will reduce annual growth by 0.7 to 0.8 percentage points in the long term. Table 12 provides an international comparison of the development of the ratios of public spending to GDP since the 1990s.

Table 12. International Comparison of Total Government Outlays as Percentage of GDP

	1991	1995	2000	2004	1991-2004 Change
Germany	46.1	48.3	45.1	47.0	0.9
Euro area	49.3	50.5	46.4	47.7	-1.6
United Kingdom	44.0	45.0	37.5	43.9	-0.1
USA	37.8	37.0	34.2	36.4	-1.4

Source: OECD (2004b).

The state share of GDP in Germany in 2004 was more or less at the level of the EU12 countries. Compared with the United Kingdom and particularly the U.S., however, the public spending ratio in Germany must be considered to be relatively high. Public spending has dynamically developed since the 1990s as well. All reference economic areas reduced their government spending ratios while the German state sector grew by about one percentage point of GDP over the period of observation. A recent study by Hauptmeier, Heipertz, and Schuknecht (2006) focuses on the widespread trend towards reductions in the share of total government outlays as a percentage of GDP in OECD countries since the 1980s. The authors use a categorisation method to identify ambitious reform phases in many OECD countries and examine these with reference to their potential fiscal and macroeconomic impact. Drawing on a descriptive cross-sectional comparison the analysis concludes that states which make substantial reductions in spending usually experience better long-term growth trends. What is more, the composition of cuts in spending appear – in combination with parallel institutional reforms – to be of decisive importance. The reform phases bringing about an improvement in the quality of the spending structure, in particular, have a positive impact on economic development.

Table 13. Composition of State Spending in International Context (as a share of total spending in each case)

	1991	1995	2000	2004	1991-2004
Germany					
State consumption spending	40.76	40.07	41.53	39.37	-1.39
of which: wages	19.10	18.14	17.85	16.15	-2.96
Public investment	5.81	4.62	3.98	2.92	-2.88
Social spending and other transfers	42.51	44.33	49.44	48.70	6.19
Subsidies	4.63	4.29	3.75	2.74	-1.89
EU15					
State consumption spending	40.09	39.80	42.21	42.37	2.28
of which: wages	22.29	21.61	22.45	21.99	-0.30
Public investment	6.45	5.22	5.39	5.05	-1.40
Social spending and other transfers	38.97	41.08	43.92	43.90	4.93
Subsidies	3.78	3.27	2.99	2.64	-1.14
USA					
State consumption spending	45.25	42.05	42.84	43.46	-1.79
of which: wages	28.81	27.39	27.30	26.82	-1.99
Public investment	9.83	8.61	9.21	8.80	-1.04
Social spending and other transfers	35.46	41.08	41.35	44.03	8.57
Subsidies	1.22	1.26	1.34	1.09	-0.12
United Kingdom					
State consumption spending	47.07	43.96	50.48	49.66	2.59
of which: wages	26.53	18.65	19.81	18.55	-7.98
Public investment	5.46	4.38	2.96	4.23	-1.23
Social spending and other transfers	37.76	41.04	44.65	39.65	1.88
Subsidies	1.40	1.56	1.27	1.05	-0.35

Source: OECD database.

Spending on the state's core tasks – such as provision of public goods in the areas of national security, the legal system and defence as well as fundamental administrative services and spending on education, basic research and the transport and communications infrastructure – are often turned to productive use while consumption spending, subsidies and social payments and state transfers are regarded as unproductive. A study undertaken by Afonso, Ebert, Schuknecht, and Thoene (2005) deals with the quality of public finance and growth and provides an overview of the empirical literature on the impact of forms of productive spending on growth. The positive growth effects of public investment appear to be a matter of some dispute. Table 13 provides an international comparison of state spending structures for the period of 1991 to 2004. The spending items in each case are shown as a percentage of total spending.

The purely consumption element of the German public budget appears to be fairly low compared with other countries at first glance. At around 40%, the ratio for 2004 was three percentage points below the euro area level. There is practically no difference in the level of subsidies between Germany and the euro area – although the United States and the UK dedicate a mere 1% of their budgets to this field. Despite a substantial reduction in 2004, the share of subsidies in Germany has been almost three times as high since the 1990s. Germany is top of the international league as far as social spending and transfers are concerned. Around half of all spending in the period under review was accounted for by this type of outlay. This area is also growing at a highly dynamic rate of almost 6 percentage points – a rate that has only been exceeded since 1991 by the United States. There has also been a noticeable drop in the share of public capital spending which, at the end of 2004, accounted for just 3% of total spending. The United States and the countries in the euro area all dedicate a considerably higher share of their national budgets to capital spending.

National Debt

Public spending can be financed by borrowing as well as from taxes and levies. In fact, extensive use has been made of the borrowing instrument in Germany since reunification. Table 14 shows that total public borrowing as a share of GDP rose by 28 percentage points in Germany between 1991 and 2004 while, at the same time, borrowing was much lower in the EU12 and OECD countries. The U.S. managed to reduce its total public borrowing, as a share of GDP, by around 7 percentage points in the same period. Despite these highly dynamic developments, Germany's public debt ratio of almost 67% is not overly unsettling when seen in an international context.

Table 14. Total Public Debt – Deficit (% GDP)

	1991	1995	2000	2004	1991-2004 Change
Germany	38.84	57.15	60.90	66.88	28.04
USA	71.29	74.19	58.78	64.13	-7.16
EU12	62.20	77.65	75.53	77.29	15.10
OECD	63.02	73.92	71.57	77.68	14.66

Source: OECD database.

In recent years many theoretical and empirical studies have examined the relationship between borrowing and long-term growth trends (refer, e.g., to Easterly & Rebelo, 1993; Tanzi & Chalk, 2000) whereby two interactions stand out in particular. The "crowding-out" effect occurs when expanded borrowing on the part of the state pushes up interest rates and, consequently, diminishes the attractiveness of private investments. An increase in public borrowing has negative effects on growth if the relevant resources are not used to finance productive investment. A second argument often wielded to demonstrate a negative link between public borrowing and growth is closely linked with the idea of sustainable fiscal policies. High and stable levels of government deficit will elicit negative rational expectations about future fiscal policy. Anticipated tax increases may result in a fall in private investment activities and a corresponding negative impact on growth. Empirical evidence for the relationship described here between deficits or public debt and long-term growth trends has been found by many studies. Both Fischer (1993) and Easterly and Rebelo (1993) confirm in cross-sectional regressions the significant influence of the balance of public spending. Easterly and Rebelo (1993) point out, however, that results need to be interpreted with care as it is very difficult to identify effects predicted by theoretical models. However, the major borrowing trends in Germany since reunification are thought to very probably have negative effects on growth.

6.4 Special Factors

In addition to the direct and indirect factors determining the long-term decline in economic growth in Germany described above, the analysis in this section now considers two important special factors that had a major impact on German growth trends in the 1990s.

6.4.1 European Economic and Monetary Union

Since the launch of Stage III of European monetary union (EMU) on January 1, 1999, monetary policy has been entrusted to the European Central Bank (ECB) which is now responsible for setting the base rate for the euro area. The European Central Bank has been criticised on many occasions for pursuing an excessively restrictive and asymmetric monetary policy which has suppressed consumer demand and investment as well as weakened growth particularly in Germany (Bibow, 2005a; Enderlein, 2006; Hein & Truger, 2002).

One of the reasons for this line of argument has been the differing rates of inflation in different euro area countries (cf. Figure 26). These persistent differences are striking when compared with other currency areas, such as the U.S., and are mainly the result of convergence processes between euro area countries in the wake of EMU, structural differences between different national economies and differing fiscal policies (cf. Sachverständigenrat zur Begutachtung der gesamtwirtschaftlichen Entwicklung, 2005; Deutsches Institut für Wirtschaftsforschung, 2005; European Central Bank, 2005).

The different rates of inflation in the euro area countries imply different real interest rates. Countries with comparatively low rates of inflation, such as Germany, have high real interest rates while countries with high rates of inflation, such as Ireland, Spain, Italy, Portugal, or Greece, have conversely low real rates of interest. Critics take the view that this inevitably leads to pro-cyclical effects: Economies with high rates of inflation and a tendency to overheat are additionally stimulated by low real rates of interest while growth stagnates in countries with low rates of inflation and weak growth (cf. Hofmann & Remsperger, 2005). In order to avoid the alleged regional disparities arising from diverging rates of inflation, some critics have proposed dropping the policy of setting uniform base rates in favour of base rates tailored to the situation in each country (Enderlein, 2006). Various publications have at least suggested that the uniform ECB policy is not capable of responding to regional differences within the EMU area and that certain countries may, as a consequence, be put at a disadvantage (cf. Hendrikx & Chapple, 2002; Wyplosz, 2006).

Fig. 26. Country-specific Development of Consumer Prices

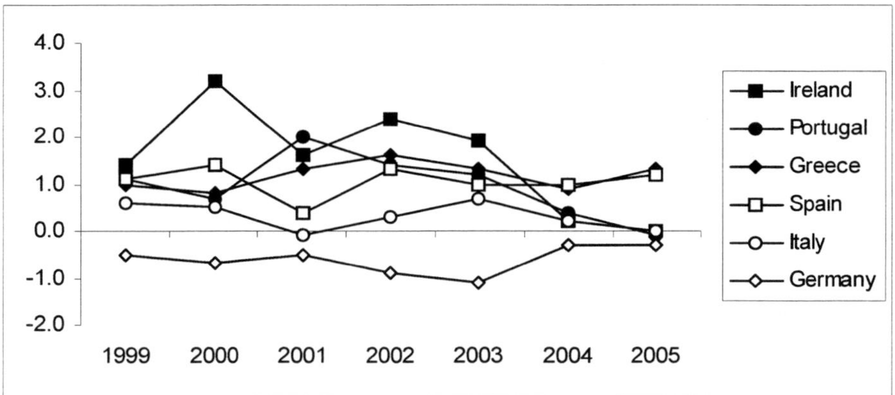

Source: Eurostat.

However, such criticism tends to overlook the issue as to which real rate of interest is decisive for consumer and/or capital spending. Economic subjects act in accordance with the ex-ante real rate of interest (nominal rate of interest minus inflation expectations) and not according to the level of ex-post real rates of interest (nominal rate of interest minus actual inflation), which is unknown at the time consumer or investment decisions are taken. Inflation expectations in the euro area countries do not differ as markedly, however, as actual rates of interest (cf. Figure 27). This means that the real interest effect does not assume the dimensions which might be suggested by the large differences in ex-post real rates of interest. Owing to the poor quality of the available data, however, analyses are usually dependent on the use of ex-post real rates of interest (cf. Deutsche Bundesbank, 2006).

The negative effect of different rates of inflation on the growth rate via real rates of interest contrasts with the positive effect of improvements in price competitiveness. In most euro area countries higher rates of inflation are combined with steeply rising real unit labour costs and comparatively low increases in productivity. These countries have poorer investment prospects and cost disadvantages with the cumulative effects on overall economic development where the effect of real rates of interest is gradually ironed out by real exchange rates.

Real rates of interest may well, of course, have been more favourable for Germany under a Bundesbank regime. However, it is important not to overlook the fact that comparatively low nominal rates of interest in the euro area in recent years have also – from a historical perspective – led to very low real rates of interest in Germany. While Germany may have forfeited the relative advantage arising from the real rates of interest it enjoyed over countries such as Spain or Portugal prior to EMU, the most decisive factor for German investments, however, is the absolute level of real rates of interest.

Another positive effect of the European Monetary Union on the economic situation of all EMU countries, including Germany, is the increase in the volume of trade. Above all, falling transaction costs, the elimination of exchange rate risks and high levels of price transparency produced by a single currency have all been responsible for the positive trade affects between EMU countries. Germany may not have experienced a significant increase in imports, but the effect on German exports has been estimated, using a gravitation model, at 18% and the expectations German exporters had prior to introduction of a single currency have been fully met (Sachverständigenrat zur Begutachtung der gesamtwirtschaftlichen Entwicklung, 2005).

In conclusion, comparatively high real rates of interest may have had negative effects on growth, but this effect is compensated, if not overcompensated, by other effects.

Fig. 27. Dispersion of Rates of Inflation and Medium-term Inflation Expectations in EMU Countries (11 Countries, Excluding Luxembourg)

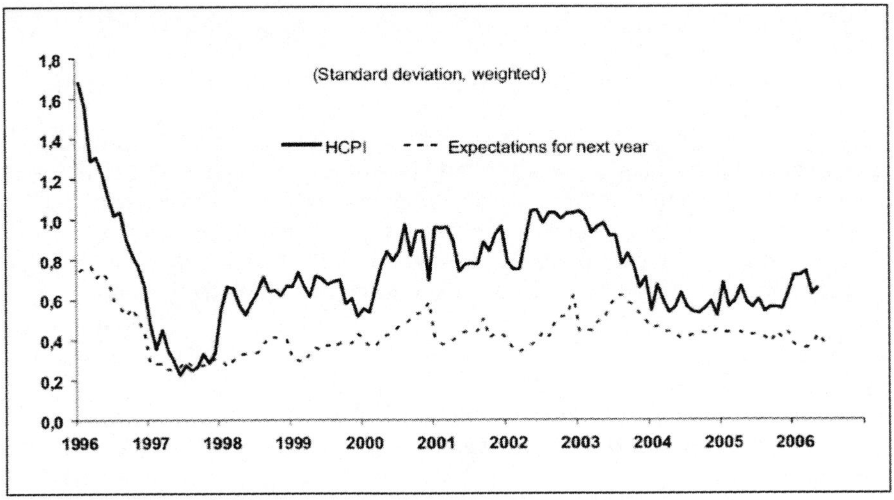

Source: Deutsche Bundesbank.

6.4.2 Reunification

The West German economy experienced sustained and dynamic growth prior to reunification. But also in the first years following reunification, real rates of growth of 5% were achieved. The "unification boom" was driven by a large volume of construction and rebuilding contracts designed to establish a functioning infrastructure in the former territories of East Germany. The situation changed abruptly, however, with the recession in 1993, and since the mid-1990s at the latest, overall German growth has been relatively low (Bibow, 2005b; European Commission, 2002).

One reason frequently identified for the low rate of growth following the "unification boom" was the very fast pace at which wages in the new eastern states were aligned with those in former West Germany. Compared with productivity levels, wage levels in the new East German states were too high and led to structural imbalances on labour markets, a development comparable with the Italian mezzogiorno problem (cf. Sinn & Westermann, 2001). Unemployment levels rose as a result and production slumped in the East German states. What is more, the consumption of resources in East Germany continued to exceed its GDP in such a way that the resulting deficit needed to be mainly financed from public transfers to East Germany in the framework of social security systems and the system of fiscal equalisation. As part of the Solidarity Pact I, around 10.5 billion euros flowed into the new East German states between 1995 and 2002 in the form of special federal supplementary payments (*Sonderbedarfs-Bundesergänzungszuweisungen*) and funds made available under the Investment Promotion Act for East Germany (IfG)[113] that were designed to close the infrastructure gap in the East and support the process towards sought-after economic convergence. Convergence did, in fact, take place in the years immediately following reunification only to tail off again from the mid-1990s and to grind to a complete halt after that. Possible explanations are identified by Sinn (2000) in both the expiry of the 1996 Development Areas Act (*Fördergebietsgesetz*) in the framework of which investments in East Germany were subsidised via the tax system as well as the real currency devaluation, which took place as a result of external transfers. The end of the convergence process could also be explained by the subsidies themselves that were so high – particularly in the framework of the Development Areas Act – that they resulted in negative capital costs. Owing to a positive substitution rate between labour and capital, however, the resulting higher capital intensity did not result in higher labour productivity (cf. Sinn, 2000; Barrell & te Velde, 2000).

---

[113] In 2001, a decision was reached during the negotiations to prolong the Solidarity Pact to transfer the targeted resources as part of the IfG as special federal supplementary payments and to document the use to which the funds had been put in "Aufbau Ost" development progress reports.

7 Alternative Methods for a Forward-Looking Assessment of Potential GDP Growth

7.1 Introduction

While the methods for assessing potential GDP growth discussed in chapter 5 were characterized by their retrospective nature, we now consider the case where forward-looking information enters the projection as well. In particular, this part of the project investigates whether information contained in the term structure of interest rates may be useful for assessing future economic growth. This part of the project is less concerned with determining potential growth itself (which is inherently unobservable). It is rather aimed at analysing the adequacy of term structure-based methods for forecasting the short- up to medium-term real development. The methodology applied in this chapter is mostly motivated from an empirical perspective and less motivated theoretically, such as the production function approach (outlined in chapter 5).

First, we provide an overview of the extant literature on the topic and briefly discuss some theoretical aspects (section 7.2). Section 7.3 discusses the empirical methodology and estimation procedure. Section 7.4 describes the data and discusses some descriptive statistics. Results of the "in-sample" and "out-of-sample" analysis are presented in sections 7.5 and 7.6, respectively.

7.2 Overview of the Relevant Literature and Theoretical Aspects

The potential benefit of using interest rates to assess the real development stems from the fact that financial variables can be characterized as forward-looking (Stock & Watson, 2003). According to the theory of efficient capital markets by Fama (1970), security prices, at a certain point in time, are a summary measure of all available relevant information for the market participants.[114] Hence, one can as-

[114] The informational efficiency of capital markets has been challenged by some authors over the last few years. This line of research (known as "Behavioural Finance") goes beyond the scope of this report.

S. Hauptmeier et al., *Projecting Potential Output*, Zew Economic Studies,
DOI: 10.1007/978-3-7908-2177-2_7,

sume that the yield curve calculated from current market prices of bonds with different time to maturity also contains the market participants' expectations about future real development.

A number of empirical studies have investigated the explanatory power of the term spread (difference between long-term interest rates and short-term interest rates) for future real activity. The predictive power of the term spread is not only well-documented for the United States[115] but also for other developed countries.[116] To the best of our knowledge, these empirical results have not been accounted for so far in projection methods for medium-term growth used by official institutions.

Contrary to section 2.3.4, we now deal less with theoretical issues but rather aim at assessing the usefulness for forecasting the short- up to medium-term real development from an empirical perspective. However, we will also briefly discuss some theoretical considerations on the predictive power of the yield curve for future real GDP growth.[117]

An informal explanation for the empirically observed connection between the term spread and output growth is that the spread is a measure of the relative stance of monetary policy.[118] The starting point of the consideration is a restrictive monetary policy of the central bank in order to curb inflation. This restrictive monetary policy leads to an increase of the interest rate at the short end of the yield curve. Whereas the central bank is able to influence the short end of the term structure, the long end is mainly determined by expectations of the real interest rate and inflation. According to the expectation hypothesis of the term structure, the long-run interest rate is the average of expected future short-term interest rates.[119] If the contractive monetary policy of the central bank is seen as effective, expected inflation as well as expected short rates should decrease or increase less quickly. This mechanism often leads to a situation where the long-term interest rate is temporarily lower than the short-term interest rate (flat or inverted yield curve). Since a high interest rate at the short end tends to slow down the economy, a positive empirical relationship between the spread and future output growth can be ob-

---

[115] For more details see, for example, Estrella and Hardouvelis (1991), Dotsey (1998), Hamilton and Kim (2002), Estrella and Mishkin (1997).

[116] For more details, see Bernard and Gerlach (1998), Estrella and Mishkin (1997), Estrella, Rodrigues, and Schich (2003).

[117] For models explaining the connection between the term spread and output growth, see, for example, Estrella (2005a) and Eijffinger, Schaling, and Verhagen (2000). A model with another focus is the consumption-based asset pricing model by Campbell and Cochrane (1999), which also contains implications for the connection between term structure and real activity. This model differs from the traditional approach basically in that, instead of the absolute consumption, consumption relative to a benchmark level (habit-level) enters into the utility function. The implications of the model for the connection between interest rates and real activity are discussed, for example, in Estrella, Rodrigues, and Schich (2003).

[118] For more details, see, for example, Estrella (2005b), Stock and Watson (2003).

[119] See section 2.3.4. A central implication of the expectation hypothesis is that the interest rate of a n-periodic bond is the average of expected (one-period) short rates plus a constant risk premium: $i_t^{(n)} = n^{-1} E_t(i_t^{(1)} + i_{t+1}^{(1)} + ... + i_{t+n-1}^{(1)}) + tp^{(n)}$.

served. As pointed out by Estrella (2005b), this reasoning is not the only possible explanation for the relationship. There are also other expectations independent of monetary policy which are important for the pricing of securities since bond prices reflect the information sets of a multiplicity of private agents.

An interesting future field of research could be the decomposition of nominal interest rates in ex-ante real interest rates and expected inflation via inflation-indexed bonds. Based on a term structure of real interest rate and expectation of inflation, it is possible to separate the predictive content of these two components of nominal interest for real activity. Given data limitations[120] and the low liquidity of the markets for inflation-indexed bonds, we do not consider this question in greater detail.[121]

Although the predictive power of the term spread has been empirically confirmed, there are several restrictions limiting the potential application of such methods. Especially in economics, one often faces the problem that historically observed relationships might be subject to temporal instability. According to "Goodhart's law" (Goodhardt, 1975), this problem particularly arises if the government or the central banks focus their economic sanctions on a single economic indicator. Further empirical studies have revealed that the stability of the link between the term spread and real economic growth may not be guaranteed[122], while other authors argue that the forecast power of the spread may depend on the monetary regime.[123] Hence, these aspects are an important caveat, which should be considered if one wishes to apply such a method.

7.3 Empirical Methodology

In this part of the project we divide the empirical procedure into two steps. First, we explore the predictive power of the term spread using the whole sample ("in-sample" analysis). The second step contains an "out-of-sample" analysis in order to assess the usefulness of the term spreads for the forecast practice. In this case, we estimate the models recursively so that only information available to the forecaster at a particular point in time enters the model.

---

[120] In the beginning of 2006, the first inflation-indexed bond was issued in Germany. Since 1997, there has been a market for TIPS (Treasury Inflation Protected Securities) in the United States. During the first years of trading, the market was very illiquid (see, for instance, D'Amico, Kim, & Wei 2008). Great Britain has the longest experience with inflation-indexed bonds (since 1981), and the British market is relatively liquid compared to other countries (see Berardi, 2005).

[121] Isolating the expectations of inflation of market participants on the bond market based on inflation-indexed bonds is problematic given time variation of liquidity premia in TIPS interest rates and the existence of inflation risk premia in the nominal term structure of traditional bonds.

[122] Compare, for example, Stock and Watson (2003) or rather Estrella, Rodrigues, and Schich (2003).

[123] See, for example, Baltzer and Kling (2007) for economic historical studies for Germany.

7.3.1 "In-Sample" Analysis

The predictive regression in its simplest form can be defined as

$$y_{t+k}^{(k)} = \beta_0 + \beta_1 \, Spread_t + \varepsilon_{t+k}^{(k)}, \tag{7.1}$$

where $y_{t+k}^{(k)}$ is the (annualised) growth rate of GDP for a period of k quarters and is defined as $y_{t+k}^{(k)} = (400/k)\ ln(Y_{t+k}/Y_t)$. Y_{t+k} is the value of real GDP in the period $t+k$. The spread is defined as the difference of long-term and short-term interest rates [$Spread_t = i_t^{(n)} - i_t^{(1)}$], where n denotes the maturity of the bond. The predictive power can be judged according to the R-square and the significance of β_1. Due to overlapping observations of the dependent variable, it is paramount that serial correlation of the error term in the equation above is taken into account. Therefore, we base our inference on t-statistics with Newey and West (1987) standard errors since they are robust against heteroscedasticity and autocorrelation.

Eq. (7.1) is estimated for different forecast horizons k in order to analyse how far the power of the term spread reaches into the future. We also analyse for which maturity n there may be a peak in the forecast power of the spreads. In order to further assess how far the forecast power of the spreads reaches into the future, we use marginal GDP growth as the dependent variable (see Estrella & Hardouvelis, 1991; Dotsey, 1998; Hamilton & Kim, 2002): $(y_{t+k}^{(1)} + y_{t+k-1}^{(1)} + y_{t+k-2}^{(1)} + y_{t+k-3}^{(1)}) / 4$. Thus, we consider in this context to what extent the "year-to-year" growth rate (realised in k periods in future) can be predicted by the term spread.

Time series variables, such as real GDP growth, usually exhibit some degree of autocorrelation. That is why it is often useful to consider lagged values as explanatory variables. Hence, it is possible to evaluate whether the spread contains information about future GDP growth beyond the information of past realisations. Since there are other (macroeconomic) variables with a certain predictive ability for output growth, it is also recommendable to consider them as control variables in the regression equation:

$$y_{t+k}^{(k)} = \beta_0 + \beta_1 \, Spread_t + \beta_2(L)\, y_t + \beta_3' X_t + \varepsilon_{t+k}^{(k)}, \tag{7.2}$$

where X_t is a vector of additional variables, which are incorporated into the analysis, and $\beta_2(L)$ denotes a lag-polynomial of order p. In this context we check whether the forecast power of the spread is robust against the inclusion of additional information.

7.3.2 "Out-of-Sample" Analysis

The majority of the empirical studies discussed in section 7.2.1 analyse the predictive content of the spread using an "in-sample" analysis.[124] For the practical applicability of methods based on the yield curve for forecasting future output growth it is important, however, to investigate the "real-time" predictive power of the

[124] Exceptions are more recent articles, e.g., Ang, Piazzesi, and Wei (2006) or Stock and Watson (2003).

spread. Hence, we estimate the forecast equation recursively and calculate "out-of-sample" forecasts for the following period. In this manner we can evaluate the predictive accuracy of term spread-based models and compare it to benchmark models. Consequently, we can ensure that only information available to the forecaster is used. For the evaluation of predictive accuracy we use the root mean squared error (RMSE) and Theil's U as described in section 4.4.1.

7.4 Data and Descriptive Statistics

The first step of our empirical analysis is to set up an adequate database for Germany. Yield curve data (zero-bond yields with maturities of 1 to 10 years) were extracted from the time series database of the Deutsche Bundesbank and were transformed accordingly. The data are calculated by the Deutsche Bundesbank on the basis of market-traded German coupon bonds using the Svensson (1994) methodology. Time series of real GDP growth and miscellaneous control variables are obtained from the data provider Reuters-Ecowin. These data were transformed accordingly (for example, correction of outliers, seasonal adjustment etc.). Non-stationary time series were transformed into stationary time series. Our sample period runs from 1972:4 to 2004:4. Detailed information on the variables and transformations of the data are available in the annex.

Figure 28 shows the evolution of interest rates of zero bonds for different maturities (1 to 10 years) together with 3-month money market rate. As the figure reveals, the dynamics of the interest rates are characterised by a high degree of co-movement. Furthermore, it is clear that the yield curve is upward sloping ("normal shape") in most periods. In several cases (especially in 1973/74, 1981, or 1993), however, an inverse shape of the yield curve (i.e. a situation in which the long-term interest rate lies below the short-term interest rate) can be observed. The figure also shows that the slope of the yield curve varies a lot over time.

Fig. 28. Term Structure of Interest Rates for Germany Over Time

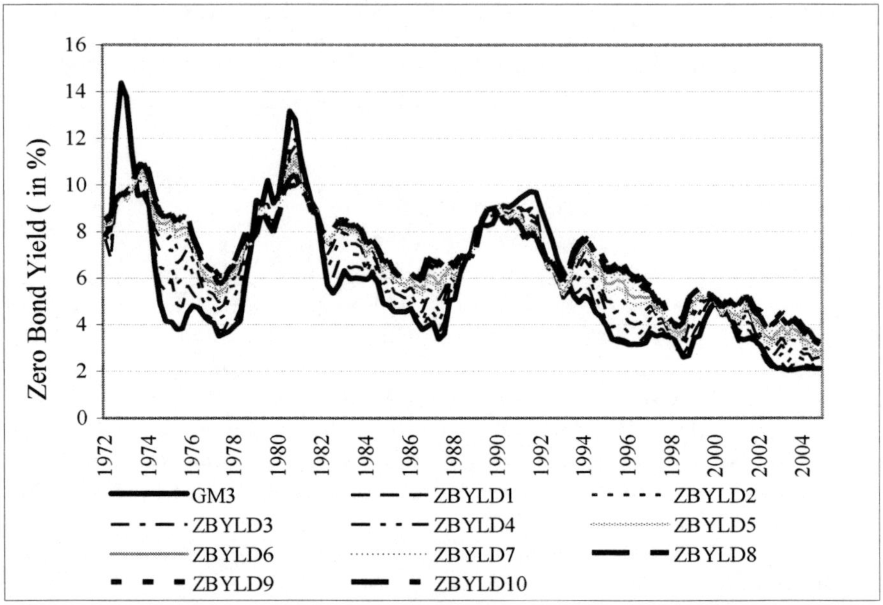

Note: GM3 denotes the 3-month money rate; ZBYLD stands for the specific zero bond yield. For example, ZBYLD10 denotes the interest rate for the zero bond with 10 years to maturity.
Data source: Time series database of Deutsche Bundesbank; authors' own calculations.

7.5 Results of the "In-Sample" Analysis

Table 15 shows results for the "in-sample" estimation of eq. (7.1). We estimate this equation for forecast horizons *k* ranging from 1 to 16 quarters. Furthermore, we use several differences between the interest rates of the (n = 1 to 10) years zero bonds and the 3-month money market rate as an explanatory variable, not just the longest maturity spread.

Table 15 reveals that cumulative growth until k = 16 periods can be explained by the term spread.[125] One can observe from the table that the estimated coefficients for β_1 decrease with the forecast horizon, but remain significant at the 5% level in all cases. The highest forecast power is obtained for 8 quarters; after this horizon the explanatory power of the term spread decreases. Furthermore, the table shows that the longest maturity spread (difference of the yield of the 10-year

[125] We confine the analysis to the period k = 1 - 16 since otherwise the overlap of observations will get very large. Furthermore, the predictive power of the spread is concentrated at a horizon from 1 to 8 quarters as shown in the next section.

bond and the 3-month interest rate) is not uniformly the best predictor for all forecast horizons.

In the following, we discuss estimation results when additional control variables are used as regressors. The question whether the spread offers a predictive power exceeding that of the control variables shall be discussed below. We employ the following (lagged) variables: return on a broad stock market portfolio (MPF), the change of the business cycle climate indicator of the ifo institute (IFOBCGR)[126], monthly inflation rate based on the consumer price index (INFLCPI), oil price changes (OILPGR) and a short-term money market interest rate (MMR). For a detailed description of the variables and data transformation, we refer the reader to the annex. Furthermore, we accommodate a simple lagged-dependent variable defined as $LDEP_{t-k} = (400/k)\ ln(Y_t/Y_{t-k})$.[127]

The results of Tables 16 and 17 reveal that for a short-term forecast horizon (k = 1 - 4) the term spread is not robust against an inclusion of additional macroeconomic variables in the predictive regression. However, lagged real GDP growth and changes of the ifo business cycle climate indicator exhibit a significant forecast power. The tables also reveal that for forecast horizons beyond 4 quarters, the coefficient on the term spread remains significant even if additional control variables are considered.

The previous estimation results refer to the explanation of cumulative real GDP growth from quarter t to $t + k$. Table 18 shows results when the dependent variable is defined as the marginal annual rate of change of real GDP (for a definition, see section 7.3.1). In Table 18 a constant and the term spread based on different maturities serve as regressors. The marginal forecast power of the term spread reaches up to 8 quarters into the future. These empirical results back the findings of Estrella, Rodrigues, and Schich (2003: 639). Contrary to our analysis, they use the industrial production growth as their measure for the real activity. One can also observe that the forecast power for the cumulative rate of change of the real GDP growth up to 16 quarters into the future shown in Table 15 is mainly due to the strong forecast power of the term spread for short-term growth (up to 8 quarters).

Tables 19 and 20 provide estimation results using additional control variables. For the short horizon of 4 quarters, only the term spread (n = 5) is significant and dominates the remaining control variables (Table 19); the spread with the longest possible maturity horizon (n = 10) is not robust against the usage of additional

---

126 Empirical studies, for example, Hüfner and Schröder (2002), also document a good predictive power of the ZEW business cycle expectations variable. However, this time series is only available from 1991 onwards.

127 To develop the optimal lag structure, the Schwarz criterion (BIC) is used. According to the BIC, a model without any lag of the dependent variable is chosen. Note that the lagged-dependent variable is important for the short-term forecast horizon (Tables 16 and 17). Therefore, we also report results using the lagged left hand side variable in Tables 16 and 17.

Table 15. Estimation Results: Term Spread as Explanatory Variable

$$y_{t+k}^{(k)} = \beta_0 + \beta_1 Spread_t + \varepsilon_{t+k}^{(k)}$$

Horizon	Term-spread (n = maturity)									
	n = 1		n = 3		n = 5		n = 7		n = 10	
	β_1	R^2	β_1	R^2	β_1	R^2	β_1	R^2	β_1	R^2
k = 1	1.037 (2.32**)	0.038	0.775 (2.81***)	0.056	0.610 (2.78***)	0.050	0.521 (2.68***)	0.044	0.452 (2.52**)	0.037
k = 4	0.950 (3.54***)	0.153	0.717 (5.06***)	0.221	0.602 (5.07***)	0.227	0.536 (4.79***)	0.220	0.477 (4.41***)	0.208
k = 8	0.837 (4.69***)	0.210	0.573 (6.20***)	0.247	0.487 (6.00***)	0.260	0.443 (5.56***)	0.262	0.403 (5.10***)	0.259
k = 12	0.465 (2.28**)	0.097	0.383 (3.53***)	0.170	0.351 (4.01***)	0.210	0.326 (4.12***)	0.222	0.300 (4.09***)	0.224
k = 16	0.286 (2.06**)	0.050	0.252 (3.15***)	0.105	0.248 (3.58***)	0.152	0.237 (3.68***)	0.170	0.219 (3.61***)	0.174

Note: *, **, *** denotes significance at the 10%, 5%, or 1% level, respectively. In parentheses, robust t-statistics (according to Newey & West 1987) are provided. R^2 denotes the coefficient of determination.

Table 16. Estimation Results: Additional Control Variables (n = 5 years)

$$y_{t+k}^{(k)} = \beta_0 + \beta_1 Spread_t + \beta_2 LDEP_{t-k} + \beta_3 MPF_t + \beta_4 \text{IFOBCGR}_t + \beta_5 \text{INFLCPI}_t + \beta_6 \text{OILPGR}_t + \beta_7 MMR_t + \varepsilon_{t+k}^{(k)}$$

Horizon	β_0	β_1	β_2	β_3	β_4	β_5	β_6	β_7	$\bar{R}^2$
k = 1	1.560	0.417	-0.174	-0.006	36.351	-0.010	0.162	0.059	0.055
	(1.15)	(0.88)	(-1.73*)	(-0.25)	(2.39**)	(-0.05)	(0.07)	(0.23)	
k = 4	1.608	0.384	0.113	0.020	11.000	0.031	-0.803	-0.073	0.248
	(1.73*)	(1.86*)	(1.00)	(1.41)	(1.62)	(0.41)	(-0.90)	(-0.50)	
k = 8	1.303	0.490	-0.010	0.019	1.940	-0.043	-0.085	0.051	0.251
	(1.41)	(2.91***)	(-0.07)	(1.72*)	(0.28)	(-0.77)	(-0.16)	(0.42)	
k = 12	1.515	0.399	-0.139	0.003	-0.176	-0.016	-0.292	0.077	0.197
	(1.57)	(2.26**)	(-1.24)	(0.31)	(-0.03)	(-0.36)	(-0.49)	(0.67)	
k = 16	1.248	0.382	-0.089	-0.002	-2.170	-0.023	-0.544	0. 119	0.151
	(0.946)	(2.44**)	(-0.53)	(-0.26)	(-0.66)	(-0.35)	(-1.01)	(1.03)	

Note: *, **, *** denotes significance at the 10%, 5%, and 1% level. The HAC-robust t-statistics (according to Newey & West, 1987) are reported in parentheses. $\bar{R}^2$ is the coefficient of determination adjusted for degrees of freedom.

Table 17. Estimation Results: Additional Control Variables (n = 10 years)

$$y_{t+k}^{(k)} = \beta_0 + \beta_1 Spread_t + \beta_2 LDP_{t-k} + \beta_3 MPF_t + \beta_4 \text{IFOBCGR}_t + \beta_5 \text{INFLCPI}_t + \beta_6 \text{OILPGR}_t + \beta_7 MMR_t + \varepsilon_{t+k}^{(k)}$$

Horizon	β_0	β_1	β_2	β_3	β_4	β_5	β_6	β_7	$\bar{R}^2$
k = 1	1.865	0.222	-0.171	-0.007	39.651	0.003	0.032	0.008	0.049
	(1.04)	(0.50)	(-1.71*)	(-0.27)	(2.68***)	(0.01)	(0.01)	(0.03)	
k = 4	1.389	0.316	0.125	0.020	12.744	0.032	-0.889	-0.053	0.242
	(1.18)	(1.42)	(1.13)	(1.37)	(1.90*)	(0.44)	(-0.96)	(-0.31)	
k = 8	0. 700	0. 477	0.008	0.018	3.659	-0.051	-0.185	0.122	0.258
	(0.68)	(2.71***)	(0.05)	(1.64)	(0.52)	(-0.87)	(-0.38)	(0.91)	
k = 12	0.730	0.447	-0.114	0.003	0.495	-0.028	-0.365	0.173	0.230
	(0.71)	(2.57**)	(-1.03)	(0.29)	(0.10)	(-0.61)	(-0.64)	(1.33)	
k = 16	0. 308	0.463	-0.053	-0.002	-1.833	-0.041	-0.593	0.233	0.217
	(0.35)	(3.50***)	(-0.33)	(-0.22)	(-0.57)	(-0.62)	(-1.16)	(2.03**)	

Note: *, **, *** denotes significance at the 10%, 5%, and 1% level. In parentheses, HAC-robust t-statistics (according to Newey & West, 1987) are reported. $\bar{R}^2$ is the coefficient of determination adjusted for degrees of freedom.

Table 18. Estimation Results: Marginal "Year-over-Year" Growth

$$\frac{1}{4}(y_{t+k}^{(1)} + y_{t+k-1}^{(1)} + y_{t+k-2}^{(1)} + y_{t+k-3}^{(1)}) = \beta_0 + \beta_1 Spread_t + \varepsilon_{t+k}^{(k)}$$

Horizon	Term-spread (n = maturity)									
	n = 1		n = 3		n = 5		n = 7		N = 10	
	β_1	$\bar{R}^2$	β_1	$\bar{R}^2$	β_1	$\bar{R}^2$	β_1	$\bar{R}^2$	β_1	$\bar{R}^2$
k = 4	0.950	0.153	0.717	0.221	0.602	0.227	0.536	0.220	0.477	0.201
	(3.54***)		(5.06***)		(5.07***)		(4.79***)		(4.41***)	
k = 8	0.720	0.085	0.425	0.073	0.367	0.080	0.341	0.085	0.319	0.088
	(3.62***)		(3.17***)		(3.27***)		(3.24***)		(3.15***)	
k = 12	-0.308	0.011	-0.012	-	0.064	-	0.081	-0.003	0.081	-0.002
	(-0.92)		(-0.05)	0.009	(0.31)	0.006	(0.44)		(0.49)	
k = 16	-0.206	0.001	-0.095	-	-0.025	-	-0.007	-0.009	-0.007	-0.009
	(-1.17)		(-0.58)	0.004	(-0.17)	0.009	(-0.05)		(-0.05)	

Note: *, **, *** denotes significance at the 10%, 5%, and 1% level. In parentheses, the HAC-robust t-statistics (according to Newey & West, 1987) are reported. $\bar{R}^2$ is the coefficient of determination adjusted for degrees of freedom.

Table 19. Estimation Results: Marginal "Year-over-Year" Growth, Additional Control Variables as Regressors (n = 5)

$$\frac{1}{4}(y_{t+k}^{(1)} + y_{t+k-1}^{(1)} + y_{t+k-2}^{(1)} + y_{t+k-3}^{(1)}) = \beta_0 + \beta_1 Spread_t + \beta_2 LDP_{t-k} + \beta_3 MPF_t + \beta_4 \text{IFOBCGR}_t + \beta_5 \text{INFLCPI}_t + \beta_6 \text{OILPGR}_t + \beta_7 MMR_t + \varepsilon_{t+k}^{(k)}$$

Horizon	β_0	β_1	β_2	β_3	β_4	β_5	β_6	β_7	$\bar{R}^2$
k = 4	1.608	0.384	0.113	0.020	11.000	0.031	-0.803	-0.073	0.248
	(1.73*)	(1.86*)	(1.00)	(1.41)	(1.62)	(0.41)	(-0.90)	(-0.50)	
k = 8	0.594	0.696	-0.165	0.012	-8.391	-0.126	0.660	0.242	0.103
	(0.56)	(3.33***)	(-1.31)	(1.25)	(-1.02)	(-1.80*)	(0.53)	(1.49)	
k = 12	0.572	0.428	-0.098	-0.020	-4.401	0.014	-1.008	0.222	0.014
	(0.33)	(1.11)	(-0.66)	(-1.02)	(-0.74)	(0.12)	(-0.99)	(0.96)	
k = 16	-0.174	0.492	-0.133	-0.013	-3.782	-0.079	-0.477	0.386	0.053
	(-0. 17)	(2.07**)	(-1.02)	(-1.38)	(-0.43)	(-0.51)	(-0.99)	(2.51**)	

Note: *, **, *** denotes significance at the 10%, 5%, and 1% level. In parentheses, HAC-robust t-statistics (according to Newey & West, 1987) are reported. $\bar{R}^2$ is the coefficient of determination adjusted for degrees of freedom.

Table 20. Estimation Results: Marginal "Year-over-Year" Growth, Additional Control Variables as Regressors (n = 10)

$$\frac{1}{4}(y_{t+k}^{(1)} + y_{t+k-1}^{(1)} + y_{t+k-2}^{(1)} + y_{t+k-3}^{(1)}) = \beta_0 + \beta_1 Spread_t + \beta_2 LDP_{t-k} + \beta_3 MPF_t + \beta_4 \text{IFOBCGR}_t + \beta_5 \text{INFLCPI}_t + \beta_6 \text{OILPGR}_t + \beta_7 MMR_t + \varepsilon_{t+k}^{(k)}$$

Horizon	β_0	β_1	β_2	β_3	β_4	β_5	β_6	β_7	$\bar{R}^2$
k = 4	1.389 (1.18)	0.316 (1.42)	0.125 (1.13)	0.020 (1.37)	12.744 (1.90*)	0.032 (0.44)	-0.889 (-0.96)	-0.053 (-0.31)	0.242
k = 8	-0.438 (-0.37)	0.716 (3.43***)	-0.144 (-1.16)	0.012 (1.12)	-6.845 (-0.85)	-0.139 (-1.89*)	0.544 (0.46)	0.368 (2.10**)	0.126
k = 12	-0.767 (-0.46)	0.580 (2.02**)	-0.076 (-0.50)	-0.019 (-1.03)	-5.177 (-0.90)	-0.009 (-0.08)	-1.063 (-1.05)	0.396 (1.72*)	0.059
k = 16	-1.485 (-1.39)	0.613 (2.92***)	-0.107 (-0.84)	-0.012 (-1.40)	-3.720 (-0.43)	-0.100 (-0.66)	-0.530 (-1.19)	0.554 (3.65***)	0.095

Note: *, **, *** denotes significance at the 10%, 5%, and 1% level. In parentheses, HAC-robust t-statistics (according to Newey & West, 1987) are reported. $\bar{R}^2$ is the coefficient of determination adjusted for degrees of freedom.

Table 21. Out-of-Sample Performance, Term Spread as Single Explanatory Variable, Dependent Variable Defined as Cumulative GDP Growth

$$y_{t+k}^{(k)} = \beta_0 + \beta_1 Spread_t + \varepsilon_{t+k}^{(k)}$$

Horizon	n = 1		n = 5		n = 10	
	RMSE model/benchmark	Theil's *U*	RMSE model/benchmark	Theil's *U*	RMSE model/benchmark	Theil's *U*
k = 4	1.768/1.852	0.955	1.708/1.852	0.922	1.740/1.852	0.940
k = 8	1.450/1.542	0.940	1.392/1.542	0.903	1.405/1.542	0.911
k = 12	1.352/1.379	0.980	1.247/1.379	0.904	1.236/1.379	0.896
k = 16	1.180/1.171	1.008	1.091/1.171	0.932	1.079/1.171	0.921

Note: the results of the Table are based on a recursive estimation of the forecast equation (initialisation period until 1979:1). The RMSE is calculated using the (pseudo) "out-of-sample" forecast. We use a naive model as a benchmark, which uses the prevailing mean of the dependent variable as forecast.

control variables (Table 20) in the short run (4 quarters). For a horizon of 8 quarters, however, the spread is the dominant forecast variable for marginal real GDP growth. It is noteworthy that in comparison to Table 18, the estimated coefficient on the term spread for a horizon beyond 8 quarters is not negative if additional control variables are added to the analysis. This may be due to a possible "omitted variable" problem that appears if other information in macroeconomic variables for a longer forecast horizon is neglected.

7.6 Results of the "Out-of-Sample" Analysis

7.6.1 RMSE and Theil's *U*

In the following, we discuss the results of the "out-of-sample" analysis. In this context, we use a recursive estimation scheme in order to calculate (pseudo) "out-of-sample" forecasts for the following periods. The accuracy of the forecasts is evaluated by the standard statistical criteria. The first 26 observations until 1979:1 were used for the initialisation. After this period, "out-of-sample" forecasts are generated in a recursive fashion. The corresponding forecasts are then analyzed according to their accuracy. A naive model, which uses the prevailing mean of the dependent variables as forecast, is used as the benchmark.

Table 21 shows that the forecast errors for cumulative growth from t to $t + k$ using the term spread model are usually lower compared to the naive model. The only exception is the model with the shortest spread ($n = 1$), which shows a poor performance for the longest horizon. These results of the overall good "out-of-sample" performance are also confirmed by the value of Theil's U, which is almost in every case less than 1.[128]

Table 22 presents results of forecast evaluation if the dependent variable is not defined as cumulative growth from t to $t + k$ but as marginal growth rate of real GDP. The term spread outperforms the naive model for a horizon of up to 8 quarters. For any further horizon beyond 8 quarters, the squared forecast errors based on the naive model are smaller (Theil's $U > 1$).[129]

[128] As our empirical analysis shows, the accommodation of many predictive variables for the forecast is not recommendable. Please see Tables AII.1 and AII. 2 in the annex. Hence, it is advisable to consider only parsimonious specifications.

[129] We used the Diebold-Mariano statistic (Diebold & Mariano, 1995) for testing if the difference of the forecast accuracy between interest-based model and alternative model is significant. See section 4.4.1 for more information. The differences were not significantly different from zero.

Table 22. Out-of-Sample Performance, Term Spread as Single Explanatory Variable, Dependent Variable Defined as Marginal "Year-over-Year" Growth

$$\frac{1}{4}(y_{t+k}^{(1)} + y_{t+k-1}^{(1)} + y_{t+k-2}^{(1)} + y_{t+k-3}^{(1)}) = \beta_0 + \beta_1 Spread_t + \varepsilon_{t+k}^{(k)}$$

	N = 1		N = 5		n = 10	
Horizon	RMSE model/benchmark	Theil's *U*	RMSE model/benchmark	Theil's *U*	RMSE model/benchmark	Theil's *U*
k = 4	1.768/1.845	0.958	1.708/1.845	0.926	1.740/1.845	0.943
k = 8	1.831/1.863	0.983	1.772/1.863	0.951	1.772/1.863	0.951
k = 12	1.968/1.968	1.000	1.996/1.968	1.014	2.014/1.968	1.023
k = 16	1.777/1.739	1.022	1.822/1.739	1.048	1.829/1.739	1.052

Note: the results of the Table are based on a recursive estimation of the forecast equation (initialization period until 1979:1). The RMSE is calculated using the (pseudo) "out-of-sample" forecast. We use a naive model as benchmark, which uses the prevailing mean of the dependent variable as forecast.

7.6.2 Predictive Power and Model Performance over Time

In order to investigate the model performance over time, we first discuss aspects of stability. Figures 29 and 30 show the estimated coefficient on the 10-year spread, which is obtained by the recursive estimation. For a forecast horizon of k = 4 quarters (Figure 29), the figure clearly shows a stable period from the beginning of the 1980s until the beginning of the 1990s. Since 1995, the estimated coefficient on the spread has declined; however, from 2000 until the end of the sample, the coefficient is fairly stable again. For the forecast horizon of 8 quarters (Figure 30), it is possible to see that there is a relative stability for the estimated parameter until the end of the 1990s. From that time until the end of the sample the coefficient has slightly declined.

Fig. 29. Coefficient on the Spread with Recursive Estimation, Forecast Horizon k = 4

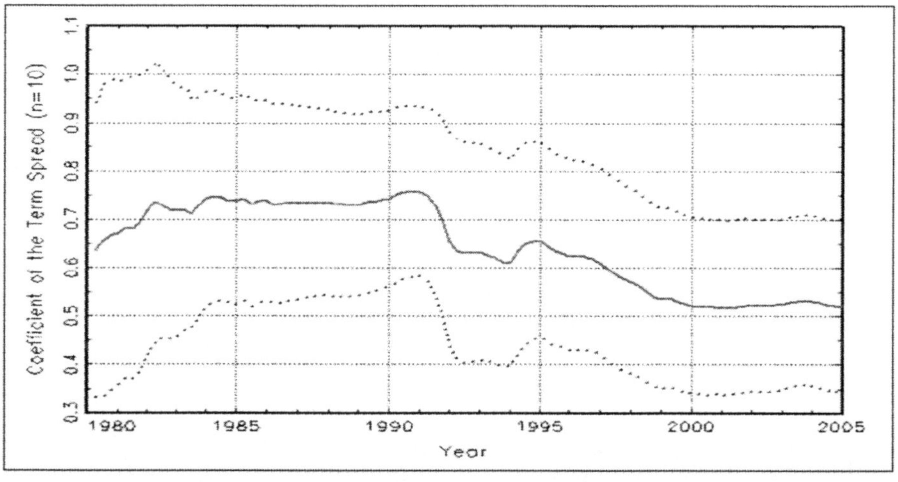

Note: The figure is based on a recursive estimation of the forecast equation (initialization period until 1979:1): $y_{t+k}^{(k)} = \beta_0 + \beta_1\, Spread_t + \varepsilon_{t+k}^{(k)}$ for a forecast horizon of k = 4 and a maturity of n = 10. The graph shows the recursively estimated coefficient β_1 over time as well as confidence bands on the basis of 2 standard deviations.

Overall, one can conclude that over relatively long periods of time, a relatively stable connection between the term spread and the real development can be observed. This corroborates the study of Estrella, Rodrigues, and Schich (2003), which is based on a sample period from January 1967 to December 1998.[130] Applying structural break tests with unknown break dates, Estrella, Rodrigues, and Schich find no evidence against the hypotheses of stability in Germany. Our fig-

[130] Estrella et al. (2003) use the growth rate of the industrial production instead of the GDP. Their estimation is therefore based on monthly data.

ures with the recursively estimated coefficient suggests, however, that in the mid 1990s until the end of the sample, the empirical connection between the term spread and projected real development decreased. Maybe the tests in Estrella, Rodrigues, and Schich could not detect this instance due to their shorter sample period.

Fig. 30. Coefficient on the Spread with Recursive Estimation, Forecast Horizon k = 8

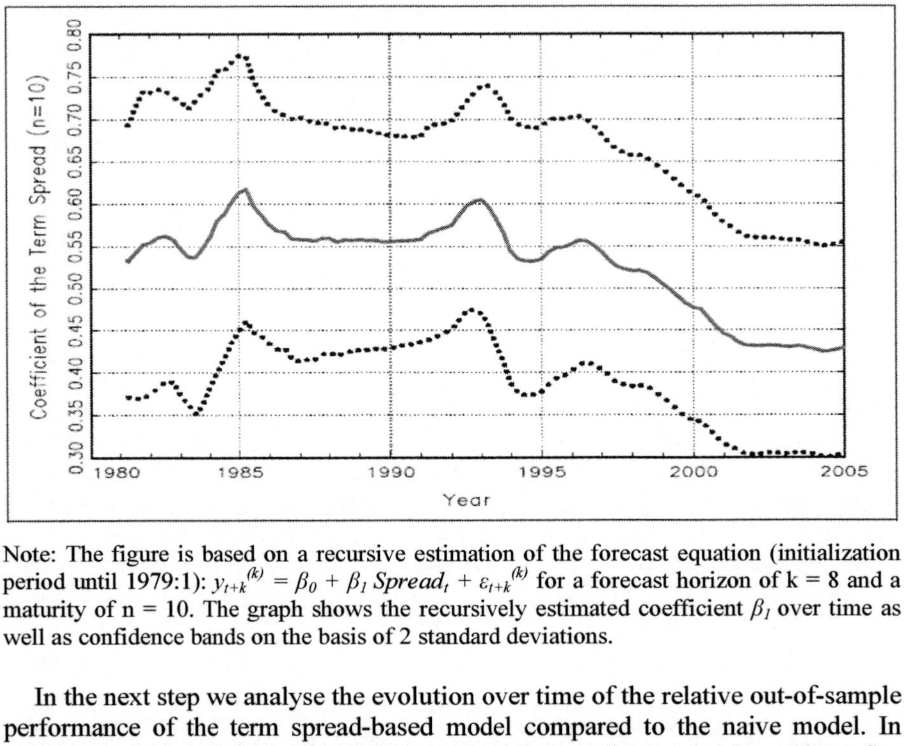

Note: The figure is based on a recursive estimation of the forecast equation (initialization period until 1979:1): $y_{t+k}^{(k)} = \beta_0 + \beta_1\, Spread_t + \varepsilon_{t+k}^{(k)}$ for a forecast horizon of k = 8 and a maturity of n = 10. The graph shows the recursively estimated coefficient β_1 over time as well as confidence bands on the basis of 2 standard deviations.

In the next step we analyse the evolution over time of the relative out-of-sample performance of the term spread-based model compared to the naive model. In analogy to Goyal and Welch (2003) we now discuss diagnostic plots. These figures show the cumulated squared errors of the naive model minus the squared error of the term spread-based model over time (Net-SSE). We define the Net-SSE at time τ as follows:

$$Net - SSE(\tau) = \sum_{t=1}^{\tau}\left(e_{b;t}^2 - e_{m;t}^2\right), \tag{7.3}$$

where $e_{b;t}$ ($e_{m;t}$) is the "out-of-sample" error of the naive model (term-spread model). A positive value of the Net-SSE at time τ indicates a better performance of the term spread-based model against the naive model at that point in time.

Fig. 31. Forecast Power Over Time (Net-SSE), k = 4

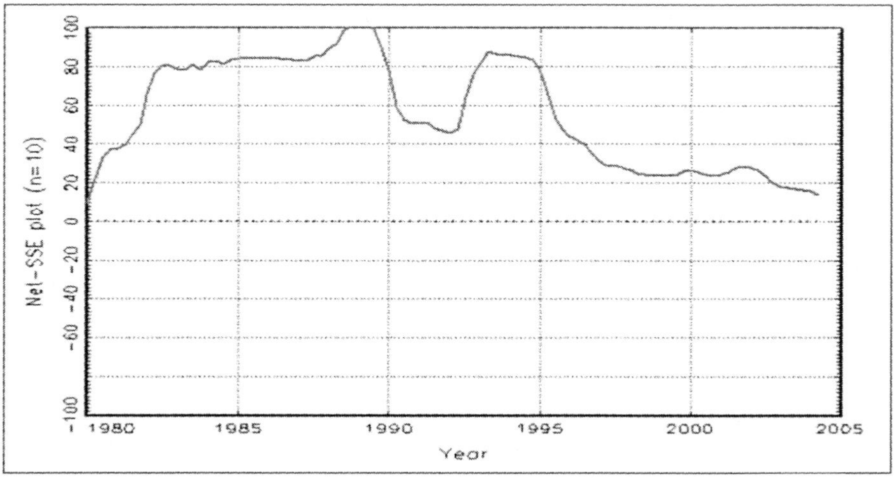

Note: The figure is based on a recursive estimation of the forecast equation (initialisation period until 1979:1): $y_{t+k}^{(k)} = \beta_0 + \beta_1\, Spread_t + \varepsilon_{t+k}^{(k)}$ for a forecast horizon of k = 4 and a maturity of n = 10. NET-SSE is computed as defined in the text.

Fig. 32. Forecast Power Over Time (Net-SSE), k = 8

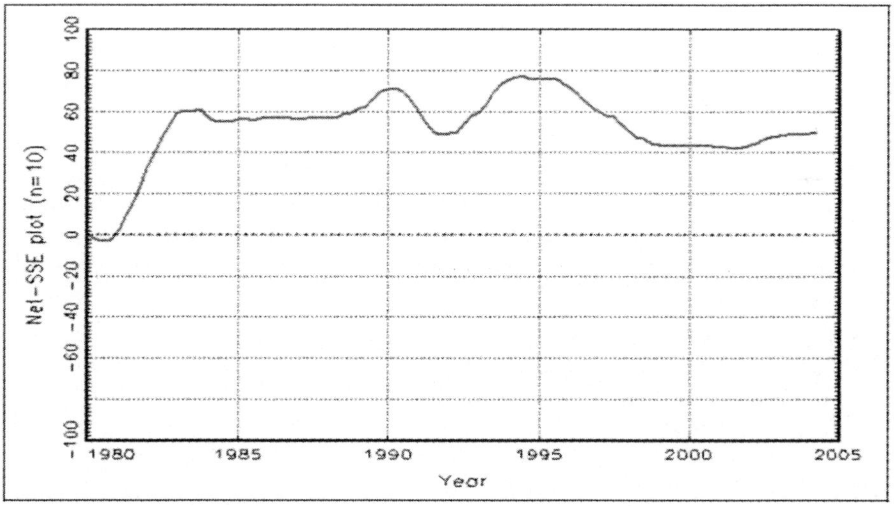

Note: The figure is based on a recursive estimation of the forecast equation (initialization period until 1979:1): $y_{t+k}^{(k)} = \beta_0 + \beta_1\, Spread_t + \varepsilon_{t+k}^{(k)}$ for a forecast horizon of k = 8 and a maturity of n = 10. NET-SSE is computed as defined in the text.

Figure 31 shows that the model based on the term spread always outperforms the naive model in terms of the cumulated squared forecast error at a forecast horizon of 4 quarters. However, one can also observe that the relative performance is fairly time variant. From 1990 until approximately 1993, for example, the performance of the model based on the spread was in fact inferior to the naive model so that the Net-SSE decreased in that period. There was also a decrease after 1995 until approximately 2000.

Even for a forecast horizon of two years, the model outperforms the naive model over time in terms of cumulative squared error (see Figure 32). The performance does not vary as much as for the k = 4 horizon. Nevertheless, a decreasing Net-SSE from 1995 until 2000 can also clearly be observed.

7.7 Conclusion

According to the empirical results of chapter 7, the German yield curve contains valuable information about the future real development. Furthermore, the “in-sample” explanatory power of the term spread for the future real GDP growth is robust against the inclusion of additional information variables. The explanatory power of the term spread is more concentrated of short- to medium-term horizons up to 8 quarters. For this reason, the suitability of the method for medium-term macroeconomic projection is obviously limited. The results we obtained from the empirical analysis suggest that term spread-based forecasts do not constitute a viable alternative for medium-term growth projection but could rather be used as a complement for conventional methods. It would make sense, for instance, to use the information in the term spread in order to check robustness of forecasts obtained by other methods, e.g., for comparing the implication with other forecast methods, in particular for the border between short- and medium-term horizons (8 quarters). Our results also indicate that the explanatory power of the spread has decreased in the 1990s. There are periods in which the naive benchmark model outperforms the term-spread model. Our empirical results also raise a warning flag. It is advisable not to solely rely on term spread-based models but on pooled information across a wider variety of variables and models. A plurality of models and methods may provide more robust projections if the explanatory power is changing over time.

8 Conclusions for Economic Policy and Empirical Macroeconomics

A central insight of the analyses in this study is that the potential output of an economy is neither theoretically unambiguously defined nor is it empirically identifiable in an uncontroversial manner. Indeed, basic static definitions such as the first definition introduced by Arthur Okun in 1962 ("the amount of output an economy can produce as it approaches full employment and full capacity utilization without raising inflationary pressure", see section 2.2) suggest a fair degree of conceptual clearness and empirical accessibility. However, the dynamic perspective, in particular, highlights the problems: Potential output on the one hand and employment, capacity and inflationary dynamics on the other hand are mutually interdependent. Furthermore, this interdependency is influenced by changing institutional environments, monetary and fiscal decisions and aggregate demand and supply shocks. Consequently, the potential output of an economy is a variable that – for theoretical reasons – cannot be fully explained nor completely projected into the future as a function of current observed data.

Artificial Dichotomy

Another closely related insight is that the conceptual distinction between "growth" and "business cycle", which is frequently made in many textbooks and economic debates, is a useful simplification for didactic purposes but is not an appropriate means of describing reality (see section 3.3). Hysteresis on labour markets caused by the rapid depreciation of human capital accompanied by persistent unemployment or the clear relation between investment activity (and, therefore, capacity expansion) and business cycles: All these are indisputable examples of how business cycles influence growth. The thinkers who lay the theoretical foundations of the concept of potential output (see chapter 2) were also largely aware of this. However, these relationships are often forgotten in current practice. Moreover, since the influence of the business cycle on growth can be exercised via the job market and the virulent problems of hysteresis affecting it, the concept of a non-accelerating inflation rate of unemployment (NAIRU) is also less unequivocal and empirically more difficult to assess than continues to be depicted in some textbooks: If a labour market is characterized by marked insider-outsider structures or other dysfunctions, a period of economic weakness can permanently shift the NAIRU to a higher level.

Hence, the better connection between business cycles and growth is one of the tasks to which theoretical and empirical macroeconomic research must position it-

S. Hauptmeier et al., *Projecting Potential Output*, Zew Economic Studies,
DOI: 10.1007/978-3-7908-2177-2_8,

self in future. In addition to these conclusions for the academic discussion, consequences arise from this analysis for economic policy and the challenges of empirical macroeconomics.

"Potential Potential Growth"

Under certain conditions Germany could achieve a higher growth path in spite of the existing estimates that quantify Germany's growth potential at merely 1%. This is a central message of this survey for economic policy in Germany. Estimates of potential growth according to presently employed estimation techniques cannot deliver a comprehensive assertion of the growth chances that would arise, for example, in succession of extensive reforms of the job markets, the tax system, the social security system and the education system. In this respect it would be wrong to conclude from the estimates circulating today that Germany is inevitably "condemned" to a growth path of around 1%.

Like economic forecasts, potential growth estimates always result in conditional statements based on a wide range of assumptions. In order to specify this idea, it may be helpful to introduce a concept such as "potential potential growth" which indicates the growth paths that would be feasible under different assumptions about institutions and the behavioural functions of important actors (monetary policy, fiscal policy and wages policy).

A report such as this is not, of course, able to extensively elaborate on how policies should be designed in detail in order to raise the German growth path. This question is basically at the heart of the ongoing economic reform debate in which there seems to be broad basic consensus (well-documented in the majority positions of the German Council of Economic Experts, for example). There are also, however, many unresolved detailed debates as well as fundamentally divergent minority opinions.

The brief digression in chapter 6 summarises the causes – which have been very well-known for some time – of the declining growth trend in Germany drawing on the available literature, without however claiming to be exhaustive:

- Growth decompositions (which, of course, are more of a descriptive tool than approaches to conduct "cause and effect" analysis) show a decline in labour input since the beginning of the 1990s. This development is usually explained by the high regulation of the German job market and with the high tax wedge on wages.
- German reunification has also had negative effects in the new federal states following the quick adjustment of wages to West German levels. This wage policy disregarded the productivity differentials between East and West Germany and led to a sustained dismantling of jobs which continues to be reflected in much higher rates of unemployment in eastern Germany today.
- Gross and net investment rates have shown a declining trend since reunification. Apart from the considerable decline in public investments, private investment has also been scarce, for which the German corporate tax system bears some responsibility which is regarded as being internationally uncompetitive.

- As far as human capital is concerned, the length of education combined with high dropout rates point to deficiencies in the university system. Comparative assessments of students' skills, such as the Pisa study, also show that the German educational system needs to be reformed.
- Unfavourable findings as far as technological progress is concerned are the low share of spending on research and development and the small number of patent applications in the field of information and communication technologies – key factors for increasing total factor productivity.
- The regulation of German product markets and high bureaucratic burdens are often identified as causes of relatively weak growth in Germany.
- Finally, a comparative analysis of German financial policy also reveals unfavourable criteria that may impede economic growth. Apart from increasing public debt, the quality of public spending has deteriorated as spending on investment has decreased while social benefits and transfers paid by the government have increased. The financial burden of German reunification has also contributed to an increase in public spending and a deterioration in public balances.
- Alongside reunification, European Monetary Union is another exceptional factor that has affected economic development in Germany since the 1990s. Comparatively low inflation rates in Germany – it is often argued – would imply a relatively high level of real interest rates and, for this reason, an obstacle to economic growth in Germany. This view, however, ignores the fact that low nominal interest rates in EMU have led to a very low real interest rate even in Germany in recent years. What is more, investment decisions are more strongly influenced by the ex-ante real interest rates that – in contrast to ex-post real rates of interest – are fairly similar throughout the EMU countries.

As eclectic and unsystematic as this short list may be, it, nevertheless, exemplifies the fields in which German economic and financial policy retains degrees of freedom, which enable it to exercise a positive influence on German potential growth. Today's potential growth estimates will almost certainly be falsified in the decades ahead if the reform process already having started in Germany proves successful in the areas referred to.

The Future of Empirical Macroeconomics

While a substantial increase in growth may be feasible under certain conditions, it is important not to confuse "conceivable possibilities" with "realities". Current estimates of potential growth should not be written off as overly pessimistic as long as substantial institutional reform continues to be put off. Realistic assessments of limited growth possibilities are indispensable, for instance, for the planning of public budgets with the aim of achieving a sustained budget policy or for firms to make correct investment decisions in order to avoid inefficient resource allocations. In this respect, apart from the methodical and empirical shortcomings of the concept of potential growth, present empirics seem to be justified.

In this context two attitudes may be taken to the objections raised against some of the current procedures (such as univariate methods) of estimating potential growth). On the one hand, it is correct that a procedure that extrapolates the development of GDP only with the help of historical time series with more or less sophisticated methods overall remains an extrapolation procedure that is not able to capture the influence of changing conditions. On the other hand, such a procedure is justified when these general conditions do not change in a country without significant reforms. Under these conditions the extrapolation may well make a substantial contribution to building up a general picture. Moreover, univariate methods can be useful if the potential component is not the main focus of the analysis. However, univariate methods are clearly not capable of fulfilling the requirements for a detailed investigation of potential output, its evolution, its determinants and derived economic policy recommendations.

It would be inappropriate to assume that the future of empirical macroeconomics depends on just one "right" method. The theoretical and empirical shortcomings inherent in each of the approaches strongly suggest using a mixture of methods. This is also confirmed by the statistical analysis of the empirical methods (see chapter 5): Even in cases where the results of the in-sample analysis show relatively high correspondence between the different methods in assessing the evolution of business cycle and trend components, considerable differences in judging the macroeconomic situation appear at single points in time. It would not, therefore, be appropriate in practice to draw on the results produced by one particular method alone to evaluate the cyclical and trend components of GDP and growth. An analogous recommendation arises from the results of the "out-of-sample" analysis (section 5.4). This analysis also suggests the use of several projection procedures to check for the robustness of the overall outcomes. According to the formal analysis of forecast precision, the production function approach showed sound practical results at least for the time periods considered in the present study for German medium-term GDP growth.

More work must be invested in extending current procedures (particularly univariate methods and production function approaches). The historical analysis of potential output growth has clarified the different theoretical approaches existing – each approach is capable of inspiring different empirical methods even though many of them are now all but forgotten. A good example of a method that has recently been rediscovered is the yield curve as a possible basis for forward-looking estimates of potential growth of the type produced in the work of Irving Fisher (see section 2.4.4). As the quantitative analyses in chapter 7 show, the yield curve contains information that can be used to estimate the future real activity of an economy. However, the predictive power of the yield curve seems to primarily apply for short- to medium-term horizons up to 8 quarters. Hence, the results suggest that yield curves-based forecasts cannot be used for the medium-term growth as an alternative rather than a complement to more traditional methods. It may be convenient, for instance, to use the information of the yield curve for robustness checks, e.g., to compare the implications to those of other projection procedures, especially with regard to the transition from short-term to medium-term horizons.

Empirical growth models on the basis of comprehensive cross-country panels may offer a promising extension of current production function-based methods (section 5.2.2). Since these procedures are capable of modelling a large variation of institutional variables and, therefore, better allow assessments of how institutional reforms influence the potential output of a country, they are also less prone to the criticism of being too backward-looking.

Annex

AI: Annex to Chapter 5

AI.1. Data Sources for Chapter 5

Table 23. Data sources for chapter 5

	Variable	mne-monic	Data source	Notes
1	Real GDP total economy	Y_t	OECD EO	Quarterly data, saisonal adjusted. West German data until 1991, German data afterwards. In order to eliminate the reunification break in the year 1991 that occurs in the linked data series, the first differences of the variable have been regressed on an impulse dummy which takes the value 1 in the year 1991 and 0 elsewhere. The level series have then been recalculated by integration of the residuals from the dummy regression.
2	Real GDP for the private sector	Y_t^p	OECD EO	Dito
3	Real GDP for the public sector	Y_t^g	OECD EO	Difference between 1 and 2
4	Unemployment rate	U_t	Database of the German Bundesbank	Seasonal adjusted, monthly data, monthly averages are used for the transformation to the quarterly frequency. Unemployment rate according to the

				definition of the German Federal Employment Agency (*Bundesagentur für Arbeit*, BA), i.e. the unemployed rate refers to the number of registered unemployed persons as a fraction of the civilian labour force.
5	Employment in the private sector	L_t^p	OECD EO	See notes to row 1
6	Employment in the public sector	L_t^g	OECD EO	See notes to row 1
7	Working age population	P_t^w	OECD EO	Number of people in the age group of 15 to 64. Also the notes to row 1 apply.
8	Participation rate	PR_t	OECD EO	See notes to row 1
9	Capital Stock of the private sector	K_t	OECD EO	See notes to row 1
10	Consumer price index	Z_{1t}	German Federal Statistical Office	The change of the index is used.
11	Crude oil price	Z_{2t}	Reuters-Ecowin	The change of the price is used.
12	Labour share	WR_t	German Federal Statistical Office	Ratio of the compensation of employees over nominal GDP

AI.2. Business Cycle Dating for Germany

Fig. 33. Business Cycles in Germany

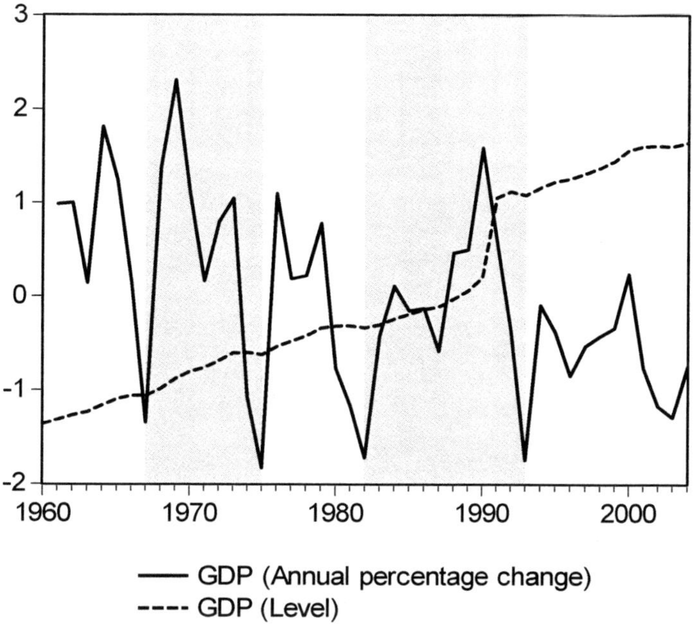

In contrast to the U.S. where the NBER Business Cycle Dating Committee classifies periods of economic expansions and contractions, no such official committee is in charge of business cycle classification in Germany. In Figure 33, the identification of expansions and contractions according to the German Council of Economic Experts (Sachverständigenrat zur Begutachtung der gesamtwirtschaftlichen Entwicklung, 2003) is shown. For the period of 1970 to 2003, three cycles are observed: 1975 to 1982, 1982 to 1993 and 1993 to 2003. A further cycle may be added for the period from 1949 to 1967 since in the year 1967 the German GDP declined for the first time after the post-war era. The period from 1966 to 1975 may also be regarded as a closed cycle. Based on this business cycle classification, an average duration of 8 to 9 years per cycle emerges. Overall, five linear trends may be fitted to the rate of GDP change.

The estimation equation for the spline regression is as follows (cf. Sachverständigenrat zur Begutachtung der gesamtwirtschaftlichen Entwicklung, 2003):

$$\Delta \hat{y} = \alpha + \beta t + \sum_{i=1}^{6} \beta_i d_{it} \;, \tag{A.1}$$

with $d_{it} = 0$ if $t < t_i$ and $t - t_i$ if $t \geq t_i$; t = time index, t_i = date of the ith break identified by the business cycle classification.

AI.3. Estimation of the Structural VAR (SVAR) Model

Methodical Overview

The following outline very briefly summarises the SVAR methodology as illustrated by Gottschalk and van Zandweghe (2001). The SVAR model of Blanchard und Quah (1989) assumes that the vector $X_t = (\Delta y_t, u_t^{-trend})$, which contains observations for the change of GDP and the cyclical component of the unemployment rate, can be regarded as the sum of past independent demand and supply shocks:

$$X_t = \begin{pmatrix} \Delta y_t \\ u_t^{-trend} \end{pmatrix} = \begin{bmatrix} \mu_{\Delta y} \\ \mu_u \end{bmatrix} + \sum_{j=0}^{\infty} \begin{bmatrix} \theta_{11,j} & \theta_{12,j} \\ \theta_{21,j} & \theta_{22,j} \end{bmatrix} \begin{bmatrix} \varepsilon_t^{Supplay} \\ \varepsilon_t^{Demand} \end{bmatrix} = \sum_{j=0}^{\infty} L^j \theta_j \varepsilon_t \,. \tag{A.2}$$

Both type of shocks are unobservable and need to be derived with the aid of an estimable unrestricted reduced form VAR model, which has the following Moving Average (MA) representation:

$$X_t = \begin{pmatrix} \Delta y_t \\ u_t^{-trend} \end{pmatrix} = \begin{bmatrix} \alpha_{\Delta y} \\ \alpha_u \end{bmatrix} + \sum_{i=0}^{\infty} \begin{bmatrix} \varphi_{11,i} & \varphi_{12,i} \\ \varphi_{21,i} & \varphi_{22,i} \end{bmatrix} \begin{bmatrix} e_t^{\Delta y} \\ e_t^{u_t^{-trend}} \end{bmatrix} = e_t + \sum_{i=0}^{\infty} L^i \varphi_i e_t \,. \tag{A.3}$$

The structural shocks, i.e. the demand and supply shocks of the structural system, can be recovered through the residuals of the reduced form since the following linear relationship holds:

$$\theta_0 \varepsilon_t = e_t \,. \tag{A.4}$$

The identification of the (4x4) matrix θ_0 is, therefore, a key element of the SVAR methodology. Three of the four required identification restrictions are provided by the assumption that demand and supply shocks are independent and by assuming normalised shock variances. The fourth identification restriction goes back to the assumption that demand shocks do not influence the level of GDP in the long run. Formally, this implies that the cumulative effect of the demand shocks is zero in the equation explaining the change of GDP:

$$\sum_{j=0}^{\infty} \theta_{12,j} = 0 \,. \tag{A.5}$$

Given these four identification assumptions, the matrix θ_0 can be determined and the demand and supply shocks can be recovered.

In order to obtain the long-run component of GDP growth, only the past supply shocks are cumulated in the structural decomposition as given by eq. (A.2). Usually, this estimated component is regarded as the potential level of GDP growth since it only comprises the long-run innovations of the system.

The forecast for the long-run GDP growth builds on the MA representation which only comprises past supply shocks:

$$\Delta y_t = \mu_{\Delta y} + \sum_{i=0}^{q} \theta_{11,i} \hat{\varepsilon}_{t-i}^{Supply} . \tag{A.6}$$

The optimal linear τ-step forecast for this process is[131]

$$\Delta y_t(\tau) = \mu_{\Delta y} + \sum_{k=0}^{q} \theta_{11,\tau+k} \hat{\varepsilon}_{t-k}^{Supply} . \tag{A.7}$$

Since for a stationary process the effect of past shocks dies out as the forecast horizon increases, the long-run forecast is dominated by the unconditional expectation $\mu_{\Delta y}$. Since the coefficients $\theta_{11,i}$ correspond to the impulse response of a unit shock, an analysis of the impulse response function in the SVAR framework helps to assess the forecasting power of the model.

Empirical Implementation

The implementation of the bivariate standard SVAR approach in the present study is based on the following data and data transformations:

- Δy_t: Quarterly changes of real GDP (differences of logarithms), 1960Q1 to 1990Q4 West Germany, Germany afterwards. Both time series are linked. The level break was removed with the aid of an impulse dummy regression.[132]
- u_t^{-trend}: See Table 23 for the data source and definition of the unemployment rate. West German and German data are linked. The unemployment rate is non-stationary according to standard unit root tests. For this reason, following Blanchard and Quah (1989), the secular increase in the unemployment rate is captured by a fitted-linear time trend regression and the fitted trend line is removed before estimation.

Augmented Dickey-Fuller tests indicate stationarity for both variables after appropriate transformations. This is an important requirement for the implementation of the SVAR Model.

The lag length of the unrestricted VAR model was chosen according to the minimum of the Schwarz information criterion. Post-estimation diagnostic statistics are generally satisfactory as far as tests on the residual serial correlation, normality and heteroscedasticity are concerned.

Figure 34 shows the impulse responses of the system to demand and supply shocks. For Δy_t the cumulative impulse response is presented to analyse the effect of the shocks on the *level* of GDP while for the cyclical unemployment rate the response to the original variable is shown. The confidence intervals which are shown in the figure are based on a bootstrap simulation with 1000 replications in each case.

[131] Cf., e.g., Kirchgässner and Wolters (2006: 70), for the derivation of forecasts that build on MA processes.

[132] Cf. Fritsche and Logeay (2002) for such a proceeding.

Interpretation of impulse responses

- The response of the GDP level to a supply shock is in accordance with theoretical considerations: A positive supply shock has a permanent effect on the level of GDP. However, the bootstrap confidence intervals are wide and imply a high degree of uncertainty of the estimated effects.
- The response of the unemployment rate (UR) is not in accordance with prior considerations that would imply a decrease of the UR in response to a positive supply shock. Gottschalk and van Zandweghe (2001) observe a comparable behaviour of the labour market in a similar SVAR model. The authors explain this kind of response of the UR with a labour supply shock caused by the German reunification, for instance. The integration of the additional labour supply into the labour market happens with a delay and initially leads to an increase of the UR. It subsequently decreases as factor prices adjust and the additional labour force integrates into the economy. In contrast, Blanchard and Quah (1989) explain such a response profile with productivity shocks. According to this view, nominal rigidities are the reason that aggregate demand does not immediately compensate the higher output and temporary layoffs and an increase in the UR arise.
- The response of GDP to a demand shock is reasonable and in accordance with the imposed restriction of long-run neutrality between demand shocks and the development of GDP.
- A significant negative response of the UR to a demand shock is observed which mirror-images the GDP response.

Overall, the impulse responses plausibly capture the dynamic interdependencies of the system variables. Therefore, this model serves as benchmark for the class of SVAR models to estimate potential output for the "in-sample" analysis and for the "out-of-sample" forecast evaluation.

Fig. 34. Quarterly Impulse Responses (---) in the SVAR and 95%-Confidence Intervals (---)

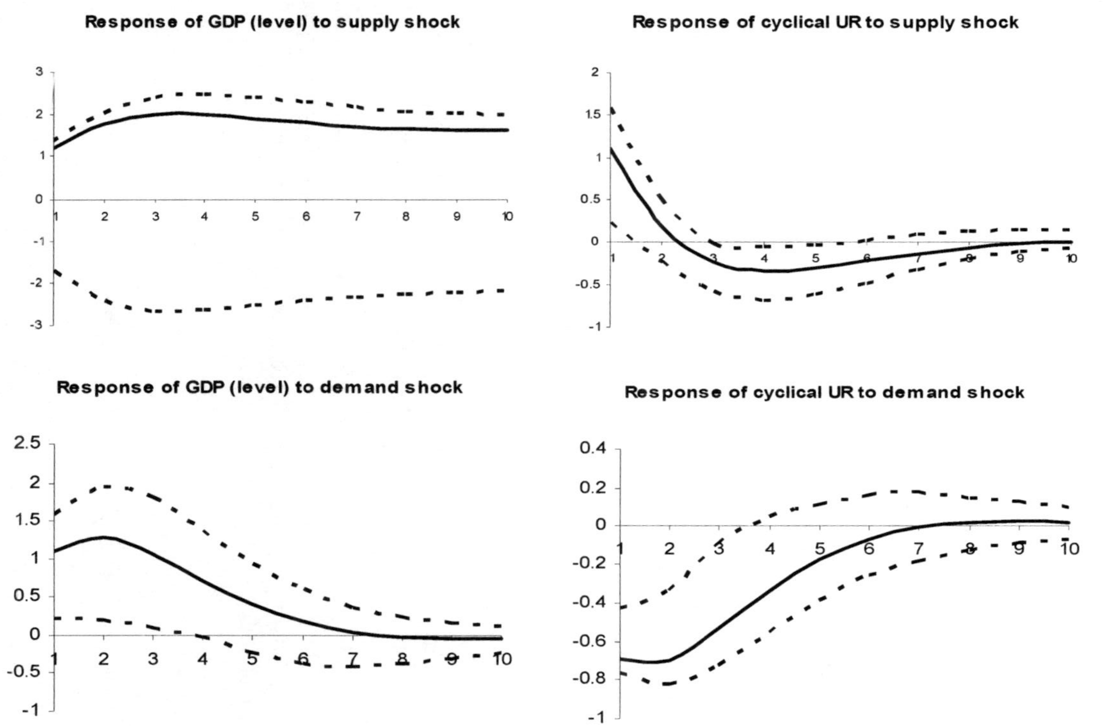

AI.4 The Production Function Approach (PFA)

Methodical Overview

The PFA builds on a standard growth accounting framework depicted in many research papers and textbooks. In the following, a formulation is adopted which is most closely related to descriptions in Giorno et al. (1995), McMorrow and Roeger (2001), and Torres and Martin (1994).

The starting point for the parametric PFA is the Cobb-Douglas production function in logarithmic form:

$$y_t^P = \alpha l_t^P + (1-\alpha) k_t + u_t . \quad \text{(A.8)}$$

y_t^P denotes real output, l_t^P labour input, k_t capital input. All variables are in logarithms and refer to the private sector. u_t is the Solow residual which captures all influences that are not explicitly modelled through factor inputs and is usually referred to as Total Factor Productivity (TFP). The coefficients α and $(1\text{-}\alpha)$ are the partial elasticities of output with respect to labour and capital which are assumed to be time-invariant in the parametric PFA. Under perfect competition, these elasticities correspond to the income shares of the inputs. In the non-parametric approach these income shares are allowed to be time-variant and contribute to output through the following linear relation:

$$\Delta y_t^P = \alpha_t \Delta l_t^P + (1-\alpha_t) \Delta k_t + \Delta u_t . \quad \text{(A.9)}$$

Potential output of the private sector in the parametric PFA is a weighted average of the potential (trend) input factors and the potential (trend) TFP:

$$y_t^{P*} = \alpha l_t^{P*} + (1-\alpha) k_t^* + u_t^* . \quad \text{(A.10)}$$

Potential trend variables are indicated with an asterisk.

Analogously, the change of potential output in the non-parametric PFA is a weighted average of the potential (trend) changes of the input factors and the change of potential (trend) TFP. In contrast to the parametric PFA, here the weights are time-variant.

Finally, potential output for the total economy is obtained by adding actual value added in the government sector to potential output of the business sector. Obviously, this implies that output of the government sector equals its potential level throughout.

Empirical Implementation

Table 23 shows the used data. For the *parametric* PFA, α is set to 0.74. The average income share over the period from 1970 to 2005 amounts to 0.72. An OLS estimation of eq. (A.8) results in a coefficient estimate of 0.76. The arithmetic mean of both estimates is 0.72, the value used in the following implementation of the parametric PFA. For the implementation of the *non-parametric* PFA, the quarterly observations for the income shares are used that have been smoothed with aid of the Hodrick-Prescott filter in order to remove erratic fluctuations.

The potential employment in the private sector is given

$$L_t^{*p} = P_t^w \times PR_t^* \times (1 - U_t^*) - L_t^{*g}. \tag{A.11}$$

P_t^w is the working age, PR_t^w is the trend participation rate and U_t^w the time-varying NAIRU. The trend value for the participation rate is obtained by applying the Hodrick-Prescott filter to the observed participation rate.

The time-varying NAIRU has been estimated with the aid of recursive OLS regressions of the "triangle model" according to Gordon (1997) which takes the influence of oil price shocks into account. See equation (5.3) for details. The recursive estimation scheme starts with a sample which covers the period from 1969Q1 to 1978Q and ends with a sample that comprises the total observation period from 1959Q1 to 2005Q4. For the period 1969Q1 to 1978Q4, the estimated NAIRU value from the first recursive estimation is used.

Fig. 35. Potential Employment in the German Private Sector

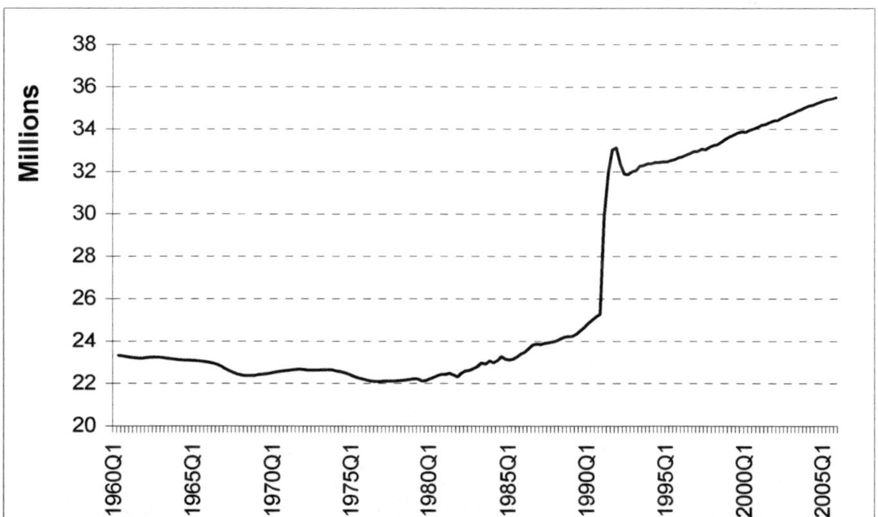

Figure 35 shows the estimated potential employment over the total observation period. The break due to the German reunification is clearly visible. In the application of the PFA, the actual capital stock is employed (see Figure 36).

Fig. 36. Real Capital Stock (Germany)

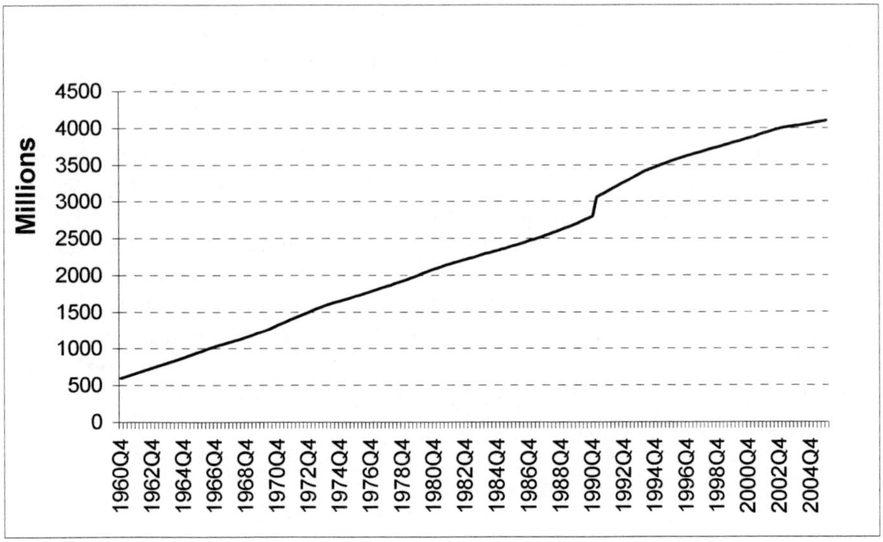

Fig. 37. Time Profile of Potential TFP (Germany)

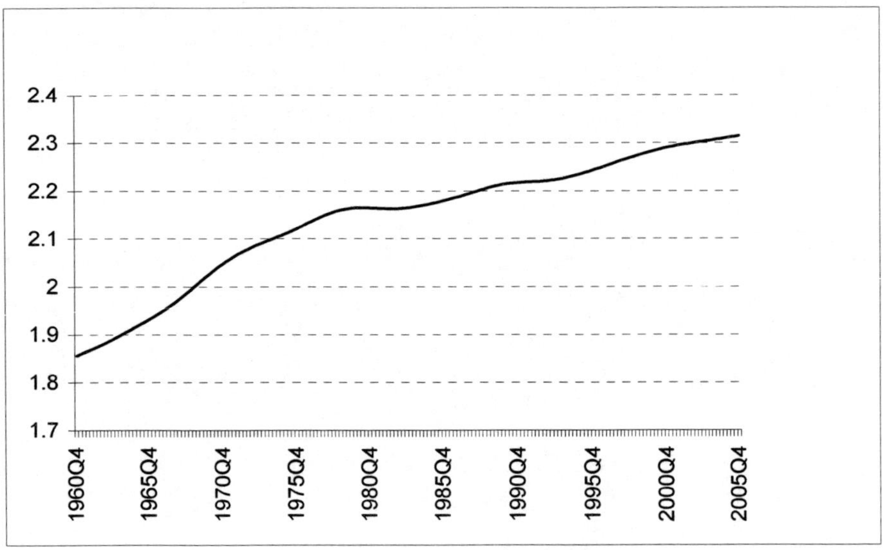

The potential TFP is obtained through the application of the Hodrick-Prescott filter to the Solow residuals of eq. (A.8). Figure 37 shows the time profile of the TFP for the parametric PFA. For the non-parametric PFA, eq. (A.9) is the basis for the computation of the TFP in differences, the rest of the proceeding is identical to the parametric PFA. Figure 37 clearly shows that the TFP was increasing sharply during the 1960s – the average growth rate amounted to about 4% p.a. – and slowing down in the subsequent periods. The average growth rate of the TFP in the period from 1990 to 2005 was only 1.6% p.a.

With the trend estimates of potential employment, the capital stock and the trend of TFP at hand, following eq. (A.10), the potential output of the private sector is readily computed. Adding the value added of the public sector gives an estimate of the *potential output for the total economy*.

Figure 38 shows the computed potential output of the parametric version of the PFA along with actual GDP. Figure 39 shows the same variables according to the computation scheme of the non-parametric PFA.[133] The variables are in logarithmic form.

Fig. 38. Potential Output and Actual GDP (parametric PFA)

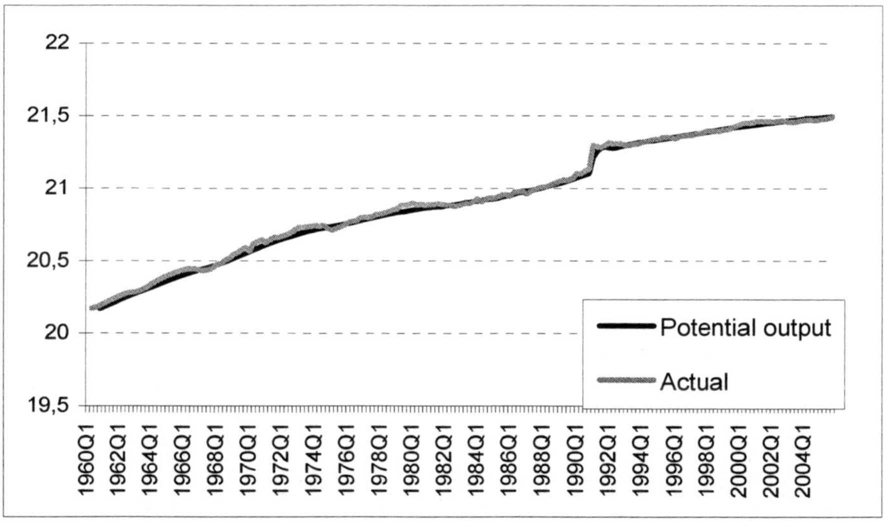

[133] The income share is not available prior to 1970Q1. Therefore, potential output based on the non-parametric PFA has been computed for the period from 1970 to 2005 whereas potential output according to the parametric PFA has been computed for the period from 1960 to 2005.

Fig. 39. Potential Output and Actual GDP (non-parametric PFA)

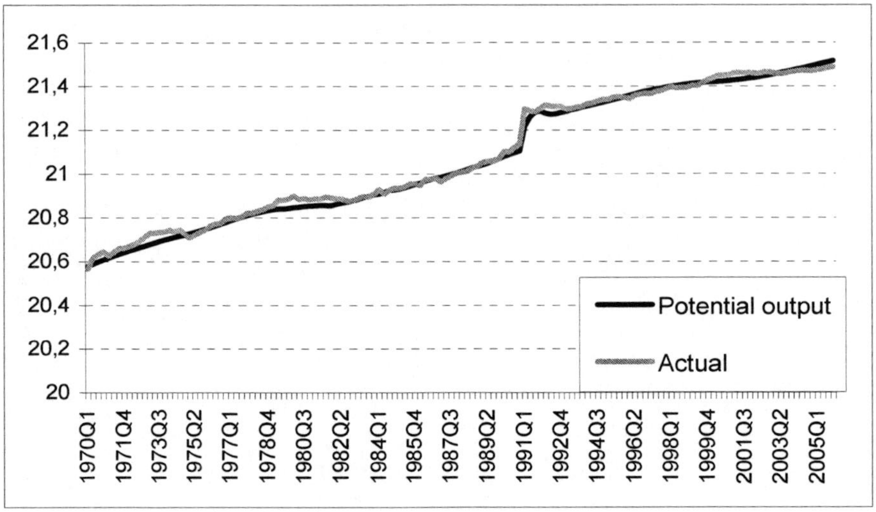

Figure 39 shows the corresponding growth rates of potential output based on both versions of the PFA along with the growth rate of actual GDP. Both estimates of potential growth have a very similar time profile. The jump of the growth rates in 1991Q1, which is caused by the connection of West German and German data, is clearly recognizable in the plot. For the computation of the "in-sample" statistics, this jump has been removed with the aid of an impulse dummy regression in order to avoid biases in the moments.

In order to derive GDP projections, the future prospects of potential output have to be assessed. Typically, this task is accomplished by extrapolating the key variables from past trends, however, it is also the stage of the projection process where judgemental adjustments usually enter the quantitative estimation by deciding whether historical trends can be sustained over the projection period or whether they should be adjusted on the grounds of additional information coming from outside the PFA framework. A neutral scenario (baseline scenario), which incorporates a no-change assumption of the evolution of the key components, builds a natural starting point for alternative scenarios in order to illustrate the range of possible outcomes and to demonstrate the uncertainties inherent to the projection.

Fig. 40. Quarterly Growth of Potential Output of the Parametric and Non-parametric PFA and Quarterly Growth of Actual GDP

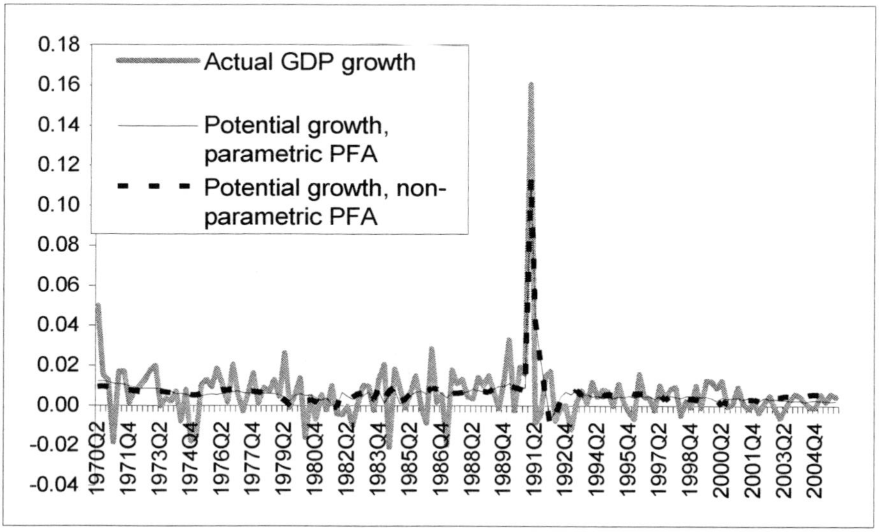

The following list explains which assumptions have been made and how forecasts for the individual inputs to the computation of a forward projection of potential output have been generated (recall equations A.8 to A.11). Note that such an analysis has to take account of the real-time characteristic of the sample data, i.e. only information that could have been known to the forecaster at the time the pseudo-forecast is produced should be employed for the prediction of subsequent potential output.

- The Total Factor Productivity is estimated as the Solow residual and is extended over the projection horizon with the aid of ARIMA-model forecasts. The HP filter is applied afterwards in order to obtain a trend value of TFP that can be fed into the Cobb-Douglas production function.
- The interdependence between GDP growth and capital investment makes it difficult to derive projections for the capital stock from a theoretical point of view. However, given the smooth trending behaviour of the capital stock data one typically observes, predicting this input variable econometrically is straightforward. Also ARIMA-model forecasts that are smoothed with the HP filter are employed for a forward projection of this component.
- Extending the number of working age population over the projection horizon is done with the aid of actual population data. No forecast is used for this variable since reliable projections of population data over medium-term horizons are typically readily available from demographic surveys to the forecaster.
- The extrapolation of the trend participation rate is also carried out with the aid of ARIMA-model forecasts and the HP filter. In practice, projecting the future evolution of this variable is typically based on extra information about whether

past trends are maintained over the projection horizon or whether trend changes are likely. However, such a proceeding is not feasible in the recursive out-of-sample analysis.

- The NAIRU is taken from the recursive OLS estimations of the "triangle model" and assumed to evolve unchanged from its last value at the period when the projection starts. For lack of alternative information, a flat extrapolation of the NAIRU seems to be most consistent with the notion of a stable long-run unemployment rate.

AII: Annex to Chapter 7

Table 24. Data Sources and Data Transformation

Variable	Code	Data Source	Details about the Transformation
Real GDP	Y	Reuters-Ecowin	We use a seasonally adjusted time series for real GDP. The outlier in the growth rate of real GDP (induced by the reunification) is corrected by interpolation (see Stock & Watson, 2003): The corresponding observation is replaced by the median of the 3 previous and the 3 following observations.
Yields on synthetic zero bonds	ZBYLD	Time series data base of the German Bundesbank	The Bundesbank calculates the yield on synthetic zero bonds on the basis of the market-traded bonds with different maturities according to the Svensson method. The monthly data are transformed into data on a quarterly base. We use annualised yields which are expressed in continuous compounding.
3-month interest rate	GM3	Time series data base of the German Bundesbank	We use interbank rates of Frankfurt Banks for 90-days' loans. The monthly data are transformed into data on a quarterly base. We use annualised rates which are expressed in continuous compounding.
Money Market Rate	MMR	Time series data base of the German Bundesbank	We use money market rates of Frankfurt Banks for overnight loans. The monthly data are transformed into data on a quarterly base. We use annualised values which are expressed in continuous compounding.

Return on broad stock market portfolio	MPF	Reuters-Ecowin	The MSCI German Gross Total Return Index is used as a broad market portfolio. We transform the monthly returns in quarterly data by summing up the monthly log-returns.
Business cycle climate indicator of the ifo-institute[134]	IFOBCGR	Ifo-institute	Until 1991:2 the indicator refers to West Germany, afterwards to the whole of Germany. We use the growth rate of the index based on quarterly data.
Inflation rate	INFLCPI	Reuters-Ecowin	The inflation rate is calculated on the basis of the consumer price index (CPI).
Oil price	OILPGR	Reuters-Ecowin	Brent Oil price. Changes of the oil price are used.

[134] We would like to thank the ifo-institute for providing the data.

Table 25. Analysis of the Accuracy of the Forecasts, Accommodation of Control Variables

$$y_{t+k}^{(k)} = \beta_0 + \beta_1 Spread_t + \beta_2 LDEP_{t-k} + \beta_3 MPF_t + \beta_4 \mathrm{IFOBCGR}_t + \beta_5 \mathrm{INFLCPI}_t + \beta_6 \mathrm{OILPGR}_t + \beta_7 MMR_t + \varepsilon_{t+k}^{(k)}$$

Horizon	n = 1		n = 5		n = 10	
	RMSE Model/Benchmark	Theil's *U*	RMSE Model/Benchmark	Theil's *U*	RMSE Model/Benchmark	Theil's *U*
k = 4	1.964/1.852	1.060	1.900/1.852	1.026	1.925/1.852	1.039
k = 8	1.675/1.542	1.086	1.610/1.542	1.044	1.601/1.542	1.038
k = 12	1.696/1.379	1.230	1.621/1.379	1.175	1.565/1.379	1.135
k = 16	1.558/1.171	1.330	1.559/1.171	1.331	1.501/1.171	1.282

Note: The results of the table are based on a recursive estimation of the forecast equation (initialization period until 1979:1). The RMSE is calculated on the basis of (pseudo) "out-of-sample" forecasts. We use a naive model as benchmark, which uses the previous mean of the dependent variable as forecast.

Table 26. Analysis of the Accuracy of the Forecasts, Accommodation of Control Variables, Dependent Variable Defined as Marginal GDP Growth

$$\frac{1}{4}(y_{t+k}^{(1)} + y_{t+k-1}^{(1)} + y_{t+k-2}^{(1)} + y_{t+k-3}^{(1)}) = \beta_0 + \beta_1 Spread_t + \beta_2 LDP_{t-k} + \beta_3 MPF_t + \beta_4 \mathrm{IFOBCGR}_t + \beta_5 \mathrm{INFLCPI}_t + \beta_6 \mathrm{OILPGR}_t + \beta_7 MMR_t + \varepsilon_{t+k}^{(k)}$$

	n = 1		n = 5		n = 10	
Horizon	RMSE Model/Benchmark	Theil's *U*	RMSE Model/Benchmark	Theil's *U*	RMSE Model/Benchmark	Theil's *U*
k = 4	1.964/1.845	1.064	1.901/1.845	1.030	1.925/1.845	1.043
k = 8	2.195/1.863	1.178	2.081/1.863	1.117	2.055/1.863	1.103
k = 12	2.265/1.968	1.151	2.480/1.968	1.260	2.386/1.968	1.212
k = 16	2.527/1.739	1.453	2.722/1.739	1.565	2.711/1.739	1.559

Note: The results of the table are based on a recursive estimation of the forecast equation (initialization period until 1979:1). The RMSE is calculated on the basis of (pseudo) "out-of-sample" forecasts. We use a naive model as benchmark, which uses the previous mean of the dependent variable as forecast.

List of Figures

List of Tables

References

Afonso, A., W. Ebert, L. Schuknecht, and M. Thoene (2005), *Quality of Public Finances and Growth*, ECB Working Paper Series No. 438, Frankfurt/Main.

Aghion, P. and P. Howitt (1998), *Endogenous Growth Theory*, Cambridge (MA).

Aghion, P. and P. Howitt (2005), *Appropriate Growth Policy: A Unifying Framework,* http://globetrotter.berkeley.edu/macarthur/inequality/papers/AghionAppropriateGrowth.pdf.

Åkerman, J. (1928), *Om det ekonomiska livets rytmik,* Stockholm: Nordiska bokhandeln (engl. version: *Economic Progress and Economic Crises,* London 1932).

Andrés, J., D. Lopéz-Salido, and E. Nelson (2005), Sticky-Price Models and the Natural-Rate Hypothesis, *St. Louis Fed Working Paper 2005-018A*, St. Louis.

Ang, A., M. Piazzesi, and M. Wei (2006), What Does the Yield Curve Tell Us About GDP Growth, *Journal of Econometrics* 131(1-2), 359-403.

Apel, M. and P. Jansson (1999), System Estimates of Potential Output and the NAIRU, *Empirical Economics* 24(3), 373-388.

Arthur, W.B. (1988), Competing Technologies: An Overview, in: Dosi, G., C. Freeman, R. Nelson, G. Silverberg and L. Soete (Eds.), *Technical Change and Economic Theory,* London, 590-607.

Arthur, W.B. (1990), Positive Rückkoppelung in der Wirtschaft, *Spektrum der Wissenschaft* 4, 122-129.

Arthur, W.B., Y.M. Ermoliev, and Y.M. Kaniovsky (1987), Path-Dependent Processes and the Emergence of Macro-Structure, *European Journal of Operational Research* 30(3), 294-303.

Ball, L. (1999), Aggregate Demand and Long-Run Unemployment, *Brooking Papers on Economic Activity* 2, 189-251.

Ball, L. and N.G. Mankiw (2002), The NAIRU in Theory and Practice, *Journal of Economic Perspectives* 16(4), 115-136.

Baltzer, M. and G. Kling (2007), Predictability of Future Economic Growth and the Credibility of Different Monetary Regimes in Germany, 1870-2003, *Applied Economics Letters* 14(6), 401-404.

Barrell, R. and D.W. te Velde (2000), Catching-up of East German Labour Productivity in the 1990s, *German Economic Review* 1(3), 271-297.

Barro, R (1974), Are Government Bonds Net Wealth?, *Journal of Political Economy* 82(6), 1095-1117.

Barro, R. and D. Gordon (1983), A Positive Theory of Monetary Policy in a Natural Rate Model, *Journal of Political Economy* 91(4), 589-610.

Bassanetti, A., J. Döpke, R. Torrini, and R. Zizza (2006), *Capital, Labour and Productivity: What Role Do They Play in the Potential GPD Weakness of France, Germany and Italy?,* Deutsche Bundesbank Discussion Paper No 09/2006, Frankfurt/Main.

Bassanini, A., S. Scarpetta, and P. Hemmings (2001), *Economic Growth: The Role of Policies and Institutions. Panel Data Evidence from OECD Countries,* OECD Economics Department Working Paper No. 283, Paris.

Batista, C. and J. Zalduendo (2004), *Can the IMF's Medium-Term Growth Projections Be Improved?*, IMF Working Paper 04/203, Washington, DC.

Baxter, M. and R.G. King (1999). Measuring Business Cycles: Approximate Band-Pass Filters for Economic Time Series, *Review of Economic and Statistics* 81(4), 575-593.

Bayoumi, T. and B. Eichengreen (1993), Shocking Aspects of European Monetary Integration, in: Torres, F. and F. Giavazzi (Eds.), *Adjustment an Growth in the European Union*, Cambridge.

Bean, C. (1989), Capital Shortages and Persistent Unemployment, *Economic Policy* 4(8), 11-53.

Bean, C. (1994), European Unemployment: A Survey, *Journal of Economic Literature* 32(2), 573-619.

Becker, S.O., K. Ekholm, R. Jaeckle, and M.A. Mündler (2005), Location Choice and Employment Decisions: A Comparison of German and Swedish Multinationals, *Review of World* Economics 141(4), 693-731.

Beffy, P.-O., P. Ollivaud, P. Richardson, and F. Sédillot (2006): *New OECD Methods for Supply-Side and Medium-Term Assessments: A Capital Services Approach*, OECD Economics Department Working Papers No. 482, Paris.

Beissinger, T. (2004), Strukturelle Arbeitslosigkeit in Europa: Eine Bestandsaufnahme, *Regensburger Diskussionsbeiträge zur Wirtschaftswissenschaft* 389.

Benes, J. and P. N'Diaye (2004), *A Multivariate Filter for Measuring Potential Output and the NAIRU: Application to The Czech Republic*, IMF Working Paper 04/45, Washington, DC.

Berardi A. (2005), *Real Rates, Expected Inflation and Inflation Risk Premia Implicit in Nominal Bond Yields,* Working Paper, University of Verona.

Berg, C. (1987), Utvecklingen av de svenska bidragen till inflationsgapanalysen, in: Henriksson, R. (Ed.): *Konjunkturinstitutet under Erik Lundbergs tid,* Stockholm, 153-170.

Bernanke, B and M. Gertler (1989), Agency Costs, Net Worth and Business Fluctuations, *American Economic Review* 79(1), 14-31.

Bernard H. and S. Gerlach (1998), Does the Term Structure Predict Recessions? The International Evidence, *International Journal of Finance and Economics* 3(3), 195-215.

Bibow, J. (2005a), *Bad for Euroland, Worse for Germany – The ECB's Record*, Working Paper No. 429, The Levy Economics Institute of Bard College.

Bibow, J. (2005b), Germany in Crisis: The Unification Challenge, Macroeconomic Policy Shocks and Traditions, and EMU, *International Review of Applied Economics* 19(1), 29-50.

Biervert, B. and M. Held (1994), Veränderungen im Naturverständnis der Ökonomik, in: Biervert, B. and M. Held (Eds.), *Das Naturverständnis der Ökonomik, Beiträge zur Ethik-Debatte in den Wirtschaftswissenschaften*, Frankfurt/Main, 7-29.

Bjørnland, H.C., L. Brubakk, and A.S. Jore (2005), The Output Gap in Norway – A Comparison of Different Methods, *Economic Bulletin (Norges Bank)* 76(2), 90-100.

Blanchard, O. (2000), What Do We Know About Macroeconomics that Fisher and Wicksell Did Not?, *Quarterly Journal of Economics* 115(4), 1375-1409.

Blanchard, O. and J. Galí (2005), *Real Wage Rigidities and the New Keynesian Model,* MIT Department of Economics Working Paper No. 05-28, Cambridge (MA).

Blanchard, O. and D. Quah (1989), The Dynamic Effect of Aggregate Demand and Supply Disturbance, *American Economic Review* 79(4), 655-73.

Boianovsky, M. (1995), Wicksell's Business Cycle, *European Journal of the History of Economic Thought* 2(2), 375-411.

Boianovsky, M. and H.-M. Trautwein (2001), Wicksell's Lecture Notes on Economic Crises (1902/05), *Structural Change and Economic Dynamics* 12(3), 343-366.

Boianovsky, M. and H.-M. Trautwein (2006a), Wicksell after Woodford, *Journal of the History of Economic Thought* 28(2), 171-185.

Boianovsky, M. and H.-M. Trautwein (2006b), Price Expectations, Capital Accumulation and Unemployment: Lindahl's Macroeconomics from the 1920s to the 1950s, *Cambridge Journal of Economics* 30(6), 881-900.

Boianovsky, M. and H.-M. Trautwein (2006c), Haberler, the League of Nations and the Quest for Consensus in Business Cycle Theories in the 1930s, *History of Political Economy* 38(1), 45-89.

Burmeister, E. and A.R. Dobell, (1970), *Mathematical Theories of Economic Growth,* New York.

Burns, A. and W. Mitchell (1946), *Measuring Business Cycles*, New York.

Campbell, J.Y. and J.H. Cochrane (1999), By Force of Habit: A Consumption Based Explanation of Aggregate Stock Market Behavior, *Journal of Political Economy* 107(2), 205-251.

Carlin, W. and D. Soskice (2006), *Macroeconomics. Imperfections, Institutions and Policies,* Oxford.

Carnot, N., V. Koen, and B. Tissot (2005), *Economic Forecasting*, New York.

Cassel, G. (1918), *Theoretische Sozialökonomie,* Jena.

Cerra, V. and S.C. Saxena (2000), *Alternative Methods of Estimating Potential Output and the Output Gap: An Application to Sweden,* IMF Working Paper 00/59, Washington, DC.

Chagny, O. and J. Döpke (2001), *Measures of the Output Gap in the Euro-Zone: An Empirical Assessment of Selected Methods,* Kiel Working Paper No. 1053, Kiel.

Christiano, L. and T.J. Fitzgerald (2003), The Band Pass Filter, *International Economic Review* 44(2), 435-465.

Claus, I. (2003), Estimating Potential Output for New Zealand, *Applied Economics* 35(7), 751-760.

Cohen, A. and G. Harcourt (2003), Whatever Happened to the Cambridge Capital Theory Controversies, *Journal of Economic Perspectives* 17(1), 199-214.

Conway, P., V. Janod, and G. Nicoletti (2005), *Product Market Regulation in OECD Countries: 1998 to 2003*, OECD Economics Department Working Papers No. 419, Paris.

Cotis, J.P., J. Elmeskov and A. Mourougane (2004), Estimates of Potential Output: Benefits and Pitfalls from a Policy Perspective, in: Reichlin, L. (Ed.), *The Euro Area Business Cycle: Stylized Facts and Measurement Issues*, London.

Cross, R. (1995), Is the Natural Rate Hypothesis Consistent with Hysteresis?, in: Cross, R. (Ed.), *The Natural Rate of Unemployment After 25 Years,* Cambridge, 181-200.

D'Amico S., D. Kim, and M. Wei (2008), *Tips from TIPS: The Informational Content of Treasury Inflation-Protected Security Prices,* Finance and Economics Discussion Series 2008-30, Board of Governors of the Federal Reserve System (U.S.), Washington D.C.

David, P.A. (1985), Clio and the Economics of QWERTY, *American Economic Review* 75(2), 332-337.

DeSerres, A., A. Guay, and P. St-Amant (1995), *Estimating and Projecting Potential Output Using Structural VAR Methodology: The Case of the Mexican Economy*, Working Paper 95-2, Bank of Canada, Ottawa.

Deutsche Bank Research (2005), The 2006 German Investment Recovery, *Current Issues* (April 27, 2005), Frankfurt/Main.

Deutsche Bundesbank (2002), Zur Entwicklung der Produktivität in Deutschland, *Monatsbericht* 54(9), 49-63.

Deutsche Bundesbank (2006), Deutschland in der Währungsunion, script of a speech from Prof. Dr. Axel Weber for the ZEW Economic Forum 2006, Mannheim.

Deutsches Institut für Wirtschaftsforschung (2005), *Auswirkungen von länderspezifischen Differenzen in der Lohn-, Preisniveau- und Produktivitätsentwicklung auf Wachstum und Beschäftigung in den Ländern des Euro-Raums*, *Politikberatung kompakt* 8.

Devereux, M.P. and R. Griffith (1999), *The Taxation of Discrete Investment Choices*, IFS Working Paper W98/16, revision 2, London.

Diebold, F.X., and R.S. Mariano (1995), Comparing Predictive Accuracy, *Journal of Business and Economic Statistics* 13(3), 253-263.

Domar, E. (1946), Capital Expansion, Rate of Growth and Employment, *Econometrica* 14(2), 137-147.

Dotsey, M. (1998), The Predictive Content of the Interest Rate Term Spread for Future Economic Growth, *Federal Reserve Bank of Richmond Economic Quarterly* 84(3), 31-51.

Dupasquier, C., A. Guay, and P. St-Amant (1997), *A Comparison of Alternative Methodologies for Estimating Potential Output and the Output Gap,* Working Paper 97-5, Bank of Canada, Ottawa.

Easterly, W. and S. Rebelo (1993), Fiscal Policy and Economic Growth, *Journal of Monetary Economics*, 32(3), 417-458.

Eijffinger, S., E. Schaling, and W. Verhagen (2000), *The Term Structure of Interest Rates and Inflation Forecast Targeting,* CEPR discussion paper, No. 2375, London.

Enderlein, H. (2006), One Size Fits None, *Central Banking* 15(4), 24-28.

Estrella, A. (2005a), Why Does the Yield Curve Predict Output and Inflation, *Economic Journal* 115(505), 722-744.

Estrella, A. (2005b), *The Yield Curve as a Leading Indicator: Frequently Asked Questions*, www.ny.frb.org/research/capital_markets/ycfaq.pdf.

Estrella, A. and G. Hardouvelis (1991), The Term Structure as a Predictor of Real Economic Activity, *Journal of Finance* 46(2), 555-576.

Estrella, A. and F. Mishkin (1997), The Predictive Power of the Term Structure of Interest Rates in Europe and the United States: Implications for the European Central Bank, *European Economic Review* 41(7), 1375-1401.

Estrella, A., A.P. Rodrigues, and S. Schich (2003), How Stable Is the Predictive Power of the Yield Curve? Evidence from Germany and the United States, *Review of Economics and Statistics* 85(3), 629-644.

European Commission (2002), *Germany's Growth Performance in the 1990's*, European Economy Economic papers No. 170, Brussels.

European Central Bank (2005), Monetary Policy and Inflation Differentials in a Heterogeneous Currency Area, *Monthly Bulletin May,* Frankfurt/Main, 65-82.

Evans, G. and S. Honkapohja (2001), *Learning and Expectations in Macroeconomics*, Princeton.

Fabiani, S. and R. Mestre (2004), A System Approach for Measuring the Euro Area NAIRU, *Empirical Economics* 29(2), 311-341.

Fama, E.F. (1970), Efficient Capital Markets: A Review of Theory and Empirical Work, *Journal of Finance* 25(2), 383-417.

Faust, J. and E.M. Leeper (1997), When Do Long-Run Identifying Restrictions Give Reliable Results?, *Journal of Business & Economic Statistics* 15(3), 345-353.

Fischer, S. (1993), The Role of Macroeconomic Factors in Growth, *Journal of Monetary Economics* 32(3), 485-512.

Fisher, I. (1896), Appreciation and Interest, *Publication of the American Economic Association* 11(4), 1-98.

Fölster, S. and M. Henrekson (2001), Growth Effects of Government Expenditure and Taxation in Rich Countries, *European Economic Review* 45(8), 1501-1520.

Franz, W. (1987), Hysteresis, Persistence, and the NAIRU: An Empirical Analysis for the Federal Republic of Germany, in: Layard, R. and L. Calmfors (Eds.), *The Fight Against Unemployment,* Cambridge, 91-122.

Franz, W. (1996), Theoretische Ansätze zur Erklärung der Arbeitslosigkeit: Wo stehen wir 1995? in: Gahlen, B., H. Hesse and H.-J. Ramser (Eds.), *Arbeitslosigkeit und Möglichkeiten ihrer Überwindung,* Tübingen, 3-45.

Franz, W. (2001), Neues von der NAIRU?, *Jahrbücher für Nationalökonomie und Statistik* 221, 256-284.

Franz, W. (2005), Will the (German) NAIRU Please Stand up?, *German Economic Review* 6(2), 131-153.

Friedman, M. (1942), The Inflationary Gap: II – Discussion of the Inflationary Gap, *American Economic Review* 32(2), 314-320.

Friedman, M. (1968), The Role of Monetary Policy, *American Economic Review* 58(1), 1-17.

Frisch, R. (1933), Propagation Problems and Impulse Problems in Dynamic Economics, in: Allen, G. and M.F. Unwin (Eds.), *Economic Essays in Honour of Gustav Cassel*, London, 171-205.

Fritsche, U. and C. Logeay (2002), *Structural Unemployment and the Output Gap in Germany: Evidence from an SVAR Analysis Within a Hysteresis Framework,* DIW Discussion Paper No. 312, Berlin.

Gärtner, M. (1997), Central Bank Independence and the Sacrifice Ratio: The Dark Side of the Force, *Schweizerische Zeitschrift für Volkswirtschaft und Statistik* 133(3), 513-538.

Georgescu-Roegen, N. (1971), The Entropy Law and the Economic Process, Cambridge (MA).

Georgescu-Roegen, N. (1979), Methods in Economic Science, *Journal of Economic Issues* 13(2), 317-328.

Gerlach, S. and F. Smets (1999), Output Gaps and Monetary Policy in the EMU Area, *European Economic Review* 43(4-6), 801-812.

Giorno, C., P. Richardson, D. Roseveare, and P. van den Noord (1995), *Estimating Potential Output, Output Gaps and Structural Budget Balances*, OECD Economic Department Working Paper 152, Paris.

Goodhart, C.A.E. (1975), Monetary Relationships: A View from Threadneedle Street, *Papers in Monetary Economics*, Reserve Bank of Australia.

Gordon, R.J. (1997), The Time-Varying NAIRU and Its Implications for Economic Policy, *Journal of Economic Perspectives* 11(1), 11-32.

Gottschalk, J. (2001), *An Introduction into the SVAR Methodology: Identification, Interpretation and Limitations of SVAR models*, Kiel Working Paper No. 1068, Kiel.

Gottschalk, J. and W. van Zandweghe (2001), *Do Bivariate SVAR Models with Long-Run Identifying Restrictions Yield Reliable Results? The Case of Germany*, Kiel Working Paper No. 1068, Kiel.

Goyal, A. and I. Welch (2003), Predicting the Equity Premium with Dividend Ratios, *Management Science* 49(5), 639-654.

Grandmont, J. M. (1985), On Endogenous Competitive Business Cycles, *Econometrica* 53 (5), 995-1045.

Green, E.J. (2005), A Review of Interest and Prices: Foundations of a Theory of Monetary Policy by Michael Woodford, *Journal of Economic Literature* 43(1), 121-134.

Greenslade, J.V., R.G. Pierse, and J. Saleheen (2003), *A Kalman Filter Approach to Estimating the UK NAIRU*, Bank of England, Working Paper No. 179, London.

Haberler, G. (1937), *Prosperity and Depression. A Theoretical Analysis of Cyclical Movements,* Geneva.

Hague, D. (Ed.) (1958), *Stability and Progress in the World Economy* (Conference Proceedings of the International Economic Association), London.

Hague, D. (Ed.) (1962), *Inflation*, Proceedings of a Conference held by the International Economic Association, London.

Hamilton, J.D. and D.H. Kim (2002), A Re-Examination of the Predictability of Economic Activity Using the Yield Spread, *Journal of Money, Credit and Banking* 34(2), 340-360.

Hahn, F.H. (1960), The Stability of Growth Equilibrium, *Quarterly Journal of Economics* 74(2), 206-226.

Hamilton, J. D. (1994), *Time Series Analysis*, Princeton University Press.

Hansen, B. (1951), *A Study in the Theory of Inflation,* Uppsala.

Harcourt, G. (1999), *The Capital Theory Controversy*, Papers 99/1, New South Wales - School of Economics.

Harrod, R. (1936), *The Trade Cycle. An Essay,* Oxford.

Harrod, R. (1939), An Essay in Dynamic Theory, *Economic Journal* 49(193), 14-33.

Hauptmeier, S., M. Heipertz and L. Schuknecht (2006), *Expenditure Reform in Industrialised Countries: A Case Study Approach*, ECB Working Paper No. 634, Frankfurt/Main.

Hein, E. and A. Truger (2002), *European Monetary Union: Nominal Convergence, Real Divergence and Slow Growth?*, WSI Discussion Paper No. 107, Düsseldorf.

Hendrikx, M. and B. Chapple (2002), *Regional Inflation Divergence in the Context of EMU, Netherlands Central Bank, Monetary and Economic Policy Department*, MEB Series (discontinued) No. 2002-19, Amsterdam.

Hicks, J.R. (1933), Gleichgewicht und Konjunktur, *Zeitschrift für Nationalökonomie* 4(4), 441-455.

Hicks, J.R. (1937), Mr. Keynes and the „Classics": A Suggested Interpretation, *Econometrica* 5(2), 147-159.

Hicks, J.R (1939), Value and Capital. An Inquiry into Some Fundamental Principles of Economic Theory, Oxford.

Hofmann, B. and H. Remsperger (2005), Inflation Differentials Among the Euro Area Countries: Potential Causes and Implications, *Journal of Asian Economics* 16(III), 420-421.

Hoover, K. (1988), *The New Classical Macroeconomics. A Sceptical Inquiry*, Oxford.

Howitt, P. (1992), Interest Rate Control and Nonconvergence to Rational Expectations, *Journal of Political Economy* 100(4), 776-800.

Hsieh, C.-Y. and M.-H. Ye (1991), *Economics, Philosophy, and Physics*, London.

Hüfner, F. and M. Schröder (2002), Prognosegehalt von ifo-Geschäftserwartungen und ZEW-Konjunkturerwartungen: Ein ökonometrischer Vergleich, *Jahrbücher für Nationalökonomie und Statistik* 222(3), 316-336.

Jevons, W.S. (1970), *The Theory of Political Economy*, Baltimore.

Kahn, R. (1931), The Relation of Home Investment to Unemployment, *Economic Journal* 41(162), 173-198.

Kaldor, N. (1940), A Model of the Trade Cycle, *Economic Journal* 50(197), 78-92.

Kamps, C., C.-P. Meier, and F. Oskamp (2004), *Wachstum des Produktionspotenzials in Deutschland bleibt schwach*, Kiel Discussion Papers No. 414, Kiel.

Kappler, M. (2004), *Determination of Potential Growth Using Panel Techniques,* ZEW Discussion Paper No. 04-69, Mannheim.

Keynes, J.M. (1930), *A Treatise on Money*, London.

Keynes, J.M. (1936), *The General Theory of Employment, Interest and Money,* London.

Keynes, J.M. (1940), *How to Pay for the War: A Radical Plan for the Chancellor of the Exchequer,* New York.

Kirman, A. (1992), Whom or What Does the Representative Individual Represent?, *Journal of Economic Perspectives* 6(2), 117-136.

Khalil, E.P. (1994), Further, *Ecological Economics* 9(3), 193-194.

Kirchgässner, G. and J. Wolters (2006): *Einführung in die moderne Zeitreihenanalyse*, Vahlen, München.

Kneller, R., M.F. Bleaney, and N. Gemmel (1999), Fiscal Policy and Growth: Evidence from OECD Countries, *Journal of Public Economics* 74(2), 171-190.

Krengel, R. (1986), *Das Deutsche Institut für Wirtschaftsforschung (Institut für Konjunkturforschung) 1925-1979,* Berlin.

Kuhn, T.S. (1962), *The Structure of Scientific Revolutions*, Cambridge (MA).

Kuhnert, S. (2005), Germany's Investment Gloom: Light at the End of the Tunnel?, *ECFIN Country Focus* 2(17).

Kydland, F. and E. Prescott (1977), Rules Rather Than Discretion: The Inconsistency of Optimal Plans, *Journal of Political Economy* 85(3), 473-491.

Kydland, F. and E. Prescott (1982), Time to Build and Aggregate Fluctuations, *Econometrica* 50(6), 1345-1370.

Laidler, D. (1999), *Fabricating the Keynesian Revolution: Studies of the Inter-war Literature on Money, the Cycle and Unemployment,* Cambridge.

Laubach, T. (2001), Measuring the NAIRU: Evidence from Seven Economies, *The Review of Economics and Statistics* 83(2), 218-231.

Layard, R., S. Nickell, and R. Jackman (1991), *Unemployment,* Oxford.

Leijonhufvud, A. (1981), The Wicksell Connection: Variations on a Theme, *Information and Coordination: Essays in Macroeconomic Theory,* New York, 131-202.

Leijonhufvud, A. (2004), The Long Swings in Economic Understanding, in: Velupillai, K. (Ed.), *Macroeconomic Theory and Economic Policy: Essays in Honour of Jean-Paul Fitoussi*, London, 115-127.

Leontief, W. (1941), *The Structure of American Economy, 1919-29*, Cambridge (MA).

Lindahl, E. (1929), Preisbildningsproblemets uppläggning från kapitalteoretisk synpunkt, *Ekonomisk Tidskrift* 31, 31-81 (trans. 1939, The Place of Capital in the Theory of

Price, in: Allen, G. and M.F. Unwin (Eds.), *Studies in the Theory of Money and Capital*, Part III, London, 269-350).

Lindahl, E. (1930), *Penningpolitikens medel,* Förlagsaktiebolaget, Malmö (trans. 1939, The Rate of Interest and the Price Level, in: Allen, G. and M.F. Unwin (Eds.), *Studies in the Theory of Money and Capital*, Part II, London, 137-268).

Lindahl, E. (1933), The Concept of Income, in: Allen, G. and M.F. Unwin (Eds.), *Economic Essays in Honour of Gustav Cassel,* London, 399-407.

Lindahl, E (1935), Arbetslöshet och finanspolitik, *Ekonomisk Tidskrift* 37, 1-36.

Lindahl, E. (1939), *Studies in the Theory of Money and Capital*, London.

Lindahl, E. (1961), Das Spiel mit dem Geldwert. *Weltwirtschaftliches Archiv* 87(1), 17-53.

Lindahl, E., E. Dahlgren, and K. Kock (1937), *National Income of Sweden, 1861-1930.* Part One, Stockholm.

Lucas, R. (1972), Expectations and the Neutrality of Money, *Journal of Economic Theory* 4(2), 103-124.

Lucas, R (1977), Understanding Business Cycles, in: K. Brunner and A. H. Meltzer, eds., Stabilization of the domestic and international economy, *Carnegie-Rochester Conference Series on Public Policy*, 5: 7-29.

Lucas, R (1981), *Studies in Business-Cycle Theory*, MIT Press, Cambridge.

Lucas, R. (1995), Nobel Lecture: Monetary Neutrality, *Journal of Political Economy* 104(4), 661-682.

Lucas, R. (2003), Macroeconomic Priorities, *American Economic Review* 93(1), 1-14.

Lucke, B. (2002), *Die Real-Business-Cycle Theorie und ihre Relevanz für die Konjunkturanalyse,* HWWA Discussion Paper 178, Hamburg.

Lundberg, E. (1937), *Studies in the Theory of Economic Expansion,* London.

Lundberg, E. (1953), *Konjunkturer och ekonomisk politik: Utveckling och debatt i Sverige sedan första världskriget*, Stockholm (trans. 1957, *Business Cycles and Economic Policy*, London).

McMorrow, K. and W. Roeger (2001), Potential Output: Measurement Methods, "New" Economy Influences and Scenarios for 2001-2010 – A Comparison of the EU15 and the US, *European Commission Economic Papers* No. 150, Brussels.

Meade, J. and Stone, R. (1941), The Construction of Tables of National Income, Expenditure, Savings and Investment, *Economic Journal* 51(202/203), 216-233.

Mirowski, P. (1984a), Physics and the Marginalist Revolution, *Cambridge Journal of Economics* 8(4), 361-379.

Mirowski, P. (1984b), The Role of Conservation Principles in Twentieth Century Economic Theory, *Philosophy of the Modern Sciences* 14(4), 461-473.

Mirowski, P. (1989), *More Heat Than Light. Economics as Social Physics: Physics as Nature's Economics,* Cambridge (MA).

Mitchell, W. (1913*), Business Cycles*, Berkeley.

Möller, J. (2005), Industrierenten und Lohnsetzungsverhalten: Gibt es Indizien für die Insider-Outsider Hypothese?, *Zeitschrift für Arbeitsmarktforschung* 38(2/3), 147-164.

Muth, J. (1961), Rational Expectations and the Theory of Price Movements. *Econometrica* 29(3), 313-335.

Myrdal, G. (1931), Om penningteoretisk jämvikt. En studie över den "normala räntan" i Wicksells penninglära, *Ekonomisk Tidskrift* 33, 191-302 (trans. 1939, *Monetary Equilibrium,* London).

Myrdal, G. (1933), Der Gleichgewichtsbegriff als Instrument der geldtheoretischen Analyse. in: von Hayek, F.A. (Ed.), *Beiträge zur Geldtheorie*, Vienna, 361-487.

Newey, W.K. and K.D. West (1987), A Simple, Positive Semi-Definite, Heteroskedasticity and Autocorrelation Consistent Covariance Matrix, *Econometrica* 55(3), 703-708.

Nickell, S., L. Nunziata, and W. Ochel (2005), Unemployment in the OECD Since the 1960s. What Do We Know?, *The Economic Journal* 115 (500), 1-27.

Nicoletti, G., S. Scarpetta, and O. Boylaud (2000), *Summary Indicators of Product Market Regulation With an Extension to Employment Protection Legislation*, OECD Economics Department Working Papers No. 226, Paris.

Njuguna, A.E., S.N. Karingi, and M.S. Kimenyi (2005), *Measuring Potential Output and Output Gap and Macroeconomic Policy: The Case of Kenya*, Working Paper 2005-45, University of Connecticut.

Nordhaus, W. D. (1975), The Political Business Cycle, *Review of Economic Studies*, 42(2), 169-90.

OECD (2001), *Measuring Capital, Measurement of Capital Stocks, Consumption of Fixed Capital and Capital Services*, OECD Manual, Paris.

OECD (2003a), *Structural Policies and Growth*, OECD Economic Outlook No. 73, Paris, 449-479.

OECD (2003b), *The Sources of Economic Growth in OECD Countries*. Paris.

OECD (2004a), *Economic Surveys – Germany*, 2004/12, Paris.

OECD (2004b), *Employment Outlook 2004*, Paris.

OECD (2004c), *Understanding Economic Growth – Macro-Level, Industry-Level, Firm-Level*, Paris.

OECD (2005), *OECD Science, Technology and Industry Scoreboard 2005*, Paris.

Ögünc, F. and D. Ece (2004), Estimating the Output Gap for Turkey: An Unobserved Components Approach, *Applied Economics Lette*rs 11, 177-182.

Ohlsson, I. (1987), Nationalräkenskaperna och den ekonomiska politiken, in: Henriksson, R. (Ed.), *Konjunkturinstitutet under Erik Lundbergs tid,* Stockholm, 35-68.

Okun, A. (1962), Potential GNP: Its Measurement and Significance. *Proceedings of the Business and Economic Statistics Section, American Statistical Association*; here cited according *to*: J.A. Pechman (Ed., 1983), *Economics for Policymaking. Selected Essays of Arthur M. Okun,* Cambridge (MA), 145-158.

Overesch, M. (2005), The Effective Tax Burden of Companies in Europe, *CESifo DICE Report 4/2005*, 56-63.

Patinkin, D. (1976), Keynes and Econometrics: On the Interactive Between the Macroeconomic Revolutions of the Interwar Period, *Econometrica* 44(6), 1091-1123.

Pesaran, M.H., Y. Shin, and R.P. Smith (1999), Pooled Mean Group Estimation of Dynamic Heterogeneous Panels, *Journal of the American Statistical Association* 94(446), 621-634.

Phelps, E (1961), The Golden Rule of Accumulation: A Fable for Grothmen, *American Economic Review* 51(4), 638-643.

Phelps, E. (1967), Phillips Curves, Expectations of Inflation and Optimal Unemployment, *Economica* 34(135), 254-281.

Phillips, A.W. (1958), The Relation Between Unemployment and the Rate of Change of Money Wage Rates in the United Kingdom, 1861-1957, *Economica* 25(2), 283-299.

Poincaré, Henri (1903), *Henri Poincaré,* Akademie-Verlag (1996 edition), Berlin.

Prachowny, M. (2000), *The Kennedy-Johnson Tax Cut: A Revisionist History,* Cheltenham.

Priddat, B.P. (1993), Nature as Subject-Matter of Economic Production, A Historical Systematic Draft, in: Dragan, J.C., M.C. Demetrescu and E.K. Seifert (Eds.), *Entropy and*

Bioeconomics, Proceedings on the First International Conference of the European Association for Bioeconomic Studies, Milan, 258-475.
Prigogine, I. and I. Stengers (1984), *Order out of Chaos. Man's New Dialogue with Nature,* London.
Ravn, M. and H. Uhlig (2002), On Adjusting the HP-Filter for the Frequency of Observations, *Review of Economics and Statistics* 84(2), 371-376.
Richardson, P., L. Boone, C. Giorno, M. Meacci, D. Rae, and D. Turner (2000), *The Concept, Policy Use and Measurement of Structural Unemployment: Estimating a TimeV-varying NAIRU Across 21 OECD Countries,* OECD Economics Department Working Papers No. 250, Paris.
Robertson, D. (1926), *Banking Policy and the Price Level,* London.
Sachverständigenrat zur Begutachtung der gesamtwirtschaftlichen Entwicklung (2002), *Zwanzig Punkte für mehr Beschäftigung,* Jahresgutachten 2002/03, Wiesbaden.
Sachverständigenrat zur Begutachtung der gesamtwirtschaftlichen Entwicklung (2003), *Staatsfinanzen konsolidieren – Steuersystem reformieren,* Jahresgutachten 2003/04, Wiesbaden.
Sachverständigenrat zur Begutachtung der gesamtwirtschaftlichen Entwicklung (2005), *Die Chance nutzen – Reformen mutig voranbringen,* Jahresgutachten 2005/06, Wiesbaden.
Samuelson, P. (1939), Interactions Between the Multiplier Analysis and the Principle of Acceleration, *Review of Economics and Statistics* 21, 75-78.
Samuelson, P. (1948), *Economics: An Introductory Analysis,* New York.
Samuelson, P. and R. Solow (1960), Analytical Aspects of Anti-Inflation Policy, *American Economic Review* 50(2), 177-194.
Santomero, A. and J. Seater (1978), The Inflation-Unemployment Trade-Off: A Critique of the Literature, *Journal of Economic Literature* 16(2), 499-544.
Sargent, T. (1973), Rational Expectations, the Real Rate of Interest, and the Natural Rate of Unemployment, *Brookings Papers on Economic Activity 1973(2),* 169-183.
Sargent, T. and N. Wallace (1975), "Rational" Expectations, the Optimal Monetary Instrument, and the Optimal Money Supply Rule, *Journal of Political Economy* 83(2), 241-254.
Scacciavillani, F. and P. Swagel (2002), Measures of Potential Output: An Application to Israel, *Applied Economics* 34(8), 945-957.
Schiantarelli, F. (2005), *Product Market Regulation and Macroeconomic Performance: A Review of Cross Country Evidence,* Boston College Working Paper 623 (rev. 11/2005), Boston.
Schumpeter, J.A. (1934), *Theorie der wirtschaftlichen Entwicklung,* 4th ed., Berlin.
Sebba, G. (1953), The Development of the Concepts of Mechanism and Model in Physical Science and Economic Thought, *American Economic Review* 43(2), 259-278.
Shannon, C.E. and W. Weaver (1949), *A Mathematical Theory of Communication,* Urbana.
Sinn, H.-W. (2000), *Germany's Economic Unification – An Assessment After Ten Years,* Working Paper 7586, National Bureau of Economic Research, Cambridge.
Sinn, H.-W. and F. Westermann (2001), *Two Mezzogiornos,* Working Paper 8125, National Bureau of Economic Research, Cambridge.
Skourtos, M.S. (1994), Vom Oikos zur Ressource – Entwicklung der Naturwahrnehmung in der Wirtschaftswissenschaft, in: Bievert, B. and M. Held (Eds.), *Das Naturverständnis der Ökonomik: Beiträge zur Ethik-Debatte in den Wirtschaftswissenschaften,* Frankfurt/Main, 30-53.

Solow, R. (1956), A Contribution to the Theory of Economic Growth, *Quarterly Journal of Economics* 70(1), 65-94.

Solow, R. (1988), Growth Theory and After, *American Economic Review* 78(3), 307-317.

Spahn, H.P. (2006), *Geldpolitik, Finanzmärkte, neue Makroökonomik und zinspolitische Strategien*, München.

Staiger, D., J.H. Stock and M.W. Watson (1997), The NAIRU, Unemployment and Monetary Policy, *Journal of Economic Perspectives* 11(1), 33-49.

Stiglitz, J. E and A. Weiss (1981), Credit Rationing in Markets with Imperfect Information, *American Economic Review* 71(3), 393-410.

Stock, J.H. and M.W. Watson (2003), Forecasting Output and Inflation: The Role of Asset Prices, *Journal of Economic Literature* 41(3), 788-829.

Svensson, L.E. (1994), *Estimating and Interpreting Forward Interest Rates: Sweden 1992-1994,* IMF Working Paper Series 94-114, Washington, D.C.

Swan, T. (1956), Economic Growth and Capital Accumulation, *Economic Record* 32(3), 334-361.

Tanzi, V. and N. Chalk. (2000), Impact of Large Public Debt on Growth in the EU: A Discussion of Potential Channels, *European Economy* 2, 23-43.

Temple, J. (1999), The New Growth Evidence, *Journal of Economic Literature* 37(1), 112-156.

Thoben, H. (1982), Mechanistic and Organistic Analogies in Economics Reconsidered, *Kyklos* 35(2), 292-306.

Timmer, M., G. Ypma, and B. van Ark (2003), *IT in the European Union: Driving Productivity Divergence?*, GGDC Research Memorandum GD-67, Groningen.

Tobin, J. (1969), A General Approach to Monetary Theory, *Journal of Money, Credit and Banking* 1(1), 15-29.

Tobin, J. (1972), Inflation and Unemployment, *American Economic Review* 62(1), 1-18.

Torres, R. and J.P. Martin (1990), Measuring Potential Output in the Seven Major OECD Countries, *OECD Economic Studies* 14, 127-49.

Trautwein, H.M. (1996), Money, Equilibrium and the Cycle: Hayek's Wicksellian Dichotomy, *History of Political Economy* 28(1), 27-55.

Trautwein, H.M. (2000), Seniors Beitrag zur Kapital- und Zinstheorie, in: *Vademecum zu Nassau W. Seniors 'Outline of the Science of Political Economy* (Klassiker der Nationalökonomie), Düsseldorf, 53-77.

Trautwein, H.M. (2005), The Loose Link: Hayek, Lindhal and Myrdal on Money, in: Bellet M., S. Gloria-Palermo, A. Zouache (Eds.),The *Evolution of the Market process: Austrian and Swedish Economics*, London, 94-113.

Turvey, R. (1949), A Further Note on the Inflationary Gap, *Ekonomisk Tidskrift* 51(2), 22-97.

Turvey, R. (1952), *Wages Policy Under Full Employment,* London.

United Nations (1947), *Measurement of National Income and the Construction of Social Accounts (with a memorandum by Richard Stone),* Geneva.

van Ark, B. and Inklaar, R. (2005), *Catching Up or Getting Stuck? – Europe's Troubles to Exploit ICT's Productivity Potential*, GDGC Research Memorandum GD-79, Groningen.

van der Ploeg, F. (2005), Back to Keynes? *CESifo Economic Studies* 51(4), 777-822.

Vanoli, A. (2005), *A History of National Accounting,* Amsterdam.

von Bertalanffy, L. (1949), Zu einer allgemeinen Systemlehre, *Biologia Generalis* 19, 114-129.

von Böhm-Bawerk, E. (1889), *The Positive Theory of Capital*, London.

von Hayek, F.A. (1929), *Geldtheorie und Konjunkturtheorie*, Leipzig.

von Hayek, F.A. (1931), *Prices and Production,* London.

Wanger, S. (2006), *Erwerbstätigkeit, Arbeitszeit und Arbeitsvolumen nach Geschlecht und Altersgruppen – Ergebnisse der IAB-Arbeitszeitrechnung nach Geschlecht und Alter für die Jahre 1991-2004*, IAB Forschungsbericht Nr. 02/2006, Nuremberg.

Walras, L. (1909), Economique et Mécanique, *Bulletin de la Société Vaudoise de Sciences Naturelles* 45, 313-325.

Weyerstraß, K. (2001), *Methoden der Schätzung des gesamtwirtschaftlichen Produktionspotenzials und der Produktionslücke*, Diskussionspapier Nr. 142, Halle Institute for Economic Research, Halle.

Wicksell, K. (1898), *Geldzins und Güterpreise: Eine Untersuchung über die den Tauschwert des Geldes bestimmenden Ursachen,* Jena.

Wicksell, K. (1911), *Föreläsningar i nationalekonomi. Första delen: Teoretisk ekonomi*, Lund: Berlingska Boktryckeriet (Trans. 1934, *Lectures on Political Economy*, London).

Wicksell, K. (1918), Karl Petander: „Goda och daliga tider“, *Ekonomisk Tidskrift* 20(2), 66-75.

Wiener, N. (1948), *Cybernetics,* New York.

Woodford, M. (1999), *Revolution and Evolution in Twentieth-Century Macroeconomics*, Paper prepared for the conference on Frontiers of the Mind in the Twenty-First Century, U.S. Library of Congress, Washington, D.C.

Woodford, M. (2003), *Interest and Prices: Foundations of a Theory of Monetary Policy,* Princeton.

Woodford, M. (2006), Comments on the Symposium on Interest and Prices, *Journal of the History of Economic Thought* 28(2), 187-198.

Wyplosz, C. (1994), Demand and Structural Views of Europe's High Unemployment Trap, *Swedish Economic Policy Review* 1(1-2), 75-107.

Wyplosz, C. (2006), European Monetary Union: The Dark Sides of a Major Success, *Economic Policy* 21(46), 207-261.

ZEW (2005), *Methoden mittelfristiger gesamtwirtschaftlicher Projektionen*, Projekt-No. 02/05, on behalf of the German Federal Ministry for Economics and Labour, Centre for European Economic Research (ZEW), Mannheim.